Surveillance, Power and Modernity

Surveillance, Power and Modernity

BUREAUCRACY AND DISCIPLINE FROM 1700 TO THE PRESENT DAY

Christopher Dandeker

St. Martin's Press, New York

First published in the United States of America in 1990

Printed in Great Britain

ISBN 0-312-04222-1

Library of Congress Cataloging-in-Publication Data

Dandeker, Christopher,
    Surveillance, power, and modernity: bureaucracy and discipline
from 1700 to the present day/Christopher Dandeker.
        p.   cm.
    Includes bibliographical references.
    ISBN 0-312-04222-1
    1. Power (Social sciences)—History.   2. Bureaucracy—History.
3. Abuse of administrative power-history.   I. Title.
HN49.P6S36   1990   89-70085
303.3—dc20   CIP

Contents

Preface and Acknowledgements

This is a book about surveillance as a means of administrative power. In the arguments defended here, the term surveillance is not used in the narrow sense of 'spying' on people but, more broadly, to refer to the gathering of information about and the supervision of subject populations in organizations. The main objective of the book is to describe and explain the ways in which long-term processes of bureaucratization have facilitated an expansion of the surveillance capacities of the strategic organizations of modern capitalist societies. By 'strategic' organizations, I mean the modern state and capitalist business enterprise. It is in the context of these two 'houses of power' and their administrative concentration of the means of production on the one hand, and the means of violence on the other, that the routines of the subject populations of modern societies are largely determined.

The analysis of surveillance offered here involves a critique of three broad traditions of social theory. Each of these can be identified in terms of the causal links which are drawn between the growth of surveillance and the other institutions of modern societies. The theory of industrial society regards bureaucratic surveillance as a rational response to the size and complexity of administrative tasks posed by science and technology. For Marxist theory, the growth of surveillance in modern societies is linked with the imperatives of capital accumulation and the class struggles focused on the business enterprise. In contrast, what I shall refer to as 'Machiavellian' theory tends to link surveillance with the geopolitical and military struggles amongst competing states.

These traditions of social theory are associated with quite different views of the connections between power and surveillance and thus how the 'triangle of power' linking central authorities, bureaucracies and subject populations in organizations should be understood. The theory of industrial society regards hierarchical systems of administrative power as inevitable features of technically complex organizations. In addition, it has always emphasized the consensual or 'power to' aspects of modern bureaucracy. On the other hand, Marxism has always placed an unwarranted emphasis on the class basis of administrative power and this is associated with the well-known difficulties it has in understanding the place of bureaucracy in socialist societies. Meanwhile, Machiavellian theory, with its view of social life as an arena of eternal struggle, has an overly pessimistic view of the inevitability of minority rule and the selfish use of administrative power in organizatior.s. I will argue that each of these traditions offers distinct advantages and limitations.

This book is a work of synthesis in two senses. First of all, it attempts to integrate these competing strands of social theory into a systematic account of the links between surveillance and modernity. In doing so, it builds on the writings of Weber and, more recently, of Foucault and Giddens. The view of surveillance developed here is characterized by a number of themes, the most important of which are:

1   Warfare and military organizations have been at the leading edge of processes of bureaucratization in modern societies. Thus, one should resist the temptation to view bureaucratic surveillance largely in terms of the imperatives of capital accumulation and the dynamics of the capitalist business enterprise.
2   The interests of bureaucratic and professional experts have been important and independent factors in the expansion of the surveillance capacities of the modern state and business enterprise.
3   Weber was right to suggest that one of the most important causes of the growth of bureaucratic systems of surveillance was an increase in the volume and complexity of administrative tasks.
4   Weber was also correct in arguing, as did Tocqueville, that in modern societies, democratization – or the demand for equality – is inextricably associated with the bureaucratization of society.
5   From a political point of view, there are good grounds for continuing to accept much of Weber's argument that it is market capitalism and parliamentary democracy rather than state socialism which offer the best defences against the excesses of bureaucracy in modern states.

This book is also a work of synthesis in the sense that I have relied on the specialist works of others. I hope I have acknowledged all of these in the notes, but it should be plain to readers how much I have been influenced by the ideas of Alfred Chandler, Stanley Cohen, Anthony Giddens, John Hall, Michael Howard, Craig Littler, Michael Mann, Sidney Pollard, James Rule and Hew Strachan.

The origins of the arguments presented here derive in part from my doctoral thesis which was concerned with an application of Weber's theory of bureaucracy to a detailed analysis of the links between the evolution of naval power and the British nation-state. I owe a considerable debt to my then supervisor and present colleague, David Ashton, who has always been willing to provide encouragement and constructive criticism. Other colleagues in the Department of Sociology at Leicester who have given invaluable advice and support include Clive Ashworth, James Fulcher, Nick Jewson, Terry Johnson and David Mason. John Scott not only cheerfully put up with a barrage of questions from me, but also offered to read the whole manuscript and made very useful suggestions as to how it might be improved. Dennis Smith and Ian Taplin have always found time to discuss my ideas and offer help. The Research Board of the University of Leicester and the British Academy provided me with financial support. The Department of Sociology, University of Maryland, College Park USA, offered me a friendly and peaceful place in which to work during the summer of 1987. I would like to thank Gillian Austen and Judith Smith for their word processing skills.

It will be evident how much the arguments defended here have drawn on the ideas of Anthony Giddens. I would also like to thank him for being, once again, such a supportive and patient editor. Last, but not least, I want to acknowledge the personal support of Anna Alexander-Williams.

Christopher Dandeker

1

Bureaucracy, Surveillance and Modern Society

Bureaucracy and Surveillance: Problems and Themes

Few would deny the claim that rational bureaucratic organization should be considered as one of the distinguishing features of 'modern' societies. Drawing on Anthony Giddens's recent work, it can be argued that rational bureaucracy comprises one of the four institutional components of modernity. These are:

1   The establishment of a durable state administration based on a centralized control of the means of violence. The political organization of the modern nation-state is normally 'democratized' in terms of either liberal or authoritarian modes of citizenship.
2   Goods and services are produced and distributed in an economic system centred on the large-scale business enterprise. In capitalist societies, the operations of the enterprise are mediated by the institutions of the market.
3   The co-ordination of the division of labour in economic and other institutions is facilitated by the use of rational technologies. Industrial technologies based on mechanical and electro-mechanical processes are increasingly being supplanted by 'post-industrial' or electronic processes and are centred more and more on information rather than on 'hard' goods.
4   In respect of the effective co-ordination of formal organizations, and

particularly of those which are central to the reproduction of power in modern societies (the state and business enterprise) rational bureaucracy is the key administrative instrument (A. Giddens 1985).

In modern societies, bureaucracy – whether private or public – is ubiquitous, and it seems to many an unloved necessity. Without it, few of the routine features of contemporary life in modern society would be possible: the collection of taxes, the provision of external defence, internal policing and welfare services, the production and distribution of goods and services at a level and regularity required for a 'reasonable' standard of living and so on. Today, one of the most obvious indicators of the pervasiveness of bureaucracy is the massive expansion of personal documentary information which is held by a range of organizations, such as the branches of the welfare state, banks, credit agencies, police authorities and so on. The age of bureaucracy is also the era of the information society.

For all the genuine contrasts that can be drawn between state socialist societies and the 'free market' societies of modern capitalism, it is difficult to imagine how the needs of those who live in the latter could be met without the guiding 'visible hand' of bureaucracy. The contrast between capitalism and socialism, at least in respect of the administrative salience of bureaucracy, would seem to be one of degree. This is the context in which Max Weber developed his bleak and ironic view of modernity as being enclosed in an administrative 'iron cage'. The members of modern societies, as products of an individualistic tradition, are increasingly dependent on bureaucratic organizations which can subject them to detailed administrative control and gather information about their lives. This idea of bureaucracy as a highly rationalized mode of information gathering and administrative control has been taken up more recently by Foucault and Giddens. They have discussed the adminstrative logic of modernity in terms of the growth of 'surveillance', understood as an expansion of the supervisory and information gathering capacities of the organizations of modern society and especially of the modern state and business enterprise. Thus modern rational bureaucracy is a highly effective and durable mode of surveillance.

The objective of this book is to explore the relationships between bureaucracy and surveillance in the development of modern capitalism, although the arguments defended here also have relevance for those interested in the nature of socialist societies and the future of socialism. The book is characterized by two broad themes. First, it analyses the nature of surveillance and the links that connect it with the phenomena of power, information and bureaucracy. It is suggested that organizations can be compared in terms of their surveillance capacities, and the general conditions

2

under which these are likely to be enhanced or inhibited are considered. Secondly, the book is concerned to outline and explain how systems of bureaucratic surveillance have become the administrative basis for the effective operation of three key institutional sectors of modern societies: the armed forces, policing and the business enterprise. The first two of these concern the external and internal organizations of the modern state, which I have already claimed to be a central component of modernity. The emergence of the armed forces as means of securing the sovereignity of the nation-state in the modern state system, can be seen as a response to the problem of *external* order. Although formally responsible for the state's dominion over its own population, this activity of routine *internal* pacification is normally performed by policing and security agencies. The third focus of the discussion concerns the evolution of the modern business enterprise, Giddens's second component of modernity, and the emergence of bur-eaucratized managerial hierarchies as means of exercising organizational surveillance. In this way, the book seeks to link an analysis of the rise of bureaucratic surveillance with changes in the overall organization of power in modern societies.

The view of bureaucracy and surveillance defended here involves a critical reassessment of three traditions in social theory the roots of which can be found in classical sociology. These traditions are Marxist theory, the theory of industrial society and neo-Machiavellianism. Each of these traditions focuses on a different aspect of modernity as the basis for constructing an explanation of the growth of bureaucratic surveillance in modern capitalism. The tendency of Marxist theory has been to view bureaucracy as a reflection of the *imperatives of capital.* The central dynamics of bureaucratic surveillance are situated within the capitalist enterprise, the prime site of the class conflict between capital and labour. The theory of industrial society has its origins in the work of Saint-Simon and was developed by Durkheim. This tradition has preferred to see bureaucracy as an administrative response to the *technical exigencies of industrialism.* Bureaucracy is an expression of modern scientific culture and is a technically indispensable form of organiza-tion in a structurally differentiated society. Classical German sociology laid the foundations of what James Burnham has referred to as the 'Machiavellian' tradition of Mosca, Sorel, Michels and Pareto, a perspective developed in the state theories of Hintze and Elias (J. Burnham 1970). This emphasizes the ways in which the technical superiority of bureaucratic modes of surveillance is revealed in the field of struggle between states. For the Machiavellians, therefore, bureaucracy is rooted in *political imperatives.*

These differences in institutional focus are also associated with quite varying views of the relationships between power and surveillance in modern society. Marxist theory situates bureaucracy in the struggles between classes and suggests that it is a strategic means for the reproduction of the power of one class over another. In contrast, the theory of industrial society, drawing on the Durkheimian tradition, has always stressed the ways in which bureaucracy facilitates collection action for consensual goals, whether in the context of specific organizations or at the level of whole societies (C. Kerr et al. 1973; T. Parsons 1969: 352–409; A. Giddens 1968; S. Lukes 1974, 1977). Meanwhile, the Machiavellians have located bureaucratic surveillance in the context of the eternal struggles for power between groups in organizations – struggles which cannot be reduced to conditions of economic scarcity or to class relations.

It should not be thought that the three traditions of social theory have developed in isolation from one another, nor that specific writers have not sought to draw on more than one of them. Nonetheless, distinguishing between these traditions does provide a means of discussing the similarities and differences between writers on these questions and of evaluating their work. It also allows us to understand and assess the ways in which particular writers have grappled with the conflicting traditions to produce powerful works of synthesis. Indeed, it is suggested that Max Weber's writings on bureaucracy can in large part be interpreted as an attempt to come to terms with all three sets of ideas. A critical evaluation of these three traditions of social theory involves a reassertion of the main thrust of Weber's argument about the relationships between capitalism, bureaucracy and surveillance. This is not to deny the significance of more recent contributions, particularly those of Foucault and Giddens. However, it will be emphasized that the significance of their work is that they share Weber's intention to consider the question of surveillance by integrating disparate strands of social theory.

The main themes of this book can be introduced by considering three related issues:

1 How the three traditions of social theory have dealt with the issue of surveillance.
2 How the surveillance capacities of an organization are enhanced or inhibited.
3 How the historical growth of bureaucratic systems of surveillance might best be characterized.

I have suggested that the problem of the relationship between bureaucracy, surveillance and modern capitalism can be approached by drawing on three broad traditions in social theory. Two of these – Marxism and the industrial society thesis – are well known and are often viewed together as defining the main axis of sociological debate about the nature of modern societies

(A. Gouldner 1970; J. Scott 1985). The third tradition – what is referred to here as Machiavellian social theory – has, until quite recently, been neglected in contemporary sociology. But there are now signs of a distinct revival of interest in the insights of this type of sociological analysis, as indicated in the works of Michael Mann, John Hall and Anthony Giddens (J. Hall 1986; A. Giddens 1985; M. Mann 1987, 1988). Although each of these traditions is characterized by a complexity of themes, distinctive theoretical views can nonetheless be discerned. These centre upon two main issues: which of the institutions of modernity are regarded as most significant in the explanation of the growth of bureaucratic surveillance in modern societies and what connections are to be drawn between power and surveillance?

The theory of industrial society can be traced from Comte, Saint-Simon, Spencer and Durkheim through the more recent 'managerialist' views of the modern business enterprise on the one hand, and the 'Whiggish' accounts of the police and welfare institutions of the modern nation-state on the other. For writers in this tradition, bureaucratic surveillance is an expression of modern scientific and humanitarian culture and is an administrative response to the technical imperatives of a structurally differentiated society. At the same time, the hierarchies of modern bureaucracies are regarded as serving consensual interests: they are viewed largely in terms of *power to* rather that *power over*. Such views are apparent in interpretations of modern business couched in terms of the 'soulful corporation', and in views of the police as servants of the neutral state battling against criminals who have opted out of society (T. A. Critchly 1967; C. Reith 1956; C. Kaysen 1957; J. Child 1969:42).

In contrast, Marxist writers have viewed modern bureaucratic surveillance in terms of the imperatives of capital accumulation and the struggles between capital and labour within the business enterprise. The centrality of class struggle is evident in diverse writings on the labour process and management (H. Braverman 1974; S. Wood 1983), the birth of the prison (M. Ignatieff 1978), the rise of the police and asylums and the general nature of the modern state (M. Ignatieff 1985; S. Cohen and A. Scull 1985). Bureaucratic surveillance is seen as contingent upon the existence of economic class division: bureaucracy will wither away with a socialist transformation of society or will at least be replaced by popular democratic forms of administration. The latter will be radically different from the centralized bureaucratic hierarchies looked on with such equanimity by industrial society theory.

Writers drawing on Machiavellian social theory have interpreted the place of bureaucratic surveillance in modern societies as stemming largely from the geopolitical and military struggles between nation-states. This is why many of the ideas in this strand of social theory have been referred to by Michael Mann recently as 'militarist' (M. Mann 1987: 54–72). As with the industrial society thesis, the administrative parallels between bureaucratic organizations in different institutional sectors are regarded as deriving from the technical advantages that bureaucracy has over other forms of administration. However, Machiavellian writers emphasize that societies should be seen in terms of conflict rather than consensus. Societies are viewed as arenas of conflict and struggles for power. Societies and nation-states are engaged in struggles with each other, and the groups which comprise those broader collectivities are involved in similar internal struggles.

Such conflicts are understood as universal features of social life. The value conflicts between collectivities have been crucial for the advance of bureaucratic surveillance as a means of administrative power. Bureaucratic surveillance is a technically superior form of administration in the modern age, and while it is bound up with the field of human struggles these cannot in any way be regarded as expressions of class relations. Writers drawing on this tradition have begun to make important contributions to the study of the organization of administrative power in modern society. Their work ranges from studies of the police, military power and war as well as the business enterprise.

Again it should be said that while these writers have drawn on Machiavellian ideas, they have also sought to integrate these with other strands of social theory. One significant Machiavellian element in their work has been an emphasis on the independent part played by the self-interest of professional and bureaucratic experts in the expansion of the surveillance capacities of the organizations in which they are based. Writings of this kind are often referred to as examples of the 'bureaucratic politics' perspective (M. Halperin 1971, 1974; D. Nelson 1975; W. McNeill 1983; A. Scull 1979; J. L. Abrahamson 1981; J. R. Lambert 1986; M. Brogden 1982; R. Reiner 1985). None of these three traditions on its own provides the basis for an adequate account of the relationships between bureaucracy, surveillance and modern capitalism. Indeed, the more sophisticated writers within each tradition have produced genuine works of synthesis. The view defended here is that such an account should draw especially heavily on the Machiavellian standpoint. The basis of such an account already exists in the writings of Weber and those who have drawn on his ideas.

Max Weber: Rationalization, Bureaucracy and Surveillance

The most thorough analysis of the relationship between bureaucratic surveillance and modern capitalism is undoubtedly that of Max Weber. Weber's discussion of this issue has often been regarded, particularly by some Marxist writers, as simply an elaboration of the theory of industrial society. However, Weber's views should be regarded as a critical departure from both these traditions, and as an attempt to incorporate some of their insights with the concerns of Machiavellian social theory.

Weber argues that the constitutive feature of modern capitalism is the institutionalization of rationality in all social institutions. This process is marked by the development of the rational capitalist enterprise, the rational-legal state, and the ethos of scientific reasoning and instrumental calculation. This rationalization of social life also provides the conditions under which sociological understanding of action as chains of practical reasoning becomes increasingly possible (A. Giddens 1971; J. E. T. Eldridge 1971).

For Weber, the modern business enterprise is different from previous economic organizations. Its peculiarities derive not from its pursuit of economic gain or its subjection of a work force in the process of production, but from its operation in conditions that maximize the rationality of its economic conduct (M. Weber 1961: 207–32). It is concerned with the systematic pursuit of profit through techniques of rational calculation, and Weber elaborates on this through a distinction between rational and irrational capitalist actions. Rational economic action involves the pursuit of favourable opportunities for profitable exchange through the methods of rational calculation, excluding all considerations extraneous to profit maximization, and this plays a part in his distinction between political and industrial capitalism. In the first, opportunities for gain are pursued through the use of political mechanisms aimed at generating a return on one's investment e.g. tax farming, piracy, speculative political loans, etc. In the second, such profits are pursued through a formally peaceful industrial enterprise with a view to exchanging the finished product on the market. It is the rationality of the entrepreneur's pursuit of profit through the exchange of goods produced in the industrial enterprise that Weber regards as a distinctive feature on modern industrial capitalism.

Profitability in the industrial enterprise is determined by a rational capital accounting system. This involves the calculation of the income yielding power of the enterprise according to the methods of modern double-entry book keeping and the striking of a balance. Rational accounting as a mode of surveillance presupposes the following conditions. First, it requires the appropriation of all the physical means of production (with the important exception of the material provision of the armed services of the state) as the disposable property of autonomous private industrial enterprises. Second, there must be freedom of market exchange, and thus the elimination of irrational barriers to economic action, for example those involving the exclusion of particular classes from types of economic activity. Third, it requires the introduction of rational technology in industrial organization. Specifically there must be a mechanization of the processes of the production, processing and distribution of goods and, as a result, the elimination of subjective factors of human mood and temperament as far as possible. Fourth, the existence of a system of calculable law and administration is presupposed. In this way, Weber sees the structure of the modern state, with its monopolization of the means of legitimate physical force in a given territory, as a precondition of rational accounting. Fifth, there must be a separation of the business accounts from those of the domestic household. Sixth, there must exist a class of formally-free labourers, a class whose members are legally free to sell their labour on the market and are compelled by their propertyless condition to do so without restriction. In this way, labour is constituted as simply another commodity for entrepreneurial use. Seventh, and finally, rational capital accounting presumes a general commercialization of economic life – or an 'enterprise culture' – established through the issue of commerical instruments to represent share rights in enterprises, and widespread property ownership.

Each of these conditions maximizes the degree to which decision-making can be reduced to problems of numerical calculation: for example in respect of which production lines should be invested in, the time needed to produce and distribute a given output, the organization of a system of production and so on. The rationality of modern capitalist enterprise is not to be equated with its efficiency, although Weber does argue that it is historically the most effective way of providing for human needs. What he means by this argument is that efficiency is a 'value concept' which presupposes the evaluative issue of which ends or goals are used in the assessment of efficiency. Therefore it cannot be discussed in a completely generalized way as a purely formal or technical matter. In addition, the question of choice between ends is not resolvable by science but is a matter of faith. The rationality of capitalism means that, in the ideal case, an enterprise can calculate exactly whether or not it is 'efficient' as determined by the value categories of, for example, providing a good service to the consumer, possessing a contented work force or whatever. On this argument, an 'inefficient' enterprise, as defined by a number of alternative value categories, could still be a rational enterprise if it could calculate precisely the nature of its problems in numerical form. This line of argument relates to Weber's contention that there are contradictions between formal and substantive rationality in modern capitalism; e.g. between the formal rationality of bureaucracy and the substantive rationality of individualism (M. Albrow 1970).

In industrial capitalist enterprises, capital accounting, the control of formally-free labour and the organization of the production process according to entrepreneurial directives are implemented by bureaucratic officials. The authority to issue commands required for the operation of the enterprise is distributed in a fixed way as official duties. Methodical provision is made for the regular, continuous performance of these activities and only persons who possess appropriate formal qualifications, as established by regulation, are entitled to join the organization.

The consequences of these arrangements for the position of individual officials are that: (1) they are personally free and subject to authority only with respect to their impersonal and official obligations; (2) they are organized in a clear hierarchy of offices – each office has a clearly defined sphere of competence in the legal sense; (3) the office is filled by a free contractual relationship; (4) candidates are selected on the basis of technical qualifications – they are appointed not elected; (5) they are remunerated by fixed salaries in money for the most part with a right to pensions; (6) the office constitutes a career, in that it is treated as the sole, or at least the primary occupation of the incumbent; (7) there is a system of promotion according to seniority or achievement or both, and such decisions depend upon the judgement of superiors; (8) the official works entirely separated from ownership of the means of administration and without appropriation of his position; (9) the official is subject to strict and systematic discipline in the conduct of the office (M. Weber 1978: 217-26).

Two aspects of Weber's discussion of the rationality of modern bureaucracy must be singled out for particular attention. First, bureaucratic decisions and calculations depend on *knowledge of the files*, that is on a mastery of the information stored centrally in the organization, rather than on tradition or charismatic inspiration. This means that administrative reasoning can in principle be understood and replicated by anyone with access to the same information. 'Bureaucratic administration means fundamentally domination through knowledge. This is the feature which makes it specifically rational.' (M. Weber 1978: 255). Second, bureaucratic administration is based on *rational discipline*. Weber argues that, in the field of administration, bureaucracy is analogous to the machine in the extent to which subjective or irrational elements of will and mood are eliminated. The official is separated

9

from the means of administration and thus fully dependent upon the employer in the same way as formally-free labour is separated from the means of production. The official's sphere of competence is clearly defined by legal rules with his or her decisions subject to scrutiny through a regular chain of command. In addition, the official is subjected to a rigorous system of technical training. This provides the means of acquiring knowledge of the files, and of instilling organizational discipline. The rational discipline of officials is further reinforced by the fact that they have contractual appointments regulated by objective criteria such as merit and seniority, rather than owing their position to political or kinship loyalties. This feature distinguishes rational officialdom from traditional, patrimonial bureaucracies in which official activities are extensions of the domestic arrangements of the head of the organization.

The most important consequence of rational officialdom is that a director of such a bureaucracy can predict, with great certainty, that his or her commands will be implemented through the chain of command, and this to a historically unprecedented extent. Moreover these activities will be based on rational calculations stemming from the institutionalization of the knowledge stored in official files. For Weber, then, *rational administration is a fusion of knowledge and discipline.*

Rational bureaucracy and the modern state

Weber identifies a number of parallels between the rational business organization and the modern state. The latter is defined, revealingly, as the rational-legal state. Like the capitalist enterprise, the modern state is a rational structure of domination and surveillance, in that it comprises a relationship between leaders and led that is mediated by a bureaucracy.

The modern state is a 'human community that (successfully) claims the *monopoly of the legitimate use of physical force* within a given territory' (H. Gerth and C. Wright-Mills 1970: 78). Weber focuses on a number of distinct features of the modern state.

It possesses a legal and administrative order comprising a body of formalized legal norms and a rational bureaucracy. The legal norms incorporate the substantive policies of the state and these can be changed only through formal mechanisms as defined in legislative and other constitutional procedures. The bureaucracy is charged with implementing such legal norms over the state's territory and population. This activity involves a permanent and continuous exercise of surveillance.

In addition, the state is a compulsory, rather than a voluntary, association. It claims binding authority over all its members, most of whom will have

10

obtained membership by birth. The state also claims authority over all action taking place within its territory.

Force is regarded as legitimate only insofar as it is permitted or prescribed by the state. 'The claim of the modern state to monopolise the use of force is as essential to it as is its character of compulsory jurisdiction and continuous operation' (M. Weber 1978: 56). As Weber points out, the surveillance capacity of the modern state is such that the distinction between the public and private realms is itself a matter of state definition. For example, in Wilhelmine Germany the power of parents to corporally punish children originated in traditional, patriarchal relations. However, under modern conditions, this became a right bestowed by the state. For Weber, the ends of the state are always a matter for empirical investigation and they can never be assumed to follow simply some ethical principle or the will of the capitalist class. Whatever may be the ends of the modern state, they are expressed in formally defined norms. The methods for changing the ends of the state are defined by legal procedures rather than by traditional norms or charismatic revelation. Changes in policy goals do not rest simply on the whim or discretion of the head of state. For these reasons, bureaucratic administration means that the subject population live under a stable and calculable political order. Whatever may be its substantive conditions of freedom or democracy, the political order permits rational calculation of the consequences of actions. In addition, political leaders can expect that commands will be implemented by their bureaucratic staff in a rationally calculable manner.

The subject population and bureaucracy obey the commands of the state for a variety of reasons, monetary reward, convenience and habit being among the more important. However, a state cannot survive without a minimal level of consent. In all systems, this stems from a belief in the legitimacy of those who give commands. The legitimacy of the modern state rests on the fact that its orders are established and exercised in a way that is recognized to be legal. Weber argues that the stability of this system of legitimation rests not on certain substantive values like freedom, democracy and so on, but on the formal logical character of legal norms which have the capacity to express and legitimate any particular substantive end as a basis for state policy. Thus it is in the formal rationalization of law rather than in the substantive rationalization of law in terms of ethical values that the fullest expression of the rational-legal state may be found. As long as state action conforms to formal legal requirements, it can adopt any policies or reflect any values without disturbing the basis of its legitimacy. Legitimacy claims based on particular values are unstable because they can always be challenged by competitors committed to alternative values. For Weber, the stability of legitimation in modern capitalism rests upon the subject population's recognition that, independently of the substantive values expressed in commands, there is an obligation to accept them as technically correct/valid (R. Cotterel in D. Sugarman 1981: 69–93).

The calculability of state administration from the point of view of the subject population is matched by the ability of the state to translate policy directives into detailed procedures and regular routines throughout its territory. Thus the state has the means of subjecting its territory and population to detailed surveillance. It can make them 'objects' of public policy through continuous administration and the consequent penetration of everyday life in ways quite unmatched by what Weber terms pre-rational political structures. Thus in ancient China, 'officials did not rule but only interfered in the event of disturbances or untoward happenings.' (M. Weber 1961: 250) This surveillance capacity of the modern state rests on its concentration of the means of administration, and parallels the power of the modern business enterprise to separate its workers from the means of production. Yet this historical parallel is also a symbiotic relationship. The business enterprise operates only within the political framework of calculability provided by the modern state, whilst the state's surveillance capacity is based upon the mobilization of resources released by the enhanced productive power of industrial capitalism.

The ethos of modern capitalism

The development of the modern state and business enterprise presupposes a rationalization of the ethos of modern capitalism. This entails the constitution of society and nature as an observable, disenchanted realm of means and ends. This process involves an expansion of 'knowledgeability', the 'demystification' of everyday life, and the increasing significance of technical rationality in the legitimation of modern capitalism.

The generalized exercise of bureaucratic surveillance in modern capitalism is associated with a transformation of the organization of knowledge. This involves a separate of the scientist, technician and scholar from the means of the production of knowledge, and their insertion as elements in bureaucratic organizations – universities and research institutes (H. Gerth and C. Wright-Mills 1970: 129–56). Such organizations are established typically as subordinate adjuncts of the state or of industrial enterprises. The proliferation of knowledge of the natural and social worlds coincides with an extension of hierarchical control over its production and distribution. The independent scholar becomes as outmoded as the self-equipped soldier, the independent tax farmer and the autonomous craftsman in the modern world of technical specialization and bureaucracy.

Although modern capitalism generates greater 'knowledgeability', this does not imply that particular individuals have a greater grasp of their surroundings than their equivalents in pre-rational societies. In most cases the reverse is true. The greater knowledgeability of modern capitalism is very much a collective rather than an individual property: knowledge is produced, stored and applied in bureaucratic organizations. For Weber, the development of scientific calculation is part of the rational mastery of the world for human ends, thus echoing Comte's dictum that to know is to control. Science and technology are inextricably connected with the rationalization of relations of domination between leaders and led on the one hand, and human societies and the natural world on the other. As we shall see, strictly *technical* imperatives demand that the natural and the social sciences become elements of hierarchical systems of command and control. This situation is constitutive of modern, industrial societies; and one which the prospect of socialism could not reverse, but would advance even further.

Weber's discussion of the organization and control of knowledge also relates to what he regarded as the pervasiveness of instrumental rationality in the everyday life of modern capitalism. Weber connected the scientific rationalization of knowledge with broader psychological problems of anxiety and meaninglessness. Science destroys the old gods, but it does not provide any new ones: it does not answer the questions of ultimate meaning. For this reason, a degree of psychological insecurity is inevitable in modern capitalism. Particularly in periods of social instability, such societies can experience periods of religious enthusiasm, reflecting the search for ultimate meaning in a meaningless world. However, in Weber's view, such movements can never match the strengths of religious feeling characteristic of pre-rational civilizations. This is because their basis is undercut by the existence of scientific enquiry and instrumental rationality. The ways in which the 'need for meaning' may be satisfied are amenable to scientific investigation, as Weber's own sociology of religion demonstrated.

The psychological anxieties associated with a demystified world are reinforced by feelings of dependence and the collapse of individual will and spontaneity in the face of modern bureaucratic order. Later, Fromm was to refer to this as a 'fear of freedom' (E. Fromm 1941). Modern society becomes a bureaucratic 'iron cage' in which people 'need order and nothing but order, who become nervous and cowardly if for one moment this order wavers, and helpless if they are torn away from total incorporation in it' (J. P. Mayer 1944: 127-8). Within this social structure, the individual – the basis of bourgeois society – becomes a regulated cog in the adminstrative machine; an implementer in detail or receiver of decisions made elsewhere at its commanding heights. This 'parcelling out of the human soul' stands in ironic contrast to the early stages of modern capitalism, when the habits of discipline and ethical duty in respect of work and the division of labour were self-imposed by entrepreneurs who were attracted to the moral values of protestantism. As Weber remarked wistfully, 'The puritan wanted to work in a calling we are *forced* to do so.' (M. Weber 1956: 181).

The only people exempt from this bureaucratic parcelling out of the soul are those in positions of leadership and responsibility such as the directors of capitalist enterprises and the modern state. The mass of the population are confined to inertia in the face of the modern bureaucratic order. Weber was aware that unsupervised bureaucracies are likely to pursue their own selfish organizational interests. However, the only way to ensure that they pursue the goals of a subject population is not through popular administration but through strong leadership from the top. The cultural pessimism evoked by this image of the 'iron cage' is countered partially with the prospect of an age of heroic leaders who may salvage a fragment of the western culture of individualism.

The preconditions of modern bureaucracy

Weber identifies four preconditions of modern bureaucracy: (1) a money economy; (2) the quantitative expansion of administrative tasks; (3) the qualitative expansion of administrative tasks; (4) the technical superiority of rational bureaucratic administration over alternative administrative structures in the three preceding circumstances. This makes the modern bureaucratic order both indispensable and indestructible. It confines realistic political analysis to questions relating to the control of bureaucracy rather than utopian schemes concerning its destruction.

A money economy is crucial in providing financial resources for paying the salaries of officials. There are, of course, exceptions, as in the later Roman Empire and the Roman Catholic Church of the thirteenth century. However, in those circumstances, officials could not be fully subordinated to rational discipline. This was because payment in kind or the bestowal of administrative rights in lieu of financial payment, as in some systems of tax farming permitted officials to evade central control. The distinctive features of rational bureaucracy compared with the administration of older civilizations (apart from technical scientific education), is the financial dependence of the official on the central authority.

The expansion in the number of tasks requiring administrative decisions establishes a favourable basis for the development of bureaucracy, as, for instance, with the expansion in the size of the territory and population of states. However, Weber argues that there are important exceptions. Large states may be held together as much by cultural homogeneity as by administrative co-ordination, as the cases of Ancient China (for long periods), and the Holy Roman Empire (in early modern Europe) illustrate. On the other hand, the power of the Roman Empire to control territory collapsed because of the administrative weight of its administrative bureaucracy in the context of the deficiencies in its economy. Nevertheless, modern industrial states have been encouraged to bureaucratize because of the increased volume of administrative tasks attendant upon the expansion of their territories and population. This process is illustrated by the transformation of political parties in the nineteenth century. The democratization of the electoral system meant that in order to 'get out the vote' political parties had to alter their organizational structures. In the early part of the century, parties were collegiate clubs with small memberships selected from privileged status groups. By the end of the period, they were mass bureaucratic parties organized on a national basis (H. Gerth and C. Wright-Mills 1970: 209–11).

Weber regarded the qualitative increase in administrative tasks and the resulting complexity of the decision-making process as the most important cause of the bureaucratization of organizations. This argument reflects his view that rational administration means administration on the basis of technical knowledge. Organizations that encounter tasks of great technical complexity have little alternative but to rely upon a bureaucracy. Its services are indispensable in the provision of military service in the industrial age; the provision of taxation and welfare systems for populations of 50 million people, or in the drafting and implementation of complex legislation.

Weber was well aware that bureaucrats have a tendency to use official secrecy as a basis for insulating their activities from external scrutiny and supervision. However, even under the most 'open' of administrative systems, the dependence of the population on administrative experts will remain great in modern society. Weber was convinced that the technical complexities which produce this dependence are aggravated by the demands of the citizens of modern democracies for public services. The popular demand for equality of social conditions merely adds to the impetus of bureaucratization.

In modern capitalism, whilst the state and the capitalist enterprise are the main sites of bureaucratization, all organizations, such as churches, voluntary organizations, political parties etc., are liable to the same process. Alternative administrative structures, e.g. amateur and collegial forms, tend to be supplanted by bureaucratic administration with its monocratic hierarchy of command. This is because Weber regarded the latter as the technically superior form of organization: 'the fully developed bureaucratic mechanism compares with other organizations exactly as does the machine with the non-mechanical modes of production. Precision, speed, unambiguity, knowledge of the files, continuity, discretion, unity, strict subordination, reduction of friction and of material and personal costs – these are raised to the optimum point in the strictly bureaucratic administration and especially in its monocratic form.' (ibid: 214)

Weber is making two judgements here: first, as was indicated earlier, modern bureaucracy, like the machine, eliminates irrational considerations by making administrative action rationally calculable. This means that substantive 'efficiency targets' can be more precisely monitored than would be the case under alternative administrative arrangements. This process is aided by modern techniques of communication which optimize the reaction time of modern bureaucracies or the time between receiving information and implementing a decision. The modern capitalist enterprise demands the calculability of modern administration from the state as a condition of its operations. Secondly, although Weber does not equate rationality with efficiency, he does argue that bureaucracy is normally the most effective means for carrying out large-scale tasks. Of course, bureaucratic administration incurs certain costs, as, for instance, in consideration of the idiosyncracies of particular cases.

Weber and his critics

Weber's somewhat gloomy analysis of the relations between bureaucratic surveillance and modern capitalism has not gone without criticism. Yet when Weber's own case against his critics is considered, the strengths of his analysis will become evident. Two related charges have been levelled at Weber: technical determinism and coercive bias. The first is made by those who draw on Marxist theory, the second by those sympathetic to the theory of industrial society.

Weber is sceptical of the possibilities of direct democracy in large-scale industrial societies. By direct democracy, Weber means a situation where everyone is qualified to conduct public affairs, where the scope of command of those in positions of authority is kept at a minimum (e.g. by delegation), and where everyone has the right of participation in public affairs. This becomes a possibility only where the organization is locally based and limited in size, where the class and status positions of the membership are not too dissimilar, where the administrative tasks encountered by the group are fairly simple and stable, and where there is a minimum level of development of universal training in the techniques of administration or in the ways of determining means and ends (Max Weber 1978: 289–92).

Some Marxist writers have argued that Weber underestimates the potential for the democratization of administration in those industrial societies where the relations of production have been socialized. For example, Hirst has questioned whether bureaucracy, which excludes mass participation in decision-making is a technically superior form of administration. He also queries whether the centralization involved in bureaucratic organization is necessarily an obstacle to popular administration and whether the complexity of the division of labour requires specialist officials insulated from the masses and likely to pursue their own selfish interests. He argues that a socialist society could diffuse knowledge to the population to a far greater extent than is possible in class-divided capitalism, where the emphasis placed on the control and supervision of the population must be greater (P. Q. Hirst 1976: 49–123).

Hirst's claim, then, is that centralization under socialism could *aid* popular administration, whereas the reverse is the case under capitalist societies. Echoing Rousseau, Hirst argues: 'If the friends of liberty have argued for centralization it is because they have argued for a quite different form from that of the centralized state operating through administrative apparatuses beyond popular control. Thus, the [Paris] communal constitution represented a national unity based on communes, upon popular executive – legislative bodies in towns and regions and not a unity of the state administration of a uniformly subordinate and politically inert countryside. The centralization of information and control, the concentration of functions in executive legislative bodies favours the control by the popular masses.' (ibid: 119)

Although the social co-ordination of a socialist society would demand the provision of specialist administrators, they could be paid wages similar to those of manual workers. Also, they could be made to perform manual work for some of the time. It would also be possible to ensure that their decisions were taken on behalf of the workforce through a system of accountable administration.

Weber has an especially powerful response to such charges. In modern industrial societies, the process of democratization involves an ever-increasing dependence on bureaucratic services. The demands for political, social and economic equality, or the rights of 'citizenship' (T. H. Marshall 1973), are associated with an expansion of bureaucratization. Equal treatment before the law presupposes the bureaucratic, universal implementation of the rule of law, whilst demands for a minimum and/or basic standard of living constrains the state to meet them through the extension of bureaucratic welfare services and planning agencies. Socialist planning merely extends this process to its logical conclusion. *The invisible hand of the market is subordinated to the 'visible hand' of the bureaucratic state* (see A. Chandler 1977). Here, Weber argues that explicit decision and co-ordination increase

17

the demand for bureaucracy compared with market systems of allocation. This is because of the volume and complexity of decisions and calculations that require administrative resolution.

Weber's analysis is similar to Tocqueville's observation of the dialectical relation between bureaucratization and democratization (A. Tocqueville 1980: 348-80). The demand for equality in mass democracies can only be implemented through bureaucratic means of intervention. Equality of condition – and thus the inevitable subservience to and levelling beneath an increasingly powerful bureaucracy – may be preferred over the value of individual liberty. Moreover, Tocqueville pointed out that the technical indispensability of bureaucracy in democratized industrial societies is also associated with an increasingly *privatized* citizenry. The preoccupation with individual material welfare, a tendency to political apathy and an instrumental, 'consumer view' of politics are linked with a waning of a vigorous pubic sphere. The result is an institutional vacuum in which bureaucracy may extend its influence (see G. Poggi 1977: 3-84).

As I mentioned earlier, although Weber was sceptical about the possibility of substituting popular administration for bureaucracy, he regarded the issue of bureaucracy and leadership as a rather more open question. Weber viewed bureaucracy's proper function as being a technical instrument for enforcing policy ends that were determined ultimately elsewhere, e.g. by the politician in the state and the entrepreneur in the business enterprise.

Weber argued that policy-making is not a technical affair and hence not the business of the civil servant (M. Weber 1978: 1403-24). Whilst directors of these organizations should rely on their bureaucracies for technical advice in the formulation of policy, the final decisions are, ultimately, matters of faith and conviction. This is because value disputes are not resolvable by scientific judgements. Their resolution requires courage, coolness of judgement and leadership skills that are quite different from those required of officials pursuing bureaucratic concerns. This contrast in skills stems largely from the different responsibilities attached to political leaders and bureaucrats. The duty of the bureaucrat is to provide technical advice and carry out policy even if he or she disagrees with it. The ultimate responsibility for the policy lies with the political leader. It is the politician who should take the praise for successful policies and resign when they are discredited. From this difference in responsibility follow distinct work practices and motives. The job of the politician is to form a following in the struggle for power and to realize his or her values in the field of policy. The task of the bureaucrat is to pursue a career of service and to provide technical advice to policy-makers. Whilst to some extent the skills of leaders and bureaucrats may overlap in terms of ambition, leadership qualities and so on, their roles are most clearly distinct from the point of view of their responsibilities. Political leaders only aquire their capacity for leadership if they are accountable or responsible for their decisions to the wider community. This is secured in the modern state by the parliamentary supervision of government ministers' conduct of affairs and that of their officials. Weber later supplemented this view with the suggestion that a head of government should be a plebiscitory leader with an electoral power base independent of Parliament (D. Beetham 1985: 215–44). This would prevent political leadership being squandered on parliamentary politics at the expense of higher matters of policy. At the same time, the existence of parliamentary supervision of government and bureaucracy would ensure that checks on government would not exclusively be plebiscitory acclamation, as this was so susceptible to government manipulation. Effectively, parliamentary supervision of government required that it had the power to investigate as a matter of constitutional right. It also needed knowledge in order to overcome the tendency of bureaucracy to evade external regulation. Bureaucracy could do this by failing to draw a reasonable distinction between technical information and official secrets. The former refers to information that legally may be seen by popular representatives and understood by those with appropriate education. The latter are items of information that are legally confined to a few authorized personnel because of the security requirements of an organization.

For Weber, a strong parliament based on 'positive politics' is a crucial means whereby the public – or its educated sections – can acquire knowledge of policy and play an informed role in its supervision. Positive politics exists when parliament has the right to supervise the budget. Ideally, it also provides the personnel for ministerial positions, or at least provides consent without which a government cannot rule. Under these conditions, responsible political decision-making and the political maturity of the population can flourish. This analysis was the basis of Weber's critical appraisal of the political systems of Britain and Germany, and his qualified approval of the former.

Weber's detailed analysis of the problems of bureaucracy and leadership seem to involve a far more realistic consideration of political issues than do schemes advocating the abolition of bureaucracy and the introduction of direct popular control.

In his analysis of economic institutions, Weber concentrates on the importance of the entrepreneurial direction of the business bureaucracy, and minimizes the significance of the accountability of the business leader to the workforce. Indeed, as I argued earlier, the rationality of modern capitalist calculation depends on the fact that, ideally, labour as a commodity should be completely subordinate to the instructions of higher authority. It should be

19

unable to provide 'irrational' obstacles to the profitable organization of production, e.g. restrictive practices. However, in Weber's discussion, there *is* a parallel between the accountability of the business leader with that of the politician. The accountability of the entrepreneur is secured through the operation of the market, and thus of the success or failure of the firm as indicated by profit and loss. Meanwhile, the interests of labour are secured in a similar way: their discontent, if serious enough, is indicated by their departure from the organization. Weber is unwilling to recognise democracy in the workplace as anything other than an irrational obstacle to rational economic conduct of the firm.

Weber was convinced that market capitalism and parliamentary democracy offer superior forms of organization for the calculation of the demands of the consumer than does a system of central planning. The latter can never overcome the irrationality of values and thus conflicts arise over the best ways of allocating scarce resources. In addition, problems of scarcity are far more likely to be met under market conditions than those of central planning because of the undoubted advantages of flexibility that markets possess over planning in relation to meeting unforeseen circumstances and changes in social conditions. The concentration of power in a socialist society would lead to the aggrandisement of power and privilege by the bureaucratic and political elite. Full bureaucratization, and the attempt to 'abolish politics', would be bound to exclude the masses from political decisions even more than is the case under capitalism. Planning gives strategic power to the bureaucratic elite who, over time, would reward themselves accordingly and do so in a secretive manner as the contrast between the vision of socialist plenty and the reality of the persistence and worsening of scarcity became manifest. Those who questioned the validity of the 'end of politics' would be labelled as subversives. The decline of politics would be associated with a repressive state (J. E. T. Eldridge 1971: 191–219).

The barriers to the bureaucratic subordination of liberty present under capitalism and, on occasion, dismissed by Marxists as 'mere' bourgeois democracy would be removed: the rule of law, freedom of speech, parliamentary government; freedom of the press; the separation of powers in the political structure; and the separation of political and economic powers of market capitalism. Weber's discussion of the probable repressive features of socialist bureaucratic societies indicates his belief that divisions of interest in societies are not contingent upon class divisions. The political aspiration deriving from Marx and before him Rousseau, to abolish conflict and realize the general will through a concentration of power would be doomed to produce a bureaucratic dictatorship.

For Weber, the supervision of bureaucracy under conditions of market capitalism and parliamentary democracy offer more opportunities for the people to play a role in policy-making than would be the case under socialism. The socialist planning of society would add to the impetus of bureaucratization. For Weber and Tocqueville, this would mean that individual autonomy would be undermined even further by the increased dependence of citizens on bureaucratic provision of services by the state. This trend would pose a threat to liberty because of problems relating to oligarchy and the abuse of all power unchecked by countervailing forces. Socialist planning would involve the merger of institutional powers that are distinct in capitalist societies. Weber believed such a structure would provide a means for the most thorough coercive and despotic power yet devised by human societies. Weber also questions the optimism of the socialist theory of administration. It is based on a failure to see bureaucracy as technically indispensable in modern society, and a conviction that conflicts of interest in society will dissolve with the abolition of material scarcity. Whilst not without its problems, Weber's case against the Marxist theory of bureaucracy has still not been satisfactorily refuted. Indeed, many Marxist writers have preferred to ignore it or label it 'technicist', arguing that 'non-Soviet' socialism would be quite different from the oppressive arrangements found there.

Critics of Weber who have drawn on the theory of industrial society have identified a coercive bias in his account of bureaucratic surveillance. Whilst they have accepted the argument that technical imperatives make bureaucracy inevitable in modern society, it is argued that Weber failed to recognize that the character of bureaucratic administration would vary depending on whether it was enforcing policies over a population rather than on their behalf. Gouldner showed in his study of an industrial enterprise that this consideration was central in determining whether orders would be obeyed without coercion, and whether the bureaucracy was open to popular control (A. W. Gouldner 1954). To some extent this argument is similar to the Marxist one considered earlier.

However it does not involve a dismissal of the technical imperatives which make bureaucracy inevitable in modern society. Rather, it questions whether bureaucracy has to be organized in as coercive a form as Weber seems to assume.

This suggestion relates to an argument made by Parsons and others concerning the relationship between bureaucracy and professionalism. Whilst it is accepted that technical conditions in modern society require a proliferation of specialist administrative officials, Weber's assumption that these have to be arranged in a strict 'top-down' hierarchy is questioned. This argument involves differentiating two components in Weber's ideal type of bureaucracy: technical knowledge and legal competence; or knowledge and rational discipline (T. Parsons 1964: 58–61; T. J. Johnson 1972; M. S. Larson 1977: 178–207).

Complex administrative tasks may be performed by specialized experts on an individual or collegiate basis as in professional occupations. Of course, historically, members of these occupations have become separated from the means of administration and housed in large corporate or state-sponsored bureaucratic organizations. However, within such organizations, 'horizontal' collegiate principles of authority persist. In addition, obedience to higher authority on the basis of the recognition of superior knowledge rather than legal power make such organizations rather different from the military model that seems to pervade Weber's writings.

In modern bureaucracies, there are areas where strict top-down hierarchies of command do not apply; for example in the employment of specialist staff personnel in organizations, and the cases of matrix and project styles of team management (M. Jelinek 1981; J. Child 1977: 95–142). Weber seems to have overestimated the extent to which the chain of command in bureaucracies operates on the basis of legal compulsion between different levels of jurisdiction. Bureaucratized organizations can be viewed as collaborative systems of experts pursuing goals which command general consensus. For Weber, bureaucracy is always a component in a structure of domination, serving the interests of leaders involved in the struggle for power. Co-operative social relations seem to be quite marginal to Weber's theory of bureaucracy and his image of the nature of social order.

These qualifications of Weber's analysis of bureaucracy are important. The character of bureaucratic surveillance is likely to be different in those organizations where autocracy prevails and in those where policies are enforced on behalf of a collectivity. Critics are also right to stress that Weber underplays the significance of co-operation and rational persuasion in the decision-making of bureaucracies. On the other hand, it would be unwise to assume that bureaucracies enforce policies which command a general consensus either within the organization, or in the wider society. Weber's discussion of bureaucracy in the context of social conflict and the struggle for power is a far more realistic one than the perspective of consensus adopted by functionalist views of modern organizations.

Weber's failure to differentiate clearly between discipline and technical knowledge in his account of bureaucratic surveillance provides a link with the more recent writings of Foucault on this issue. Like Weber, Foucault's work may be regarded as a synthesis in social theory from a neo-Machiavellian standpoint. There are also some important contrasts between their views.

22

Foucault: Knowledge, Power and Surveillance

Foucault regards discipline and bureaucratic surveillance as constituitive features of modern capitalism. Weber's rationalization thesis is echoed in Foucault's analysis of the rise of 'disciplinary society'.

Foucault argues that power is not a thing possessed by an individual or group, but a *strategy*, the effects of which are realized through a network of relations and tactics. This network is in a constant state of tension, owing to the resistance of those subjected to it, and so power is always in the process of being achieved. Power involves a constant process of struggle, reaching into the depths of the social structure. Foucault also rejects the separation of power from knowledge. He advocates that we 'abandon a whole tradition that allows us to imagine that knowledge can exist only where power relations are suspended, and that knowledge can develop only outside its injunctions, its demands, its interests' . . . 'We should admit rather that power produces knowledge . . . that power and knowledge directly imply one another; and that there is no power relation without the correlative constitution of a field of knowledge, nor any knowledge that does not presuppose and constitute at the same time power relations.' (M. Foucault 1979: 27)

The history of power strategies, e.g. modes of punishment and social control is simultaneously a history of the forms of knowledge which constitute the mental assumptions and categories of both the subject populations and those in strategic positions of power. Central to Foucault's writings on bureaucracy and surveillance is the claim that there are close parellels between the surveillance and disciplinary systems of the modern prison, the factory, the hospital and military organizations. Whilst having complex historical roots, each reflects a *general* social transformation.

Forms of knowledge such as penology, criminology, medicine and military science are not simply useful adjuncts to power strategies but are the very social products of the technologies of power. In turn, these forms of knowledge are means for developing power relationships.

Foucault's analysis of the rise of disciplinary society in western Europe focuses on the sixteenth and seventeenth centuries. Significant innovations in surveillance were made in the military, religious, educational and penal institutions. During the eighteenth and nineteenth centuries, with the explosion of population, urbanization and industrialization, bureaucratic surveillance spread from these early institutional locations and became a constituitive feature of modern capitalism, penetrating thoroughly the whole social structure.

This can be seen in Foucault's analysis of the prison. He argues that

23

prisons were not a principal means of punishment before the nineteenth century. The new schemes for penitentiaries advanced in the late eighteenth century involved a break with existing prison regimes, and the application of surveillance techniques and forms of knowledge which had been pioneered in military and other organizations in the classical period of the sixteenth and seventeenth centuries. 'The classical age discovered the body as object and target of power . . . the great book of man the machine was written simultaneously on two registers: Descartes' anatomico–metaphysical and the techno-political . . . which was constituted by a whole set of regulations and by empirical and calculated methods relating to the Army, school and hospital for controlling or correcting the operations of the body.' (M. Foucault 1979: 136) What is reflected here is Foucault's emphasis on the social uses of the human body.

Power-knowledge relations are involved in a political economy of the body. 'Power relations have an immediate hold upon it; they invest it; mark it; train it; torture it, force it to carry out tasks, to perform ceremonies to emit signs.' (M. Foucault 1979: 25) In the field of punishment, a corpus of techniques and scientific discourses is formed and becomes entangled with the practice of the power to punish – providing a structure with parallels in other institutional spheres.

These disciplinary practices were both the products and the means of accummulating knowledge about individual behaviour in the form of documentary evidence. The history of the tactics of discipline is also the history of the knowledge 'disciplines' of penology, medicine and branches of military science.

The age of science in the sixteenth century illustrates Foucault's contention that the evolution of power and knowledge are two developments on the same axis: man was constituted as machine in knowledge as discourse and as a productive cog in a machine for the exercise of power as for example in the execution of war, or the education of particular populations.

The novelty of this new discipline of the body lay first in the scale of control exercised. Populations were not managed *en masse* but individually and in detail in regard to specific bodily movements and gestures. Moreover, the objective was to control behaviour by a discipline of the body rather than through a process of persuasion. Discipline was exerted through a continuous, uninterrupted process of supervision of the activities of the body according to arrangements that involved the partition of time, space and bodily movements. This new bodily discipline was structured through the organization of space and time in which the collectivity was broken up into manageable sections. The organization of space through the partitioning of 'barracks', 'wards' and 'prisons' created physically distinct locations within which people could be controlled. This partitioning of space was associated with the classification of populations into ranks and grades organized in systematic networks of lateral and vertical relations. The detailed military hierarchies of officers, non-commissioned officers and men, and emergent hierarchies in business are examples. These techniques facilitated individualized discipline and assessment. Discipline was also achieved through the creation of time tables which excluded idleness by defining a division of labour and a regular programme of routines and education. For example, in the field of military discipline, the drill of marching in step which, in time, made individuals components of a machine. Discipline was organized into distinct spatial and temporal structures, and, as a result, power became internalized and so became, to a considerable extent, invisible. Power as 'visible coercion' was supplanted by detailed disciplinary practices and the sustained observation and monitoring of conduct.

The regulation of behaviour was further secured through a 'panoptic' system of surveillance, which transformed the relationships between observer and observed. Surveillance was organized in such a way that each individual subjected to discipline was 'totally seen without ever seeing, whilst the agents of discipline see everything without ever being seen' (M. Foucault 1979: 202). 'Panopticism' is a system for ensuring the automatic operation of power. The principles of panopticism were laid down in the classical age in specific institutions – barracks, schools and workshops. Since the seventeenth and eighteenth centuries, modern discipline has spread throughout the whole social body, and this is best seen in the new prisons:

each individual in his place is securely confined to a cell from which he is seen from the front by the supervisor, but the side walls prevent him from coming into contact with his companions. He is seen but does not see; he is the object of information never a subject in communication . . . If the inmates are convicts there is no danger of a plot, an attempt at collective escape, the planning of new crimes for the future, bad reciprocal influences; if they are patients there is no danger of contagion; if they are madmen there is no risk of their committing violence upon one another; if they are school children there is no copying, no noise, no chatter, no waste of time; if they are workers there are no disorders, no theft, no coalitions, none of those distinctions that slow down the rate of work make it less perfect or cause accidents. The crowd, a compact mass, a locus of multiple exchanges, individualities merging together, a collective effect is abolished and replaced by a collection of separated individualities. From the point of view of the guardian it is replaced by a multiplicity that can be numbered and supervised; from the point of view of the inmates by a sequestered and observed solitude. (ibid.: 200-1)

How does Foucault explain why panopticism became the basis of the carceral, disciplinary societies of modern capitalism? Foucault's answer to this question illustrates a basic tension in his social theory. On the one hand, the new disciplinary strategy is understood in terms of the removal of monarchical privilege by bourgeois class culture. On the other hand, this strategy is a response to technical conditions in respect of the scale and complexity of administrative tasks. It is an extremely effective way of co-ordinating large masses of people. These 'general formulas, techniques of submitting forces and bodies . . . could be operated in the most diverse political regimes, apparatuses and institutions' (ibid: 221). The localized innovations of the classical period involved technical and epistemological discoveries relating to the effective exercise of power. Their spread is accounted for in terms of both technical superiority and class advantage.

The birth of the prison, for example, was linked with the class struggles of the late eighteenth century. Popular illegality constituted a politically serious challenge to bourgeois class power, as working-class criminality became fused with wider political struggles and challenges to the social order.

These developments led to 'a great fear' amongst those who sought to defend the emerging bourgeois order, and to a conviction that far from criminality being a political tendency in all citizens party to the social contract, it was almost exclusively a feature of a certain social class (ibid: 275). Criminals who were once to be met within every social class now emerged almost always from the bottom rank of the social order.

Foucault argues that the main functions of the modern prison are not to detach the criminal from contaminating moral influences (thus safeguarding the community) and to subject him or her to a discipline that produces a useful member of society. Rather, it stabilizes the system of bourgeois class power by separating 'criminality' from political opposition. Imprisonment results in a 'manageable delinquency', detached from emerging working-class struggles against modern capitalism. With the assistance of other institutions of social control, a swarming mass of a population practicing occasional illegality, which is always likely to spread and to become a formidable *political* force of class struggle, is replaced by a 'relatively small and enclosed group of individuals on whom a constant surveillance may be kept' (ibid: 275). In addition, delinquents could be directed to less dangerous and more manageable forms of criminality, confined to the fringes of society, limited in their power to attract popular support, and so rendered politically harmless and economically negligible. Meanwhile, the control and surveillance of manageable delinquency provides an opportunity for the policing and surveillance of the general population, through the search for dangerous groups or challenges to the existing order. The prison then, is the focus for the administrative production of a divided and more easily manipulated working class.

During the nineteenth century and beyond, 'the techniques of the prison [spread] to the entire social body' (ibid: 298). As a result, discipline concerned not simply the punishment of offences, but the deviation from normative standards in the regimes of the school and the asylum. In doing so, the disciplinary network of society does not simply await the arrival of the offender against the legal code. Rather, the institutions of almshouses, prisons, hospitals, apprenticeships, penal colonies, established a curriculum and a network of disciplinary practices that produced a docile deviant population. In modern society, the legitimacy of power to discipline the body is not centred on the legal apparatus but spreads throughout the 'carceral archipelago'. The proliferation of disciplinary networks such as social work outside of the prison, means that the prison loses its role as the core of the disciplinary society.

For Foucault, the emergence of bourgeois society is founded simultaneously on formal social and legal equality on the one hand, and a regime of the disciplines and substantive socio-economic inequalities on the other. All citizens are equal before the law, yet the criminality of the disadvantaged classes is identified as *the* principal area of criminality that requires the imposition of discipline. Similarly, formally-free labour in the capitalist economy encounters employers in a free contract, yet the appropriation of surplus value requires a disciplined subjection of the workforce in the capitalist business enterprise.

Whilst Foucault's account of the emergence of disciplinary society derives in part from Marxist social theory, it links even more closely with Weber's analysis of capitalism and surveillance. Although Foucault argues that the new disciplines were produced in the context of class struggles he also suggests that their main objectives were: (1) the exercise of power at minimal costs in terms of economic expenditure, political visibility and amount of resistance provoked; (2) to bring the effects of social power to maximum intensity, and to extend them throughout society without failure or interval; (3) to link the economic growth of power achieved by the discipline of different organizations so as to increase the utility and docility of the system as a whole.

27

Foucault does not, however, indicate clearly how this process of the 'parcelling' or partitioning of the human soul by the disciplines is linked with class struggle and the technical conditions of modern society. In addition, he attributes the disciplinary innovations of the classical age to an 'epistemic shift' or ideological transformation which enhances the production of social power, as with the new techniques of military organization. It is unclear how these different principles of explanation link together in Foucault's account of surveillance. There are uneasy relations between an idealist history of knowledge, a focus on class struggle, and the functional or technical imperatives of modern societies.

The key to this confusion is indicated by the presence of neo-Machiavellian elements in Foucault's writings. This seems to be the context for Foucault's suggestion that power pervades all social life, including knowledge. As with Weber, struggle is a constitutive feature of social life. It is not reducible to class analysis and economic scarcity despite Foucault's gestures towards Marxist theory. This position allows Foucault to argue that the capitalist enterprise, modern military organization, the hospital and the prison possess homologous disciplinary systems. They do not simply revolve around the central axis of the capital-labour relation.

The basis of Foucault's whole argument is power itself. He appears to argue that given the universal struggle for power, epistemic shifts such as those of the classical age have major social effects because they prove to be technically superior for the realization of power in a range of institutions. *Modern* surveillance techniques are inevitable because of their technical superiority in controlling mass populations.

However, this argument reverses the political optimism of Marxist social theory. The 'disciplinary cage' of modern society is regarded as all of a piece (A. Giddens 1981: 172–3). Foucault does not draw sufficient distinctions between the disciplinary practices of different institutions within capitalism, as, say, between the prison, military organization and the capitalist enterprise. There are distinctions to be drawn between the insitutions of bourgeois parliamentary democracies and those of fascist dictatorships; or between Stalinist socialism, and the market socialisms that have been developed partly in response to the traditional structures of the Soviet Union. In addition, the whole question of the relationship between interests and the disciplinary structures is pushed to the margins of Foucault's concerns.

If bureaucratic surveillance is constituitive of modern society, then it is difficult to see from Foucault's analysis how a socialist transformation of society would involve any major social change. Perhaps this is why, despite Foucault's positive gestures towards the struggles of the working class, his programme of political action is based on an anarchistic and individualistic critique of the discipline that pervades contemporary society. Foucault's politics is one of pessimism and inaction – a mirror image of his undifferentiated view of power and discipline (A. Giddens 1982: 215–30).

Foucault has made a major contribution to the social analysis of the relationships between surveillance and the rise of modernity, particularly in respect of characterizing the historical changes involved and exploring the links between power and knowledge. His insights need to be used to complement those generated by other strands of social theory. However, on the issues of the causes of surveillance and how some of its excesses might be countered, Weber's approach has a number of advantages. Weber argued that, for technical reasons, bureaucracy was inevitable in modern society. However, this did not preclude discussions of how bureaucracy could be supervised and directed. Whilst Weber exaggerated the degree to which bureaucracy was neutral in respect of class relations, he was concerned to discriminate between the administrative systems of capitalist and socialist societies. Furthermore, Weber's analysis of the development of bureaucratic surveillance is not couched in terms of a generalized will to power or an idealistic history without a subject, but in relation to historically specific struggles between classes, status groups and states. On these issues, Weber is specific where Foucault is rather vague.

Anthony Giddens: Surveillance, Power and Modernity

One contemporary writer who has sought to make the issue of surveillance a central problem in modern social theory, and to link it with an analysis of violence and warfare, is Anthony Giddens. His work is significant in that he seeks to synthesize elements drawn from each of the three traditions of social theory. Giddens notes how far the theory of industrial society and Marxism have dominated the agenda of modern sociology and argues 'with notable exceptions neither the expanded role of surveillance nor the altered nature of military power with the development of the means of waging industrialized war has been made central to formulations of social theory' (A. Giddens 1985: 294–51).

The sociological neglect of military organization and surveillance is not accidental (M. Howard 1981; M. Mann 1985, 1987; C. Ashworth and C. Dandeker 1987). As a number of writers have suggested recently, both the industrial society thesis and Marxist theory regard war as a transient phenomenon which will disappear with the maturation of modern society.

For the former, the normal development of the division of labour in and between societies ensures that peaceful activities of production and exchange supplant warfare as the dominant social activities. Relations of global interdependence provide conditions under which a peaceful concert of liberal nation-states can thrive. Aggressive nationalism will wane with the rise of a united humanity and the triumph of reason over tradition and the affectual aspects of human behaviour. So argued Durkheim, Spencer, Cobden and Bright.

In contrast, Marxist social theory regards warfare and military organization as aspects of the development of political struggle. This means that far from being a constituitive feature of a world of competing states, or in the modern age, nation-states, war is contingent on the existence of class divisions. Socialization of the means of production, and thereby the abolition of class divisions, preferably on a world scale, would remove the socio-economic basis of war and military organization and would preface a peaceful confederation of socialist states. This view constitutes a mirror image of the liberal vision to be found in the industrial society thesis. For one, capitalism is the root of war; for the other, it is the basis of peace.

The sociological neglect of war is, rightly, linked by Giddens to a similar point in relation to surveillance and administrative power. However, the view here is not that the two traditions of theory ignore surveillance and war; it is rather that these phenomena are considered as epiphenomena of other social forces. Surveillance, as a means of domination over other people, is regarded as a transitory phase of history. According to the theory of industrial society, the maturation of modernity will see the administrative co-ordination of social life undertaken by a technocratic elite, acting to supplement the operations of the market in pursuit of the common interest. For the Marxist theory of capitalist society, this role will be played by socialist planners, who will establish a framework of regulations within which many administrative functions will have, in any case, been returned to popular control. In both scenarios, the abolition of economic scarcity, albeit by different institutional means, heralds the end of fundamental human conflict and the beginning of an era of the administration of people over things rather than over other people.

These two accounts of modernity both hinge on teleological conceptions of social change – the dialectic of class on the one hand and that of scientific and technological progress on the other. The possibility that assymmetrical relations of administrative power and conflict between rulers and ruled are not contingent on economic scarcity or economic class division, but are independent elements in the structuring of human societies – a central theme in Max Weber's use of Nietzsche against Marx is hardly recognized.

In order to understand the proper significance of military power and surveillance in modern societies, Giddens considers 'right liberal' or conservative social theorists such as Weber and Hintze. They have focused on the state as a war-like entity. Furthermore they show a reluctance to view relations between rulers and ruled in economic terms preferring to regard struggles for power within societies and the division of modern humanity into competing and potentially warring nation-states as inevitable. In addition, it should be noted that these writers have often stressed the ways in which war has played an important part in the expansion of the surveillance capacities of the modern nation-state. This theme is in stark contrast with modern liberal writers, like Bendix and Marshall, who, in relying more heavily on the theory of industrial society, prefer to view the modern state as a 'political community within which citizenship rights may be realised, not as the bearer of military power within a world of other nation states' (A. Giddens 1985: 29).

Although recognizing the importance of 'Machiavellian' ideas in providing an overdue corrective to sociological orthodoxies, Giddens has three serious reservations about them. The first concerns their inadequacies in respect of identifying the peculiar features of the modern nation-state and the ways in which it connects with capitalism and industrial technology. Here, Giddens stresses that this is where the theory of industrial society and Marxism have advantages in showing how modern technology and market society introduced new sources of social change and provided the basis for the distinctive community of the democratized nation-state. The second weakness of conservative ideas is that there is a tendency to regard violence and war as inescapable elements of the human condition. The struggles between absolute values can only be resolved by the ultimate arbiter – force.

The third criticism of Machiavellian social theory is that while Marxist and industrial society theories have an unwarranted optimistic view of the nature of surveillance and administrative power, Machiavellian theory has an unnecessarily pessimistic, oligarchical conception of the relations between rulers and ruled. There is little scope in this analysis for determining the ways in which changes in economic relations and political power can effect genuine advances in the democratization of organizations.

Notwithstanding these three critical reservations, Giddens's recent writings seek to incorporate Machiavellian insights into a broader synthesis. Central to his current concerns is the idea that the contemporary world is constituted by a network of competing nation-states. The now universal appeal of the nation-state as a type of human community still seems robust in the face of the corrosive effects of global industrialism, the spread of market relations or of socialism. Giddens argues, further, that the means of violence and military power are fundamental features of human societies and will not wither away with the further development of modernity. They are, in particular, fundamental to the nation-state. Systems of administrative power, furthermore, cannot be conflated with economic class relations and, by implication, power and conflict more generally cannot be understood in terms of the conditions of economic scarcity or pre-scientific modes of thought. Giddens argues that modern social theory should break with its tendency to study societies as isolated entities and should instead locate them in the wider context of the emergent world system. Indeed, it is only in terms of this level of analysis that the development and current problems of nation-states as reflexively monitored organizations and the capitalist economic system can be properly understood. Contemporary social theory should also break with evolutionary assumptions and recognize the contingent or conjunctural nature of historical change. In this context, Giddens defends what he defines as a 'discontinuist' radical break with the past. One of the most important features of this break concerns the surveillance capacities of the most pre-eminent organization of modernity – the bureaucratic nation-state.

As was indicated earlier, Giddens argues that surveillance involves two activities: the accummulation of coded information and the exercise of direct supervision. Surveillance is a means of administrative power and, as such, is a means of establishing 'power containers'. Power containers are defined as 'circumscribed areas for the generation of administrative power' (A. Giddens 1985: 13). A locale can be converted into a power container if it 'permits a concentration of allocative and authoritative resources' (ibid.) i.e., means of controlling nature and people respectively. Such a process of concentration is favoured by a number of conditions, and Giddens focuses on four such factors. The first of these concerns the possibility of exercising surveillance within different types of setting. Echoing his defence of a discontinuist view of modern history, Giddens argues that non-modern societies are character-ized by very limited surveillance capacities, with the exception of cities. This situation is in stark contrast with modernity, which comprises an age of organizations. Here 'either large segments of the daily lives of social actors (as in factories or offices) or substantial periods of their lives in a more total setting (as in prisons or asylums), can be subject to more-or-less continuous surveillance.' (ibid.: 15)

The other three factors relevant to the transformation of a locale into a power container are specialization, sanctions and ideology. Drawing on Weber's discussions of the presuppositions of bureaucracy, Giddens points to the significance of a money economy in allowing the specialization of administrative officials who are not directly involved in material production. In highlighting 'the facilitation of the scope and intensity of sanctions, above all the development of military power' (ibid: 16). Giddens again echoes Weber in his view of the mobilization of disciplined force as the basis of the modern state. As a system of rule, the nation-state is quite different from the segmental structures of non-modern political forms, in which there remain significant sources of armed opposition to the central authorities. Thus, the differentiation of internal police surveillance from a predominantly external facing military power is a novel administrative achievement of the modern nation-state. The fourth factor relating to the development of power containers is ideology. Here Giddens is referring to the extent to which the symbol systems of the ruling authorities can gain sway over subject populations. This process can be encouraged by surveillance activities, e.g. through the mobilization and deployment of a literate class by means of a formal education system.

Giddens's discussion of power containers is linked with his classification of societies into three types – tribal, class-divided, and the class societies of modern capitalism. He contends that, although surveillance is a generalized feature of social systems, its significance as a mechanism of societal integration reaches its highest point in the age of modern capitalism. In tribal societies, 'tradition and kinship hold sway as the basic media of societal integration' and there is a minimal differentiation of system and social integration (A. Giddens 1981: 161–2). That is to say, these simple societies are reproduced primarily through face-to-face encounters amongst actors, rather than through the relations of institutional interdependence more characteristic of larger, more complex societies (D. Lockwood 1964; N. Mouzelis 1974). In class-divided societies, tradition and kinship remain as important mechanisms of societal integration but, in addition, the differentiation of 'social' and 'system' integration remains limited. The face-to-face, communal basis of existence is 'left relatively untransformed by the mechanisms of state administration and surplus product exploitation' (A. Giddens 1981: 162). Nevertheless, the emergence of propertied and ruling classes is, here, more strongly defined. The locus of power of these ruling classes lies in the city, as the principal power container. In the larger imperial types of class-divided societies, military power is of great importance as a mechanism of integration. Notwithstanding the development of central government, in the form of tax and military bureaucracies, subordinate populations are not subjected to regularized police surveillance: military power is crucial in overcoming armed opposition to the central authorities in what remains, in large part, a segmental social organization.

It is in the class societies of modern capitalism that surveillance is, in its bureaucratic modes, a principal means of integration, as it is in this context that the differentiation between social and system integration is most strongly defined. In addition, capitalist societies are pervaded by rationality, as is indicated by the rationalization of political authority and the spirit of calculation induced by the process of commodification in the economy. As an economic system rooted in the transformation of Europe in the sixteenth century, modern capitalism is defined in terms of commodity production. Two features of this 'commodification' mark it out as distinctively modern. First, the extent to which historical limits and inhibitions on market operations and the alienability of property rights have been overcome, and, second, the extent of the commodification of labour power.

Modern capitalism, as a global commodity system, is an age in which capitalist societies emerge. This is because such societies are also industrial systems and nation-states. A capitalist society is characterized by a capitalist economic system comprising an institutional differentiation of and insulation between economy and polity. In addition, the character of the state, although autonomous, is conditioned by the capitalist socio-economic order. As was indicated earlier, the distinctive relationships between state and society are viewed in terms of the principles of separation and surveillance. The state is a separate political and administrative order, but is able to supervise market society through bureaucratic surveillance in ways quite unmatched by other types of society. In the separate economic sphere, formally-free labour is disciplined by the increasingly bureaucratized management structures of the modern capitalist enterprise. However, the asymmetrical relations between capital and labour, rooted in the production relations of the enterprise, are mediated by the bureaucratic state. Both organizations are expressions of the impersonal character of modern capitalism as a class society.

Although capitalism is a global system of commodity production and exchange, capitalist societies are 'bounded entities'. Modern capitalism is, as it were, bigger than the nation-state. No single political authority can subordinate the global operations of the world system to overall administrative control. This is because capitalist development, and the social changes it has brought about, occurred in the context of the pre-existing, absolutist state system. The latter provided the political and military framework in which the modern nation-state could emerge. The wealth of capitalism and the industrialization of technology which it engendered enabled ruling classes to build new power containers that surpassed the capacities of the non-capitalist cities.

The modern nation-state is a 'bounded power container' (A. Giddens 1985: 120). It exists in a complex of other nation-states and comprises 'a set of institutional forms of governance maintaining an administrative monopoly over a territory with demarcated boundaries its rule being sanctioned by law and direct control of the means of internal and external violence' (ibid.: 121).

In the power container of the modern nation-state, surveillance is a principal medium of integration. It connects the economy and polity, and it operates also as a medium of administrative power in the control of formally-free labour within the business enterprise.

The main thrust of Giddens's analysis of the relations between surveillance and modernity has involved a critique of Marxist and industrial society theory. But he also draws on Machiavellian ideas, while at the same time revising some of their claims. Although Giddens has always been impressed by Weber's critique of Marx's theory of surveillance and administrative power, he wishes to distance himself from the pessimism dictated by Weber's own position, particularly in respect of the supposed inevitability of violence in human society and the indestructible iron cage of bureaucracy which appears to encase modern societies. In this context, Giddens reconsiders Marxist theory to counter Weber's reliance on Nietzche and to avoid Foucault's even stronger drift in the direction of Machiavellian social theory and its consequent one-dimensional view of the ubiquity of power (ibid.: 29-30). Thus, because power is 'everywhere', Foucault is unable to understand the peculiarity of the nation-state as a hierarchy of power and he is even more prone than Weber was to consider the possibility of democratizing power relations as closed rather than open to historical change.

The crux of Giddens's neo-Weberian analysis is his attempt to unite the competing claims of the three traditions of social theory. This is a worthy, but hardly unproblematic exercise. With Marx, Giddens argues that the capitalist enterprise, with its asymmetrical class relations between capital and labour, is a major arena for the contestation of power in modern capitalism. In addition, class conflict is seen as one of the central mechanisms accounting for the development of bureaucratic surveillance within the modern business enterprise. Nevertheless, the rise of bureaucracy within the firm was connected with the technical conditions of modern industrial production and emergent occupational struggles for power. These must be expected to occur whatever forms of property relations prevail. While Giddens does suggest that future advances in the democratization of the workplace are, in part, contingent upon changes in class relations, he has no illusions about the weaknesses in Marxist accounts of workers' control. However, at the same time, he castigates the attempts of Weber and Michels to apply the 'iron law of oligarchy' to these issues. Here Giddens appears to be approaching some of the recent ideas of Bobbio (N. Bobbio 1987).

While the capitalist enterprise and class relations have a broader social impact beyond the enterprise, struggles between capital and labour do not constitute the principal axis of modern societies. Giddens argues that such relations have a bearing on the form and content of state power, both internally and externally. However, in the area of external relations, in particular, he stresses that interests stemming from control over the means of violence cannot be reduced to those attendant upon possession of the means of production. Recent Marxist discussions of the 'autonomy of the political' are simply semantic attempts to square Marxist theory with the realities of power.

On the other hand, Giddens is suspicious of any idea of the interests of the nation-state as being completely above or separate from society and its economic class divisions, and most of all of the tendency to regard potentially violent conflict as an inescapable part of the human condition. However, by linking state power to class conflict, particularly in the field of internal relations (although there appears to be little reason to accept this particular argument), Giddens is careful to suggest that non-class forms of conflict are of equal significance in the contemporary capitalist order. Whatever the precise nature of the relationships between political order and class and other forms of groups conflict in society, Giddens appears to be sceptical of the possibility of removing either the relationships between rulers and ruled in any viable 'modern' social system, or the role of bureaucracy in mediating those relations. As will be seen later, here Giddens broaches issues of political theory, and particularly of the competing claims of liberalism and Marxism to offer a realistic model of what constitutes a 'good society' in an age of surveillance.

In conclusion, Giddens's account of the relationships between surveillance and modernity attempts to combine quite different strands of social theory. He seeks to analyse the ways in which economic class relations condition systems of administrative power yet also to recognize that the relations between rulers and ruled in organizations have their own logic and generate divisions of labour and power struggles which cannot be understood in the terms of Marxist analysis. However, in defending this position he wishes to distance his analysis from Foucault's view of power as ubiquitous. Foucault breaks the connection between economic class and political power that is so central in Marxist political theory. Giddens sees this as unhelpful to social analysis and as equally one-sided as economic determinism. To use his own terminology, if Foucault stands closer to Machiavellian ideas than does Weber, Giddens seems to place his own work closer to Marx than Weber himself thought prudent. In what follows, although Giddens's ideas are drawn on, they are used in such a way that the result is to turn social analysis back towards Weber's own project.

2

Surveillance: Basic Concepts and Dimensions

In this chapter, two themes are explored. First of all, the basic elements of surveillance activities are outlined. Second, I present the general argument that, with the rise of rational bureaucracy, the organizations of modern capitalism – particularly the modern state and business enterprise – have greater surveillance capacities than those characteristic of other types of society.

Surveillance, Rule and Organizations

In a general sense, surveillance activities are features of all social relationships. The exercise of surveillance involves one or more of the following activities: (1) the collection and storage of information (presumed to be useful) about people or objects; (2) the supervision of the activities of people or objects through the issuing of instructions or the physical design of the natural and built environments. In this context, architecture is of significance for the supervision of people – as for instance in prison and urban design; (3) the application of information gathering activities to the business of monitoring the behaviour of those under supervision, and, in the case of subject persons, their compliance with instructions. (Surveillance activities need not always be linked with relations of supervisory discipline; information gathering may simply be the means of constructing knowledgeable courses of action in relation to persons or objects which are autonomous from supervisory control. Military intelligence gathering by one state in relation to another normally takes this form.) However, here surveillance as information gathering and as supervisory discipline are to be considered as mutually reinforcing. When these activities endure over time they can be said to comprise the administrative basis of a relationship of domination between ruler and ruled. In this context, surveillance is not simply an aspect of all social relationships but an administrative means of reproducing a social system of rule. Although it is difficult to avoid tying the concept of rule to that of state, following Weber, the term is used here to refer to a durable system of domination whatever its institutional location.

Two further preliminary observations should be made at this point. First, as surveillance involves a deliberate attempt to monitor and/or supervise objects or persons, it is to be found in its most developed froms in formal organizations, which possess an explicitly stated goal(s), together with a formal administrative structure for achieving those goals, including arrangements for maintaining the boundaries and passages between the organization and outsiders. In this context, Giddens has referred to organizations as a type of human collectivity, 'in which knowledge about conditions of system reproduction is reflexively used to shape or modify that system reproduction' (A. Giddens 1985: 12). It can be said that modernity comprises an age of bureaucratic organizations. This is one indication of the long-term process of the rationalization of social action observed by Weber.

The second observation to be made concerns the issue of power and surveillance. Although surveillance is understood here as the administrative basis of systems of rule and particularly of rule in organizations, the temptation to consider rule by definition as always being exercised 'over' subject populations should be avoided. Indeed, organizations vary in respect of the power resources available to rulers and their administrative staffs; the accountability of rulers and staffs to subject populations; the type of information on subject populations that may be collected, the rights of subject populations to view that information and so on.

In the context of formal organizations, a number of connections can be traced between the three related meanings of surveillance outlined earlier and the concept of rule. A point of departure is to view the problem of how to reproduce a system of rule from the standpoint of a ruler and his or her administrative staff.

A system of rule involves durable, routinized relationships of command and obedience. As Weber suggested, rule implies that there is a high probability that commands will be obeyed in a stereotyped or predictable manner (M. Weber 1978: 53-4, 212-16; A. Giddens 1985: 7-17).

To achieve the objective of a compliant subject population, a ruler can use a range of sanctions stemming from control of economic, coercive or normative resources (cf. A. Etzioni 1975: 3-22). In constructing a system of rule, these resources can be mobilized around two related strategies: (1) to maintain and deploy punitive sanctions against rule breakers – this constitutes a power to punish after the event; (2) to devise mechanisms of excluding potential rule breakers from the opportunity to disobey instructions; this is a preventative power of control. The more successful the second strategy is, the less a ruler would have to rely on the first. This argument can be illustrated briefly by referring to some recent debates in the UK on the merits of the new community charge or 'poll tax'. Some have suggested that, from an administrative point of view, one advantage of the current rates system is that being levied on fixed property it is much more difficult for taxpayers to avoid payment than would be the case under the community charge. The latter system, being levied on every person, would provide far more opportunities for rule breaking in the form of tax evasion, even if the cost to the individual would be effective disenfranchisement. The greater opportunities for tax evasion would be likely to lead to an increase in the resources devoted to keeping track of individuals in order to reduce their chances of evading payment quite apart from the resources that would be required to punish those who succeeded in doing so. Yet the very nature of the new tax would make the provision of such administrative resources extremely costly as a proportion of the amount of revenue actually realized.

In any event, as has been argued in a neglected work (J. B. Rule 1973), neither of the strategies of gaining compliance outlined above is of much use without the administrative support of a surveillance system: the first entails a 'means of knowing when rules are being obeyed, when they are broken, and most importantly who is responsible for which' (ibid. 21–3). The second requires an 'ability to locate and identify those responsible for misdeeds of some kind' (ibid.). In the exercise of control, surveillance involves 'activities having to do with collecting and maintaining information' (ibid.). Acknowledging the difficulties involved, Rule seeks to draw a distinction between processes of surveillance and the exercise of powers of control. The latter are concerned with the 'actual management of behaviour through sanctioning or exclusion' (ibid.).

However, whilst there is a genuine distinction to be drawn here, following Foucault and Giddens, it seems more useful to consider the supervision or management of behaviour and the collection of information as two different types of surveillance activities. Particularly in the context of formal organizations, systems of rule are reproduced through these two mutually reinforcing surveillance activities: the very collection of information normally presupposes a certain capacity to supervise and manage behaviour and vice versa.

While surveillance activities are implicated in the reproduction of systems of rule, organizations vary considerably in respect of their surveillance *capacities*. It is difficult to point to concrete examples of 'total surveillance systems' except in the fields of literature and of sociological speculation about the authoritarian potential of modern societies (whether capitalist or socialist). However the outline of such a hypothetical system can be described as follows. From the standpoint of a subject population,

> there would be but a single system of surveillance and control, and its clientele would consist of everyone. This system would work to enforce compliance with a uniform set of norms governing every aspect of everyone's behaviour. Every action of every client would be scrutinised, recorded and evaluated both at the moment of occurrence and for ever afterwards. The system would collate all information at a single point, making it impossible for anyone to evade responsibility for his past by fleeing from the scene of earlier behaviour. Nor would the single master agency compartmentalise information which it collected, keeping certain data for use only in certain kinds of decisions. Instead it would bring the whole fund of its information to bear on every decision it made about everyone. Any sign of disobedience – present or anticipated – would result in corrective action. The fact that the system kept everyone under constant monitoring would mean that, in the event of misbehaviour, apprehension and sanctioning would occur immediately. By making detection and retaliation inevitable such a system would make disobedience almost unthinkable. (ibid.: 37)

From this hypothetical system can be derived four criteria with which to measure the surveillance capacities of different organizations and to specify what the expansion of those capacities entails. By implication they also point to the factors which might prevent the administration of an organization from approximating a total surveillance system. These can be referred to as:

1 The size of the files held in a surveillance system.
2 The centralization of those files.
3 The speed of information flow.
4 The number of points of contact between the system and its subject population.

The size of the files held in a surveillance system refers to the numbers of persons and items of information about them that can be stored. This information may be relatively simple and crude or, as will be observed in the

40

case of modern bureaucratic systems, more 'fine-grained' or precise and discriminating. Other things being equal, the more precise the information the greater the capacity of an organization to construct precise and subtle interventions of monitoring and/or control, as is well known to, for instance, those responsible for screening the credit-worthiness of modern consumers, market researchers and so on.

When the information files of an organization are highly centralized, it is possible to gather information on a person at any point in the system and then to use it to control that person at any other point. As will be seen in a later discussion, the cross-referral capacities of some modern computer systems or their capability of integrating knowledge from formally separate systems is regarded by some observers as indicative of a trend towards a more authoritarian state and the emergence of a 'society under surveillance' (p. 131).

The speed of information flow concerns the time taken for information on subject populations to be gathered, transmitted to a central point, processed and then used to supervise or manage their behaviour. Finally, organizations will vary according to how many points in the lives of their subject populations are available for the collection of information and the supervision of behaviour. In addition, systems will vary in respect of the ease with which deviants can be identified and their behaviour monitored consistently and continuously. These considerations involve the capacity to maintain a constant and detailed connection between an individual and his or her record or file.

Bureaucracy, Power and Surveillance: Towards a Typology of Surveillance Systems

Personal and bureaucratic surveillance

The main concern of this book is to analyse the development of bureaucratic systems of surveillance in the key organizations of modern society and, as a result, to show how these organizations expanded their surveillance capacities in terms of the dimensions outlined above.

This long-term process involved what Weber referred to as a shift from personal and patrimonial forms of administration to the rational and bureaucratic organizations of modernity. In the former, rulers have few means of controlling their subject populations beyond their personal powers of supervision and information gathering. They have no reliable, disciplined administrative staffs who can act on their behalf at a distance. Circuits of administrative control and information-flow are therefore extremely limited in terms of spatial and temporal extent. In respect of political structures, these limits have been breached by rulers through the adoption of a number of strategies: the delegation of administrative powers to members of the ruler's household, as in the creation of patrimonial regimes, or the delegation of administrative rights to autonomous power-holders in exchange for military service and loyalty, as in feudal patterns of rule. A third strategy involved the creation of rationally disciplined bureaucracies (M. Weber 1978: 255-65).

Modern bureaucracies are extremely durable structures. The economic and technological resources of modern industrial society provide the means of establishing permanent and rationally disciplined bureaucracies to an extent which would have been the object of envy to all pre-modern rulers for whom bankruptcy and administrative weakness or disintegration were routine features of the political landscape. Their resilience through time is matched by their surveillance capacities or the effect with which they can integrate and administer mass populations across vast spaces: for instance, compare the areas occupied by the contemporary USA and Soviet Union with the effective jurisdictions of the great agrarian empires of China and India (J. Hall 1986: 173-92). In this context, one should refer to 'time-space' as each dimension implies the other. For example, the barrier which spatial distance can pose to rulers who wish to ensure that their instructions are complied with by subject populations, can only be determined by considering the time required to ensure that sufficient resources are mobilized and delivered to any points of disobedience. Depending upon the social structure, 100 or 1,000 miles can have similar consquences in terms of the ease with which rulers can supervise their subjects. Modern systems of transport and communication have overcome natural barriers in ways quite beyond the capacities of non-industrial civilizations. Such conditions enable modern rulers to have a high 'presence availability' at the most distant points of their administrative networks (A. Giddens 1985: 172-91). Indeed, in many respects, industrial states, once defeated, are easier to administer than non-industrial ones simply because it is easier to identify strategic points which, when captured, are decisive for the effective control of a state.

Modern bureaucratic systems of surveillance not only provide effective means of administering subject populations; they also constitute a basis for 'willing the future'. This involves the collection of information from diverse time-space locations, including scientific forecasts of projected trends in order to plan the future of an organization. Thus the process of bureaucratization can be viewed in terms of an extension of the strategic horizons of the rulers of those organizations which undergo it at the same time as subject populations are increasingly made the objects of rulers' policies.

Surveillance in Autocratic and Liberal Systems of Rule

While the process of bureaucratization is central to a discussion of the growth of the surveillance capacities of the organizations in modern society, a second issue cuts rights across it. This concerns the connections between power and surveillance.

As I indicated earlier, in considering the ways in which surveillance activities reproduce systems of rule, a distinction needs to be drawn between rule over and rule on behalf of subject populations. This dichotomy derives in part from Mosca's social theory. In autocratic systems, the authority of rulers is generated at the top of the society as in doctrines of the divine right of monarchs. In what Mosca referred to as 'liberal' regimes, authority derives from the lower reaches of society and is couched explicitly in terms of the voluntary consent of the subordinate population (R. Bellamy 1987: 50-1). At this point it is necessary to clarify some terminological issues. The distinction between autocratic and liberal principles encompasses two related issues:

(1) the degree to which the ruled can exercise supervision over rulers and their administrative staffs;   (2) the extent to which the prerogatives of rulers are concentrated so as to facilitate arbitrary rule.

Mosca was careful to point out that, as he viewed it, 'democracy' cut right across the contrast between liberal and autocratic systems. That is to say, it is possible for rulers in both types to be recruited from a relatively narrow (aristocratic) or broad (democratic) social base. For example, he pointed to Imperial China and the Venetian Republic as examples respectively of autocratic democracy and liberal aristocracy.

However, as will be observed in more detail later, there is a sense in which 'democracy' is constitutive of modernity if, following Tocqueville, this term is used to refer to the condition of social and political equality. In this context, the rise of the masses as participants in the modern state has been associated with both liberal and autocratic systems, (what Tocqueville viewed as republican and despotic regimes). For Tocqueville, as for Weber, modern democracy in this sense is 'Janus-faced' and can be expressed in bureaucratic dictatorship or the rational-legal bureaucracies of liberal capitalism (J. Stone and S. Mennell 1980: 348-80).

As Hall and Mann have argued recently, although it is possible to identify a long-term trend in the growth of the surveillance capacities, or 'penetrative' and supervisory powers of the modern state, the spectre of totalitarianism in the twentieth century indicates that the same cannot be said of a shift from autocracy to liberal structures (J. Hall 1985; M. Mann 1988). This argument echoes Tocqueville's view: it is one thing to establish a bureaucratic state but it is quite another to establish durable arrangements under which rulers act on behalf of a subject population yet are also prevented from using the 'tyranny of the majority' (as in the one party state) to rule arbitrarily and to exclude the interests of large sectors of society.

Hall uses some of these ideas as the basis for a discussion of capstone and organic government and links this with a broader argument concerning the 'uniqueness of the west' and the rise of modernity (J. Hall 1986; C. Ashworth and C. Dandeker 1986). An organic system is strong in terms of its surveillance capacities; however this administrative power is made to serve interests that express a fairly broad social consensus. In contrast, capstone government is arbitrary in terms of the narrow range of social interests it serves yet severely limited in its capacities to gather information about and supervise the subject population. Hall uses the contrast between capstone and organic government to explain how modern capitalism, based on the primacy of the market and private business enterprise, developed so vigorously in north-western Europe. Crucial in this development was the impact of organic government. Modern capitalism flourished in the context of the adminis-trative and legal framework of the early modern state. The surveillance capacities of the state evolved especially in the fields of taxation, law and military administration.

Two conditions prevented the development of bureaucratic despotism or autocracy and the dysfunctional consequences of such arrangements for market capitalism. First, the marked rivalries between nascent western nation-states prevented the formation of a despotic hegemonic empire in Europe along the lines of Imperial China. Second, for reasons explored by Max Weber, the west was characterized by more liberal political structures, particularly from the standpoint of the capitalist classes. States either accommodated the interests of these classes, or, if political conditions for capitalist enterprise worsened in one society, the rivalry between nation-states enabled entrepreneurs to move to those states prepared to offer more favourable conditions for capitalist economic activities.

In the early modern west, a rare institutional complex thrived: this comprised 'strong' government in terms of its administrative power to 'penetrate' society – not so strong as to inhibit enterprise and initiative, yet not so weak as to discourage market transactions altogether. At the same time, this administrative power was linked with more liberal political structures than those prevailing in, say, Imperial China.

The conclusion to be drawn from the preceding discussion is that surveillance systems can be analysed in terms of two cross cutting

	Personal Administration		Bureaucratic Administration
Autocratic Interests	Petty tyranny		Bureaucratic dictatorship
		Patronage	
Liberal Interests	Direct democracy		Rational–legal

FIGURE 2.1 Systems of rule

dimensions: first whether their capacities are rooted in personalized or bureaucratic administrative structures; and second whether those systems reproduce autocratic or liberal systems of rule. These dimensions provide the basis of a typology in terms of which the main themes to be explored in this book can be defined.

In figure 2.1, four modes of surveillance are distinguished in ideal typical form. These can be described as petty tyranny, bureaucratic dictatorship and rational-legal bureaucracy. Petty tyranny and direct democracy will be referred to briefly before turning to the issue of patronage and what are viewed as the two main types of modern bureaucracy.

Under a petty tyranny, autocratic power is exercised over a subject population by a single person whose means of supervision and information gathering do not extend much beyond his or her own personal capacities. Their limited reach confines the realistic ambitions of such a person to a local area and population. As Weber argued, charismatic warrior bands, religious groups and criminal gangs through the ages have, on occasion, approximated to these arrangements (M. Weber 1978: 241–54).

45

In direct democracies, surveillance activities are carried out by all members of the collectivity in pursuit of popular interests, although this may result in the tyranny of the majority over the liberties of particular individuals or minorities. As is the case with petty tyranny, the means of surveillance are personal and informal; for example, in the ways in which some communities rely on gossip networks to ensure general compliance with normative standards (N. Elias 1965). In this context one can also refer to some anthropological discussions of the processes through which simple, stateless societies maintain social order without recourse to bureaucratic administrative structures (see S. Roberts 1979). In both petty tyrannies and direct democracies, surveillance activities are performed with little or no recourse to intermediate specialist officials.

Patronage and Surveillance

What has been referred to in figure 2.1 as the zone of patronage concerns transitional modes of surveillance that fall mid-way between personal and bureaucratic systems on the one hand and autocratic and liberal principles on the other. Under arrangements based on patronage, surveillance activities and the reproduction of systems of rule are tenuous social processes characterized by personalism as well as the anonymous or impersonal features more prevalent in modern societies. At the same time, surveillance activities are performed by specialist intermediaries who are autonomous from both the controls of the subject population and of the discipline normally imposed by modern bureaucratic systems.

The term patronage is used here in two senses: to refer to a social relation and to a social system (T. Johnson and C. Dandeker 1989). In all societies, one can identify patronage relations defined as durable, reciprocal relations of vertical or lop-sided friendship. As Bourne has argued, the essence of patronage comprises inequality of power resources, the reciprocity of services and the intimacy of friendship (J. Bourne 1986: 5). To this should be added the principle of voluntarism as the social basis for participation in patronage relations. These features distinguish relations between patron and client from those between lord and serf, master and slave and the contractual relations between employer and employee characteristic of modernity.

However, the social significance of patronage in societies fluctuates. In some societies, patronage relations play a strategic role. Here one can identify a patronage system defined not as a relationship but as complex, hierarchically organized chains of such relationships that provide the socio-economic and administrative basis of a system of rule: here patronage constitutes a means of surveillance.

There are two important structural features of patronage systems: (1) the dominance of vertical over horizontal relations of social solidarity; and (2) the effects of voluntarism in inhibiting the formation of inherited forms of power holding.

The existence of vertical relations connecting patrons with clients in a deferential social hierarchy inhibits the social significance of class or status forms of horizontal solidarity as well as undermining the potential legitimacy of egalitarian forms of ideology. Communal, status or class actions are not unknown but patronage ties and loyalties reduce the salience of these forms of group mobilization and integration.

Similarly, the institutionalization of personalized ties which are in principle the outcome of individual choices has the generalized effect of undermining the emergence of stable, hereditary structures of power holding. The incorporation of voluntarism into a system of resource allocation introduces a destabilizing factor as patronage operates as a competitive and pluralistic system: patrons are dependent on maintaining a high level of client support in a situation where clients are neither owned nor totally controlled and where client choice is a significant resource and dynamic in the system. In a deferential social order, the subordinate population can shift their client loyalties or have multiple patrons. At the same time, patrons as 'entrepreneurs' can compete for clients and are neither members of a hereditary status group nor disciplined bureaucratic subordinates of a ruler.

Societies based on patronage are associated essentially with transitional phases in state development and the wider process of modernization. Patronage provides the administrative basis of systems of rule where, 'political integration and social mediation are limited by the weakness of market forces and the ineffectiveness of central government' (J. Bourne 1986: 8). It emerges to facilitate economic and political relationships where the personal ties of kinship are no longer effective and the integrative and distributional effects of the market and rational-legal state cannot operate.

To refer briefly to material considered in detail later, (pp. 111-16) in England 'the vertical links of mutual dependence and obligation which we call patronage were . . . the natural cement of society in the middle years of the eighteenth century' (N. A. M. Rodger 1988: 275). Patrons were those in a position to bestow favours by reason of their property and control of appointments to places in estates, household service as well as official positions in Church and state. Clients were those who could claim to be friends and kinsmen of a patron, claims which rested on property and personal connection either directly, or through the activity of third parties (brokers).

Notwithstanding the hegemony of the landed class – sometimes referred to

47

as the Whig oligarchy – fluidity was a key feature of the social structure of England in the eighteenth century, as with any other system of rule based substantially on patronage. There were four principle sources of this fluidity: first the great landed families did not constitute a unified elite but were divided into factions competing for power and therefore for clients. Second, patrons did not constitute a closed society. Entry to their ranks could be gained through the accummulation of wealth. Third, the landed class led a society characterized by a complex social hierarchy with multiple sources of patronage (H. Perkin 1969; N. A. M. Rodger 1988). Fourth, and most important for the argument here, the hegemony of the landed class was diluted by the existence of what, from an administrative point of view, was a relatively weak state structure, and a division between central and local patronage powers.

Bureaucratic surveillance was not the principal means of sustaining the system of rule: as a formal organization, the state was ill equipped to supervise and gather information about the subject population, processes which rested on the more personal and informal basis of the patronage system. In this context, no patron could claim to monopolize the control of scarce resources in any social hierarchy be it the church, army or navy. For instance, the Royal Navy, as the most developed formal organization of English society at the time, in large part comprised a decentralized club of more or less important patrons each with their followers or dependents stretching from senior officers down to the ordinary seamen. The admiralty was not a monopolistic agent in the distribution of scarce organizational resources as it came to be in the Victorian age of bureaucracy. In this regard, the navy was simply a microcosm of the broader social realities of England in the eighteenth century (N. A. M. Rodger 1988: 273–302; C. Dandeker 1978).

At the same time, the patronage system was characterized by the predominance of vertical over horizontal principles of group formation and allegiance. As Perkin has suggested, 'class remained latent in the old society.' (H. Perkin 1969: 2) Thus, notwithstanding the existence of a broad horizontal division between gentle and common this was overlaid by complex grada-tions. In addition, the groups to be found at each level in the social hierarchy had more in common with their social inferiors and superiors who shared the same functional interests and activities than with others on the same broad social level. The possible exception to this was the elite despite their factional clashes. Those in the middle and lower reaches of the social structure, in seeking protection and advancement for themselves and their families, looked 'upwards' to patrons for assistance rather than 'outwards' to those on a similar social level in order to pursue a strategy of collective class action.

From the patron's point of view, clients were mobilized as resources in the competition for power in society and as security for their own positions in it through the exercise of personalized supervision or surveillance over their social inferiors. Yet this supervision was always tenuous because of the fluidity of a system of relations partially dependent upon the market. For this reason, patronage in the eighteenth century meant a social structure in which the subject population at one and the same time had many liberties and encountered a savage penal code.

Bureaucracy and surveillance

Attention can now be turned to the other two modes of surveillance indicated in figure 2.1. In modern societies, surveillance of subject populations is performed largely by bureaucratic officials in the context of formal organizations. However, two broad variants of modern bureaucracy need to be distinguished, each reflecting the broader institutional differences between capitalist (with the exception of fascist or similar authoritarian regimes) and the great majority of state socialist societies. These two administrative structures are defined respectively as rational-legal public bureaucracy and bureaucratic dictatorship.

Clapham has discussed the differences between these systems in terms of two conditions: first, the effective enforcement from above of a public ethic of correct behaviour; that is to say, a legal code commanding general acceptance which requires officials to administer the population impersonally through the application of abstract, formal rules to particular cases. Second, the enforcement from below of the accountability of the bureaucracy to the subject population. As Clapham argues,

> either the ruler or the public have an interest in bureaucracy run on correct Weberian lines: the ruler because it promotes effective hierarchical control and efficiency in carrying out the agency's defined task; the public because the rules reduce the opportunities for bureaucrats to exploit the clientele. Meanwhile, the bureaucratic officials, in the middle so to speak, possess considerable scope for discretion in respect of the gap between their actual powers, deriving from occupancy of their official positions, and the formal rules which define their use. (C. Clapham 1982: 26)

In circumstances where neither the ruler nor the bureaucracy itself are accountable to the subject population through some robust system of interest representation, the possibility of impersonal control of the bureaucracy and of the way it supervises the subject population will decline. The ruler is likely to become in practice accountable only to the bureaucracy itself on which he or she depends for the maintenance of a system of rule, rather than to the subject population. In other words, if all the bureaucracy has to fear is the wrath of the ruler, its power will be greater than in a system where the subject population also has the means of ensuring the accountability of bureaucratic behaviour. And then the bureaucracy itself will be able to maximize its powers of manoeuvre and, as in the context of the administrative history of the Soviet Union, become 'the sole corporation, whose interests . . . [the ruler] . . . cannot afford to offend while as the agency for implementing the ruler's policies, it will be well placed to block any initiatives which threaten it' (ibid.: 26–8). Furthermore, in order to carry out any policies at all, the ruler may have to reconcile him or herself to a strategy of patronage as a means of overcoming sources of bureaucratic resistance.

Of course, in the relational sense defined earlier, patronage is a universal feature of bureaucratic organizations; the key issue is whether patronage is the key or strategic principle of organizational behaviour. In bureaucratic dictatorships, it is likely that the autocratic ruler(s) may be forced into patronage as the principal way of managing the bureaucracy. Meanwhile, the subject population, armed with few means of guaranteeing the accountability of the bureaucracy to themselves, have only the choice of accepting its arbitrary behaviour or joining in the patronage game of bribery and corruption in order to divert scarce organizational resources their own way.

In bureaucratic dictatorships then, personalism and competition pervade the system; factionalism operates in such a way that the ruler cannot relate to the bureaucracy as if it were a dependable administrative machine.

This line of argument has important implications for a view of modern totalitarian systems of rule (A. Giddens 1985: 294–341). If a given system has little or grudging consent from the subject population, then while the latter might experience bureaucratic administration as arbitrary and something over which they have little control, the rulers themselves would have little effective means of supervising or knowing about what was carried out in their name. If consent is a significant factor in the maintenance of a system of rule, the possibilities for control over and knowledge about a subject population, somewhat paradoxically, would be rather limited from a ruler's point of view. Indeed it might be suggested that the scope for effective action by autocratic rulers would be relatively less than those situated in a rational-legal system and who, in principle, could command the more willing consent of broader sections of the population. In the former, bureaucratic surveillance would be ineffective but arbitrary; in the latter the reverse would be the case.

Thus in systems of rule reproduced by rational-legal bureaucracies, both ruler and bureaucracy are accountable effectively to the subject population and distribute resources according to a widely held ethic of acceptable bureaucratic behaviour. The ethic is enshrined in the legal and wider value system and secured through liberal structures of interest representation.

It should be borne in mind that the contrast between bureaucratic dictatorship and rational legal bureaucracy is an ideal typical one. It is a means of contrasting the different ways in which bureaucratic surveillance can reproduce systems of rule in different types of society – liberal capitalist, state socialist, authoritarian capitalist. Moreover, its purpose is to define the framework in terms of which more substantive themes can be considered below. The view to be defended here is that the organizations of modernity in the west have managed to come closer to approximating the ideal type of rational-legal bureaucracy than their equivalents in state socialist societies have managed to do so far.

Surveillance and Modernity

As I indicated earlier, the rise of bureaucratic surveillance in modern societies can be viewed in terms of three institutional contexts. Two of these concern the nation-state: they involve the part played by military power in the management of its external relations and the significance of police surveillance in the internal pacification of subject populations.

As Giddens has suggested, sociology and its object of study – society – are in large part the products of modernity (A. Giddens 1985: 172). If by society one means a clearly demarcated and internally well-articulated social entity, it is only relatively recently that large human populations have lived under such arrangements; and these have been the administrative achievements of modern nation-states. From a political point of view, the modern world comprises a network of competing nation-states and collectivities aspiring to that status.

Modern nation-states have well-developed bureaucratic systems for the internal policing of their populations as well as for the management of their external relations. Their systems of rule are legitimated in terms of the politics of citizenship and the bonds of national solidarity as expressed in language and customs, although of course, many nation-states are multi-ethnic or multi-national units. These distinctive features of modern nation-states can be outlined in more detail before focusing more specifically on the

51

impact of war and military organization on the development of their surveillance capacities.

The nation-state: bureaucracy, citizenship and military power

Bendix has argued that, 'the central fact of modern nation building is the orderly exercise of a nation wide public authority' (R. Bendix 1969: 22). In the west, there were four aspects of this political transformation. First, there was a long-term concentration of political authority. The political structure of absolutism anticipated one of the constituitive features of modern nation-states: 'where all people have rights, where all are subjects of one king; where the king in turn exercises supreme authority over everyone, we get a first intimation of national citizenship and one supreme authority over all public affairs' (ibid.: 57). With the French revolution, the 'democratic' will of the people replaced monarchy as the agency that wielded nation-wide political authority.

Second, the concentration of political authority was accompanied by a shift from functional to more individualistic systems of political representation with the extension of citizenship rights. In this context, Bendix, Marshall and, more recently, Giddens have discussed three types of citizenship rights: civil rights are those concerned with freedom of association, movement (including the right to sell labour and own property), freedom of speech and the rule of law. Political rights are concerned with the participation of subject populations in the exercise of political power and thus in the supervision of rulers. In contrast, economic rights 'concern the right of everyone within a state to enjoy a certain minimum standard of life, economic welfare and security' (A. Giddens 1985: 201).

Bendix argues that in the modern nation-state, 'each citizen stands in a direct relation to the sovereign of the country, in contrast with medieval polity' (R. Bendix 1969: 89–90). Although Bendix recognizes the importance of Marshall's discussion of three types of citizenship rights, in his own analysis he focuses mainly on the extension of civil and political rights to the lower classes. This process meant that wider sections of subject populations could speak for their own interests rather than depending on the patronage of their social superiors in whose houses or estates they served.

For Marshall, the emergence of citizenship involved a sequential development of civil, political and social (or what Giddens prefers to call economic) rights. Thus, in the British context, the civil rights realized in the seventeenth and eighteenth centuries provided the basis for an extension of political and economic rights in the nineteenth and twentieth centuries respectively.

Giddens's analysis of citizenship draws on Marshall's discussion but also departs from it in three important respects. Empirically, Giddens suggests that the extension of citizenship rights has been a more complex process than Marshall acknowledges. For instance, in Britain some civil rights were not extended until the twentieth century while yet others have been diminished. In Germany, Bismark's social reforms – the extension of welfare or economic rights – were instituted in order to forestall concessions on the political front (A. Giddens 1985: 205).

Secondly, Giddens prefers to view citizenship rights not simply in terms of phases of social development but rather as recurrent 'arenas of contestation' between rulers and ruled. Each cluster of rights is focused on a particular organizational and thus surveillance context: the police and society (civil rights); the electorate and the political organs of the state (political rights); and the relations between capital and labour within the business enterprise (economic rights). Thus in modern capitalist societies, a crucial area of citizenship rights are 'beyond' the state and anchored in an organization based on private property.

Thirdly, in explaining the rise of modern citizenship, Giddens departs from both Bendix's and Marshall's views. In sharp contrast with Marxist analysis, Bendix relegates class conflict to the periphery of his discussion of political modernization. On the other hand, Marshall views modern citizenship rights as providing a basis of (social democratic) compromise between the main classes of modern capitalism. Although Giddens accepts Marshall's view of some of the consequences of modern citizenship, he prefers to interpret class conflict as a medium for the extension of citizenship rights. This is in contrast to both Marshall's own suggestion that such rights have 'blunted' class divisions, and Bendix's marginalization of class in the social analysis of these issues. In the present argument, one qualification of Giddens's analysis will be to suggest that a significant motive for the extension of citizenship has been competition for military and economic power amongst states as well as struggles between classes within states.

The extension of citizenships rights in the modern nation-state has been dependent on the concentration of political authority: the allocation of equal rights to more and more citizens presupposes the development of an agency 'above' those individuals. However, the extension of citizenship rights is connected not only with this process of concentration but also with other features of the modern nation-state. These concern two aspects of modern bureaucracy: as a mode of public administration and as a means of surveillance.

In the modern nation-state, the administrative instruments of power become the property of the public rather than being privately owned by the monarch. The impersonal, public authority of the state is extended in modern polities and this process entails an institutional separation between state and society. The administrative functions of government generally become 'removed from the political struggle in the sense that they cannot be appropriated on a hereditary basis by priveleged estates and on this basis parcelled out among competing jurisdictions' (R. Bendix 1969: 128-9). This entails the 'development of a body of officials whose recruitment and policy execution were separated gradually from the previously existing involvement of officials with kinship loyalties, hereditary principles and property interests' (ibid.). As was observed earlier, this change means that patronage declines as the strategic mechanism in the recruitment to and operation of the administrative structures of the modern nation-state (pp. 46-9).

The fourth attribute of the modern nation-state concerns its surveillance capacities: these are produced by the use of rational bureaucracy for the administrative penetration of society. As Giddens and Poggi have argued, this development suggests a quite different meaning of separation from the one referred to above as a way of analysing the relationships between the modern state and society (A. Giddens 1981: 169-81; G. Poggi 1978: 92-116).

The modern state is separated from society in respect of the emergence of a public power from pre-existing patrimonial regimes. However, from an administrative point of view, pre-modern states and their rulers were far more separated from their societies than are their modern counterparts. They could not subject their populations to the fine mesh of bureaucratic surveillance evident in modern states.

In the context of the European ancien regime, the rulers of even the most absolutist states found it difficult to supervise and gather information about their populations. The presence availability of rulers was limited by a number of conditions.

A series of technical problems shortened considerably the radii of effective administration from a central point. Poor transport and communications, with roads impassable to wheeled traffic for much of winter made it difficult to administer subject populations in any detailed way. This remained the case until the end of the eighteenth century.

Demographic considerations were also significant: the population was small compared with those characteristic of modern societies, and widely dispersed in relatively self-sufficient communities. Only a small proportion lived in towns and cities. The limited social division of labour favoured a disperal of effective administrative control to the localities.

Economic factors reinforced transport and demographic limitations. The economy produced only a limited surplus for the tax system to channel into state coffers. Here was a vicious circle from the standpoint of rulers: limited economic resources made it difficult for rulers to build (expensive) reliable tax and military bureaucracies. In turn, limited bureaucratic development meant that it was difficult to channel those resources that the economy could produce into the hands of the state. Major state functions such as taxation and military force were, in varying degrees, decentralized to private contractors. This process of 'sub-contracting', and, in the absence of strategic financial control by the state bureaucracy, the corruption that went with it, constituted important obstacles to the will of the central authorities. However, this line of argument is not to deny the genuine advances made in central government administration during the late seventeenth and eighteenth centuries (pp. 62–3).

A further limitation on the administrative penetration of society by the central state was that the political aspirations of rulers encountered the jealously guarded prerogatives of local power-holders – in particular, agricultural landlords and city elites. In conjunction with the other limitations, this factor meant that the manner of state penetration depended largely on the form in which local and central powers were articulated (J. Hall 1986: 187–90).

Two broad patterns can be distinguished: on the one hand, local areas were subordinated politically and monitored by agents of the central authorities. However, for practical as well as political reasons, these arrangements were not accompanied by administrative supervision through rational bureaucracy. Central supervision of what went on in the localities depended upon the co-operation of local power-holders. This was tempered by their connivance at their own subordinates' reluctance to let the rulers divert local resources away from their own hands into those of the central state. Localism existed despite impositions from the centre. Coupled with the tendency towards autocracy, these emergent despotic arrangements were characteristic of absolutist France.

On the other hand, as in England, colonial and post-colonial America, the political and administrative powers of local privileged classes were held relatively independently of the sanction of the central state. The latter was even more delimited in its surveillance capacities and political prerogatives. Its aspirations were confronted by the self-confident independence of the localities. In addition, the central power was more amenable to influence by the middling orders of society than was the case in the more despotic or autocratic regimes. For this reason these arrangements can be defined as a liberal set of institutions.

However, in both patterns, central governments were relatively weak in respect of their surveillance capacities. The real differences between them concerned the degree to which they could monitor and manipulate local power-holders and make themselves susceptible to popular interests. In both cases, the state was relatively separate from society from the point of view of its surveillance capacity. Of course, as Hall has suggested, this may have meant that liberal structures could achieve more in respect of mobilizing resources for war or other collective actions than other more autocratic systems (see also N. A. M. Rodger 1988: 164–204).

The emergence of the modern nation-state can then, be identified in terms of a combination of four attributes: the concentration of political authority; citizenship as the political basis for the relationships between rulers and ruled; administration by public bureaucracy rather than by patronage; and administration of society through bureaucratic surveillance.

In this overall process, war and military organization were of central importance. First of all, the armed forces constituted the most significant branch of the early modern state in terms of relative size, organizational complexity, consumption of state expenditure, and means of power projection – both internally and externally. Second, war was the most important motive for the establishment of the modern state as a durable and well-articulated social entity. As Paul Kennedy has argued, 'the post 1450 waging of war was intimately connected with the "birth of the Nation state" ' (P. M. Kennedy 1988: 70). The bureaucratization of military power in the west was connected symbiotically with the development of the capitalist economic system: an expansion of military power depended on the technical, financial and organizational resources of commercial and industrial enterprises; at the same time military power, and especially naval weaponry, aided the global economic expansion of the west overseas in respect of new markets for raw materials and exports. It also provided an important stimulus to capitalist industry and commerce by way of demands for textiles, timber, iron and later steel, chemicals and other goods. All these resources of the capitalist system were channelled into military activities through loans raised by states on the developing financial markets and revenue secured through the tax system (W. McNeill 1983: 79–101; C. M. Cipolla 1965; M. Howard 1976: 38–74).

Bearing in mind this symbiotic relationship between economic and military resources, war was an important motive for the conduct of the state and military organization the most important feature of its administrative structure. Thus, military organization provides a clear example of the association between bureaucratic surveillance and the modern nation-state.

There were distinct phases in the bureaucratization of military power. In the argument defended here, particular attention is paid to the effects of what Roberts has called the 'military revolution' of the late sixteenth and early seventeenth centuries (M. Roberts 1958). During this period, the foundations of the modern armed forces as a fusion of professional and bureaucratic principles were laid. This process can be discussed by focusing on changes in the relationships between three groups: the central authorities, the officers' corps, including the important NCO or supervisory class, and the ordinary soldiers and sailors themselves. The state transformed military organization from a system comprising autonomous, largely self-equipped mercenary formations, employed by contracting captains, to one based on professional servants of the state, disciplined in a bureaucratic hierarchy and owing allegiance to the state alone. This process constituted a shift from a system based on petty and competing patrimonialisms to a unified rational-legal order for the administration of military violence. By 1700 the outline of all that is modern about the modern armed forces was visible (M. Howard 1976: 54).

By the eighteenth century,

the enhanced authority and resources of the state ... gave to their armed forces a degree of permanence which had often not existed earlier ... Power was now national power, whether expressed through the enlightened despotisms of eastern Europe, the parliamentary controls of Britain or the later demagogic forces of revolutionary France. (P. M. Kennedy 1988: 75–6)

In the nineteenth century, further developments in the bureaucratization of military discipline can be linked with the impact of the industrial and democratic revolutions. In that context, attention can be focused on the ways in which modern technology and the national citizenship state altered the relationships between military organization and society and increased substantially the capacity of the state to deploy bureaucratized military power.

In the twentieth century, two particular aspects of the bureaucratization of military power stand out: first, the relationships between modern technology and surveillance in military organizations; and second, the impact of the demands of war on the growth of state surveillance beyond the military sphere into the wider society.

During the two world wars and beyond, the seemingly ever-increasing pace of technological change continued to enhance the capacities of the state to mobilize, deploy and control military power. The technical demands of war not only led to an enhancement of the ability of the state to exercise surveillance over its armed forces but also to a tightening of the networks of surveillance over the rest of society. Although this process was rooted in the industrialization of war in the nineteenth century – particularly in the equation linking citizenship and military service – the main connections between war and what is referred to here as the rise of the 'security state' were forged during the two world wars and the subsequent nuclear age. Whilst some of the advanced societies have lessened their dependence on mass conscripted armies, it remains the case that defence and security issues have provided important grounds for supervising the civilian population in time of war or threat of war.

The bureaucratization of military power has, then, been an important aspect of the rise of the modern nation-state. War has been perhaps the most significant motive for the formation of the modern nation-state in the west, and military organization its most crucial arm, particularly of course, in the field of external relations (M. Mann 1988). Yet as was pointed out earlier, the institutional differentiation of internal and external relations was itself an achievement of the nation-state. As Giddens has suggested, the process of modernization is accompanied by a decline in the routine use of military power within the territorial boundaries of states and an increased focus on police surveillance as a means of supervising subject populations (A. Giddens 1985: 103–21, 172–92). This issue provides a second substantive theme in the overall view of surveillance to be defended here.

The nation-state: surveillance and policing

The rise of the modern nation-state is marked by the development of specialized bureaucratic organizations concerned with the management of its emergent external and internal boundaries. With the process of modernization, the focus of the armed forces is increasingly on external matters while the populations within the boundaries of the nation-state become the subjects of police surveillance.

The flourishing of capitalist institutions based on the primacy of the market not only released resources for state bureaucracy in the field of tax and military administration; it also undermined the social basis of traditional structures of law and order, the core of which comprised face-to-face community sanctions. In the mid-seventeenth century, law and order rested on a combination of traditional mechanisms and those expressing the new authority of the central state. They comprised an amalgam of military violence, a spectacular and brutal penal code and a deferential social hierarchy of patronage constituted by personalized relations of dependence and surveillance. Within these structures of social control, subject populations had routine freedoms from the surveillance of state administrators because the impact of market society was more than the traditional structures of community regulation and the new penal powers of the state could accommodate. This situation was in sharp contrast with the everyday life of those who live under the fine administrative nets characteristic of the modern nation-state.

The conjunction of the capitalist market and the industrial revolution in the late eighteenth and nineteenth centuries altered dramatically the social and spatial structures of populations and created a more impersonal society; one that Ignatieff has referred to in a telling phrase as a 'society of strangers' (M. Ignatieff 1985). These social changes ensured that the mechanisms of law and order inherited from the pre- and early modern periods were called into question. The outcome was a wholesale rationalization of social relations: the military and tax officials were joined by police, prison and other state bureaucracies concerned with the surveillance of the subject populations of modern nation-states.

Modern industrial capitalism not only created a society of strangers; it also gave rise to the 'birth of class' (H. Perkin 1969: 176-217; A. Giddens 1973: 132-5; 1981: 157-81). As Giddens has suggested, the peculiarity of modern capitalist societies derives not simply from the existence of class relations but also from the ways in which class structuration operates to connect economic inequality and social solidarity with political order. In this context, the distinction between class and class-divided societies becomes relevant. The similarity between the two relates to the inequalities of power deriving from property relations. The difference is that in the former these inequalities are mediated by a market that constitutes them simultaneously as horizontal ties of solidarity and vertical relations of antagonism. As Marx once put it, in a sense capitalism and the bourgeoisie created class society (A. Giddens 1973: 32). The extension of the market in the industrial age ensured that the potential for conflicts between capital and labour shifted from unconnected local struggles to more nation-wide encounters between classes and their political organs. With modern industrial capitalism, the potential for such vertical and horizontal class relations in both rural and urban contexts undermined the vertical connections and horizontal rivalries of the patronage system. Class politics became matters of the autonomous self-expression of interests rather than the heteronmous issues of paternalism and patronage. As will become evident in the more substantial discussions of policing later, an adequate view of the nature of police surveillance in the modern nation-state would have to connect its emergence with both the impersonality as well as with the class nature of the contemporary social order.

In this book, the main focus in respect of police surveillance concerns the impact of the birth of class and a society of strangers on the structures of law and order in the old society of the eighteenth century and the processes through which new police organizations were constructed. The administrative systems of what are termed 'indirect rule' within the old society were supplanted by bureaucratic control: local community based and semi-privatized means of administration were substituted by formal bureaucratic state organizations. The rise of a separate public power was linked with a more detailed bureaucratic penetration of society by the state. A number of processes need to be distinguished (S. Cohen 1985: 13–29; M. Ignatieff 1985).

First, there was a decline in the public infliction of corporal punishment and the emergence of imprisonment as a means of punishing criminal offenders. Second, the birth of the prison and a rationalized legal code were aspects of the emergence of a more consolidated state, armed with the means of penetrating society in ways quite unmatched in previous eras. A continuous, rational, discipline of society by the state replaced the arbitrary, and, ironically, permissive regimes of brutality characteristic of the old society. An important component in this new system of rational discipline was the new police force.

Third, the emergence of the prison as a state controlled formal organization for the housing of criminal offenders was accompanied by a panoply of other bureaucratic organizations concerned with the reprocessing and incarceration of deviant populations. The asylum was one important example. Such organizations came to share a similar administrative routine despite their distinct social functions.

Fourth, as in the sphere of military organization, the growth in the bureaucratic surveillance of subject populations was simultaneously a matter of discipline and knowledge. Discipline was based in part on the collection, storage and application of knowledge about individuals. The exercise of supervision and the accumulation of information became the occupational basis for a range of bureaucratically controlled professions. Again, as in the military sphere it will be suggested that these emergent professions were not simply creations of the state, nor could they be construed as servants of the dominant economic class. Rather, their interests and expanding influence in the institutions of what was to become a 'disciplinary society' (J. O'Neill 1986) were to a substantial degree self-determined and outcomes of opportunism.

Capitalism, surveillance and the business enterprise

In the account of modernity and surveillance defended here, a third focus of discussion concerns the bureaucratization of the capitalist business enterprise. Recent attempts to explain the rise of the west have focused on two features of European societies: the intense military and geopolitical rivalries between nation-states, and the economic struggles amongst capitalist enterprises for markets and profits (J. Hall 1985; M. Mann 1987; W. McNeill 1983). These two arenas of struggle have been interlocked in such a way as to provide the institutional basis for the dynamics of western capitalist societies. On the one hand, the struggles between nation-states prevented the establishment of a hegemonic empire and the consequent bureaucratic stifling of capitalist enterprise; on the other hand, political fragmentation was limited in extent: the European system of nation-states pacified territories and provided a political and legal framework for stable markets and capitalist activities. Capitalism extended in parallel with the expansion of western military and political power beyond the European context. For the last 300 years the capitalist economic system has always been 'bigger' than the nation-state and thus able to both rely on its political guarantees yet not be subordinated to a single regulating agency (A. Giddens 1981: 182–202). The growth of the modern business enterprise should be located in this broad institutional context and the bureaucratization of its surveillance capacities can be linked specifically with two phases in the development of the capitalist economic system. These are referred to as competitive and organized capitalism respectively (J. Habermas 1976).

In the context of a more 'directing' rather than 'facilitating' state, the economic system of modern capitalism centres less on the small and medium sized firm and more on large business enterprises operating in more administered markets. As in the discussion of the nation-state, the business enterprise is approached from two somewhat artificially divided perspectives: first, the external relations of the firm with its environment, particularly the consumers of its products and business competitors; second, the internal administrative structure of the firm. Again, within the enterprise, as with military organization, the focus is on the relationships connecting three principal actors: the directors of the enterprise, the emergent managerial hierarchy and the labour force. The growth of bureaucratic surveillance within the firm involved a shift from personal to bureaucratic control: entrepreneurial ownership and direct control of small enterprises (often approximating petty tyranny) gave way to the impersonal control of large enterprises by a directorate employing a managerial hierarchy.

This broad development was linked with the movement from competitive to organized capitalism. It was characterized by distinct phases which are discussed here from the point of view of both external and internal exigencies of the business enterprise. Focusing on external constraints, the growth of the firm can be viewed in terms of Chandler's idea of the 'visible hand' of management (A. Chandler 1977). This refers to a process of the internalization of market transactions amongst autonomous enterprises and their subjection to managerial control through bureaucratic procedure in the

61

context of a single firm. The invisible hand of the market is supplanted by the visible hand of bureaucratic management. This process meant that the organizational boundaries of the firm, or the divisions between internal and external, changed over time.

The emergence of a managerial hierarchy involved an occupational differentiation of functions once performed by a single individual. This division of labour resulted in a separation of line and staff and, again in parallel with military organizations, the development of corporate planning of the firm's operations and strategy.

The growth of the firm and the visible hand of management were linked with a shift to a more collectivist economy, dominated by a relatively small number of large corporations, and characterized by a more directing state. At the same time, the social and geographical basis of capitalist production and distribution altered. The orbit and interests of the larger firms encompassed ever-wider areas; from regional to national to international and global concerns for the very largest enterprises.

As firms expanded and internalized operations, often through acquisitions, a number of strategies were adopted by their directorates in order to exercise control over subordinate managers in the increasing number of organizational units. In the case of direct acquisitions, there was usually an extension of bureaucratic control. Under cartel systems, more informal collegial relations were constructed with other enterprises in respect of fixing prices, production quotas and market shares. In the case of holding companies, control was exercised largely on the basis of financial influence rather than administrative commands. In each case recourse could be had to systems of interlocking directorates to ensure that a parent company or its 'dominant coalition' could control the policy of subordinate managers (J. Scott 1985).

While bureaucratic control through direct acquisition provided the tightest form of surveillance, its exercise did not imply a unilinear process of centralization. Some firms resolved the problem of controlling very large, and functionally and geographically diverse enterprises by introducing administrative techniques already developed in military organizations. Primary amongst these was the divisional system. This involved the decentralization of operational management to autonomous divisions and the centralization of strategic planning and financial controls in the head office of the enterprise. The emphasis on strategy and accounting controls in such enterprises added a further impetus to the occupational differentiation and professionalization of management.

While the large companies grappled with the administrative problems attendant upon an increase in the number, diversity and dispersal of their organizational units, they also sought to monitor and influence other aspects of their external environment. Other than the state itself, principal amongst their concerns was the behaviour of the consumer. A focus on the behaviour and intentions of consumers was linked with attempts by enterprises to benefit from the economies of large-scale production and regular volumes of market demand. In the USA the large firms, particularly in the field of motor cars, pioneered the modern techniques of advertising, after-sales service, market research, the trade-in, consumer credit and brand loyalty, now common features of the contemporary economic order, yet quite novel in the 1920s. The creation of a network of bureaucratic surveillance over consumer behaviour had two important consequences. First, the creation of additional occupational specialists in this area of 'consumer management', as well as in that of strategic planning, i.e. of future operations products etc. Second, the growth of vast amounts of information on consumer behaviour, which recently have become valuable commodities in themselves in the form of mailing lists, files on credit worthiness and so on.

A second view of the relationship between bureaucratic surveillance and the modern business enterprise can be developed by studying the internal administrative structure of the firm where the focus is on the changing relationships connecting the directors of the enterprise, the emergent managerial hierarchy and the labour force. In this context, issues relating to the management of labour are central although not the only concerns. Indeed the argument to be defended here is that one of the major weaknesses in many Marxist discussions of these questions is the quite mistaken view that problems of management are largely to do with the 'labour process'. As in the study of the nation-state, Marxist analysis has all too often focused on internal at the expense of external relations and constraints.

A number of phases can be identified in the shift from what can be termed the petty tyranny of many of the early personal enterprises of competitive capitalism to the deployment of complex managerial hierarchies in modern corporations.

Despite the administrative achievements of the early industrial enterprises – they marked a break with many typical eighteenth-century business practices – their surveillance capacities were quite limited. New forms of bureaucratic discipline co-existed with systems of 'indirect rule' (deriving from occupational traditions of the old society) in the industrial enterprises of mid-nineteenth-century capitalism. An analysis of sub-contracting reveals that these systems of indirect rule were structurally similar to those identified in the discussion of the emergence of the modern state. During the period 1890–1930, these structures of indirect rule were replaced by more extensive systems of bureaucratic surveillance as a result of the introduction of systematic or scientific management.

Although this change has been linked by many writers to the process of 'de-skilling', it was a far broader development than that: scientific management cannot be understood solely in terms of the struggles between capital and labour. Nevertheless, one result of scientific management was the achievement by the directorate of enterprises of a far more detailed surveillance over the whole process of production.

Since that period the managerial surveillance of the labour process has extended beyond the area of work roles more narrowly conceived. Firms have sought to extend their surveillance powers into the social and psychological context of workers' lives, particularly in the spheres of 'morale' and career regulation.

To sum up, the analysis of surveillance defended here draws on the ideas of Weber, Foucault and Giddens. The growth of surveillance in modern societies is understood in terms of a growth in the surveillance capacities of organizations. This process is understood in terms of a shift from personal to bureaucratic control via intermediate forms of patronage. In modern capitalist societies, bureaucratic surveillance comprises a combination of control over and on behalf of subject populations. This is certainly not to underplay the hierarchical nature of surveillance in these societies, but it is to draw a distinction between the systems of administrative power in liberal capitalist, authoritarian capitalist and state socialist societies. This was the point of the dichotomy between liberal and autocratic principles.

The growth of bureaucratic surveillance can be explored in three broad institutional contexts: the external relations of the nation-state and the field of military power; the internal relations of nation-states and the formation of police surveillance; and the business enterprise in the modern capitalist system.

Capitalism – that is to say, generalized commodity production as the economic core of class societies – has been a central force in these administrative developments. Its importance can be seen in the establishment of the feedback loop between military and economic power and thus the formation of modern nation-states; in the undermining of patronage and personalized forms surveillance as the principal media of societal integration and thus in providing the material basis of police surveillance; and in creating the mass markets for labour and other commodities as a context in which the modern bureaucratic business enterprise could flourish.

While capitalism was a major force behind the growth of bureaucratic surveillance, bureaucracy was also linked with other features of modernity: the constraints of industrial technologies, the power interests of professional occupations linked with emergent bureaucratic organizations; the power needs of states; and, of course, as Weber stressed, the inherent technical advantages and momentum of bureaucracy itself.

The more detailed analysis of surveillance takes as its point of departure the 'old societies' of western Europe in the eighteenth century. These were class-divided societies in which, despite the achievements of the previous two centuries, the organizations of the state had quite limited surveillance capacities. On the other hand, it was the state rather than the economic sphere which was at the leading edge of bureaucratic development.

3

Military Power, Capitalism and Surveillance

In this and the following chapter, the relationships between surveillance and the modern nation-state are explored. As I indicated earlier, the distinctive features of the nation-state derive from an emergent division between external and internal relations together with a corresponding specialization of bureaucratized military power on the one hand and police surveillance on the other. Here, the focus is on the development of the armed forces as a bureaucratized arm of the modern state.

In this context, three related historical themes are explored. First, the division between external and internal relations involved a monopolization of the means of violence by the state. The corollary of a predominantly externally facing military organization is a pacified domestic population. In the domestic sphere, the population does not, as a matter of routine, provide sources of collective armed opposition to the rule of the central authorities. In this sense, war and peace are two sides of the same coin (M. Howard 1983: 7–35; A. Giddens 1985: 103–15). This process was a long-term development characterized by the phases of feudalism, absolutism and the modern nation-state. The starting point here will be the eighteenth century – a point at which this process was well advanced, particularly when one compares the organization and role of military bureaucracies at that time with their counterparts during the era of the Thirty Years War.

This point provides a link with the second historical theme: the bureaucratization of the armed forces. This process involved a transformation of the relationships connecting the central authorities, the emergent military profession and the other ranks. Personal and patronage forms of administration were replaced by bureaucratic systems of surveillance. The monopolization of force was achieved through bureaucratization. There were a number of phases in this development. With the triumph of absolutism in the sixteenth and seventeenth centuries, mercenary service gave way to the principle of exclusive service to the state. By 1700, the basic characteristics of the modern military had been established: a state machine responsible for and capable of maintaining a full-time force in war and peace, paying, feeding, arming and clothing it; and a coherent hierarchy of men with a distinct sub-culture of their own, set apart from the rest of society not only by their specialized function but by their habits, privileges and responsibilities (M. Howard 1976: 54; W. McNeill 1983: 117–43; M. S. Anderson 1988: 24–134).

Standing armies and navies meant that the organizational forms developed by mercenary forces could be transformed by systematic drill into military discipline. In this way, soldiers became component parts of a military machine which, through a hierarchy of command and control by officers and their subordinates, could be readily manipulated by generals in the field. Similar developments occurred in relation to the formation of specialized fighting navies. Important changes after 1700 involved the prevention of officers from offering their military services to other states, the full establishment of regular salaried employment, and a general subordination of their occupation to state bureaucratic regulation with respect to recruitment, training, promotion and compulsory retirement (N. Elias 1950; C. Dandeker 1978).

In the nineteenth and twentieth centuries the modern officers' corps was constituted by its sponsoring client, the state, as a fusion of profession and bureaucratic organization (G. Teitler 1977; J. A. A. Van Doorn 1965; M. Janowitz 1960). An expert officers' corps was organized into a bureaucratic hierarchy of powers of command. This was in contrast to other professions whose early development, while facilitated and guaranteed by the state, was not directly sponsored and controlled by it in the same way. Of course, in the twentieth century the age of the independent lone professional in non-military fields has also waned in the face of the emergence of bureaucratic employing organizations. Now no profession can escape what the military experienced from an early stage – increasing intervention from business enterprises or from the state itself. (T. J. Johnson 1972; M. S. Larson 1977: 178–207).

Parallel with the emergence of the military profession was a bureaucratization of the authority relations between officers and other ranks. This involved the emergence of forms of rational-legal discipline within military organizations; a process that was connected with the emergence of a 'citizenship state' and the shift from class-divided to the class societies of modern capitalism. That is to say, the military systems of western societies in the twentieth century have relied less on physical coercion and more on normative means as 'social order has come to rest on the consent of the subordinate population' (S. Wesbrook 1980: 250; C. Dandeker 1985).

The third historical theme in this chapter concerns the relationships between bureaucratized military power and modern capitalism, together with the ways in which these were mediated by the tax systems of the modern state. The monopolization of force and the establishment of the professional military as an agency of the state was facilitated by the reciprocal relationships between war and wealth which were the basis of the growth of western global power. The process of commodification released liquid wealth which the central authorities could tax and use to build expensive military bureaucracies. Particularly in the field of naval warfare, military power provided a basis for the further expansion of commodification, which in turn released more resources for building the political and military power of western states. This reinforcing 'feedback loop' or cycle of development was particularly well defined from the sixteenth century onwards (W. McNeill 1983: 63–117).

By the eighteenth century, European societies had constructed substantial military bureaucracies together with the tax and logistic structures on which they depended. However, there were a number of limits on the surveillance capacities of these military organizations. These limits or sources of friction were not simply problems of military administration, but were connected with the broader organizational features of class-divided societies.

The Military Revolution in Western Europe and the Foundations of the Modern State

If one surveys the European scene in the eighteenth century, despite their administrative limitations, the armed forces of states were probably the most developed organizations from the standpoint of surveillance. By the end of the seventeenth century, Europe comprised a number of competing dynastic states. Their political authorities had largely subordinated the feudal lords, often employing them as paid officials in their burgeoning central administrations. At the core of these states were the emergent tax and military bureaucracies which had been forged during the period 1550–1700. As a result of this process, the mercenary systems of military organization which had flourished in Europe with the revival of the market and subsequent corrosion of feudal social relations, had been in large part supplanted by those of professional military organization under state management (M. S.

Anderson 1988: 13-134; M. Howard 1976: 38-74; W. McNeill 1983: 63-143).

By the end of the seventeenth century, then, European states had acquired sufficient control of their territorial resources to maintain standing armed forces and to wage prolonged campaigns, almost as a matter of routine. These permanent forces were also subjected to a rationalization of discipline. Roberts has conceptualized these social processes as a 'military revolution' (M. Roberts 1958). Their importance lies in the fact that they provided the material basis of the modern state as a surveillance machine. For as Gilpin has suggested, 'in conjunction with what has been called the military revolution the modern bureaucratic state also came into existence . . . the exercise of military power became an instrument of foreign policy; war was no longer the (unrestrained) clash of societies' (quoting M. Howard 1983: 15) that was characteristic of warfare in the ancient and medieval worlds (R. Gilpin 1988: 607).

According to Roberts, there were four aspects of this military revolution: (1) the tactical organization and control of manpower; (2) strategic development and the formation of the professional officers' corps; (3) the scale and intensity of warfare; and (4) the burden on the wider society in terms of cost and administrative implications. For the present argument, emphasis will be placed on the first and second developments. Both relate to the extension of surveillance over military organization by the state.

In relation to tactical matters, smaller sub-units were trained to co-operate in more complex patterns of organization, instead of the simpler mass organization of pike squares with protective sections of muskets. Maurice of Orange recognized that firepower was the decisive element, rather than the shock of mass pikes. He devised tactical formations composed of lines of co-ordinated musketeers as a means of maximizing the regular delivery of firepower against an opponent. This focus on sub-units and their co-ordination made military force less like a mere massed body and more akin to a complex machine of closely co-ordinated cogs and mechanisms. Linear deployment and the dependence of officers on subordinates to manipulate sub-units of men allowed the co-ordination of the various specialized arms and the maximization of the delivery of firepower. This system was established on the basis of a ruthless period of discipline in which, through repeated drills, men were trained to obey orders unquestioningly and in a rationally calculable manner. It was no mean feat to train men to load, fire, march back a set number of paces to let another row of men fire their own guns, reload their weapons, and then march forward in order to fire once more, all in the face of the death and destruction around them. Firearms and rational discipline meant that a continuous and regulated stream of fire could be delivered against an opponent and that, when necessary, men could be ordered to dig defensive positions to protect themselves.

The drills established in this period were remarkably similar to those canvassed by F. W. Taylor in the industrial sphere 250 years later, and there is little evidence to suggest that such disciplinary mechanisms are an invention of modern industrial capitalism. The act of loading and firing a gun was broken down into a number of simpler actions, each of which was to be learned in a manner laid down in detail and in advance by a higher authority. Each movement was then to be enacted in sequence, immediately on receipt of an order or number. Continuous repetition of the sequence made the soldier more efficient in the firing of weapons. He also became an element in a system of gunfire controlled by higher authority and co-ordinated through an elaborate administrative hierarchy of commissioned and non-commissioned officers which controlled the sub-units of military force – the companies and battalions. It should be noted that armies comprised a combination of professionals, mercenary forces and volunteers, usually drawn from the most disadvantaged sectors of society. This was because in a society where political rights were the prerogative of the few, the state preferred not to require the majority of the tax payers to serve in the military. Rather it wanted them to stay in the economy producing the wealth required for war (H. Strachan 1983: 8–22).

This social basis of military organization meant that, without rigid discipline, any initiatives by the men would tend towards desertion or plunder. The machine-like standing armies of the late seventeenth and eighteenth centuries could not rely on the initiative of the ordinary soldier in combat. The 'soldier as automaton' was confined to a limited number of pre-learned soldierly routines. The power of a disciplined infantry was allied to a similarly disciplined shock cavalry and more mobile artillery on the battlefield. One symbol of the new discipline of precision drill was the introduction of the uniform. This expressed the administrative dependence of the soldier on the funds and supplies provided by the state, and was also an additional means of ensuring that the soldier subsumed his identity beneath that of the military organization.

The second important aspect of the military revolution concerned the growth of bureaucracy and the professionalization of the military. The rationalization of discipline provided the central authorities with a means of constructing far more ambitious strategies of military operations. A whole sequence of large-scale movements in space and time could be designed and executed without the fear of one's forces running away. However, the rational discipline of soldiers and their use for more adventurous strategies presupposed the subordination of officers to a more bureaucratic chain of command. This bureaucratization of the upper levels of the chain of military command transformed officers from a collection of ill-disciplined military captains into an officer corps of graded service ranks subject to a corporate military discipline of their own. Officers lost their autonomy in respect of the recruitment, payment and administration of their units. As a result they became bureaucratic servants instead of powerful, independent patrons. This process was not completed until the nineteenth and twentieth centuries. However, major advances were made in this period. As Howard argues in relation to the French army in the 1640s, 'senior officers were aristocrats reluctant to acknowledge any allegiance to the Crown, refused to serve under each others' command and conducted their quarrels flamboyantly in public and on occasion on the battlefield itself.' (M. Howard 1976: 63) However, by 1700, France and other states had ensured that, whilst commanders of regiments remained responsible for recruiting and paying their men, they lost their control of supply and equipment to the administration of the central authorities. In addition, they were required to account in detail for their military expenditures. Meanwhile, their professional training was supervised more effectively. Insubordination was punished, and disciplinary standards improved generally. The new uniform of officers had an equivalent symbolic significance to that worn by the men – the subsumption of their identity in military organization. A more disciplined officer corps constituted the means of command and control by which monarchs implemented their strategic demands through military operations.

With the pressure of war amongst the competing states of Europe, the advantages of the 'new discipline' meant that all states which could afford to do so and pursued power, adopted it. The United Provinces was joined by England, Sweden and Brandenburg as the military revolution spread in Europe. Accordingly, the scale of warfare increased. By the eighteenth century, warfare had become a subtle game with well-defined principles based on the rational discipline of standing armies, siegecraft, lines of communication and the art of logistics or supplies for the men in the field. By this time, warfare was an activity carried out by monarchs according to established procedures with dependable specialized instruments of force relatively insulated from the tax providing civilian sphere. States had managed to mobilize violence through the pacification of their territories and the regulated projection of force to external enemies.

Despite the advances achieved during the period 1650–1700, the officer corps in the eighteenth century was not a rational bureaucracy. Recruitment, training and discipline were only partially bureaucratized. Although the regimental units were equipped by the state, they were raised, paid and administered by their commanding officers. Originally they had paid the ruler for the privilege of raising a military unit. They gained a return on their investment by husbanding the resources received from the state to pay the men, and by engaging in more or less corrupt dealings with supply tractors to the armed services. As with the rest of state administration, corruption was a serious drain on the financial means of military organization.

These 'irrational' elements in the bureaucratic military organizations of the eighteenth century were linked with other obstacles that inhibited the state's surveillance capacity in this area. Three of these were of particular significance. First was the problem of logistics – that of supplying, maintaining and transporting troops, supplies and equipment. To equip up to 70,000 men in the field with food and supplies required careful planning and meant that food stocks (gathered in the previous harvest) had to be placed at fortified positions in advance of the route of campaign. Of course, during all campaigns troops, where possible, lived 'off the land' or through plunder. Thus armies tended to campaign in areas of potential agricultural surplus. Yet the limitations of agricultural productivity ensured that armies could not give up their reliance upon the umbilical cord of supply. This limited their movement.

Second, these difficulties of supply were reinforced by the impact of poor road communications and the limitations which the horse and foot placed upon the mobility of armies. These logistic and communications difficulties ensured that, despite the destructive firepower provided by rationalized discipline, warfare depended on the art of siegecraft, march and counter-march, the mastering of communications, and the ability to endure in the field longer than the opponent. Wars were won and lost not so much through the destruction of an opponent's forces (though there were on occasion destructive bloody battles), but through logistic and financial exhaustion. The latter could be inflicted without the risk of the destruction of one's own expensive forces, and thus with experience came to be regarded, not unreasonably in the circumstances, as a very effective way of fighting a war (H. Strachan 1983: 8–22). Wars were thus 'limited' in the sense that states were quite unable to mobilize the resources of their whole societies for war (even should they have wanted to) and those resources were quite limited despite the advance in commercialization. In the field, logistic and communications difficulties ensured that the chances of the potentially destructive meeting of massed forces were not high, unless one or other opponent was fairly sure it had the advantage. A third source of friction related to the command and control of military forces. Mechanical discipline meant that the initiative of the soldiers could not be relied upon. Indeed, without this discipline the tendency to desert was high. Deployment of troops in battle took a great deal of time, quite apart from the problems of supply and

72

movement. Thus, flexibility on the battlefield was not a distinctive feature of eighteenth-century warfare. Military discipline was secured through a command and control system which relied on oral and written instructions carried by aides of senior officers, whose intelligence gathering rested on reconnaisance troops, occasional recourse to spies and their own eyesight aided by telescopes.

Important changes in the command and control of armies occurred in the latter half of the eighteenth century, particularly in France. These became elements of a further military revolution which was implemented by Napoleon in the context of the nationalist upsurge released by the French revolution. These changes concerned techniques of command and control, organization structure, logistics, the importance of initiative and firepower. As a result, the relationships between force and surveillance were transformed in ways which to some extent anticipated the industrial age of total war in the twentieth century.

The command and control system was improved with advances in intelligence gathering. Map reading and topographical techniques raised the strategic awareness or horizon of commanders and of course greatly assisted in the more effective planning of compaigns. Detailed plans were committed to paper and transmitted to subordinates by officers specially trained in staff work, i.e. the movement and supply of troops and thus overcoming of time and space. Although these early developments in staff work did not replace the personalized planning of compaigns by individual generals, they aided the flexible control of force (D. D. Irvine 1938).

A further improvement in command and control systems concerned the divisional system. This was a means of subdividing an army into autonomous units, each relatively self-sufficient in respect of all the various arms, and thus able to act independently and defend itself if caught on the move. The divisional system allowed a commander to subdivide his army, so allowing the components to use different roads and supply routes from one another, and so avoiding the congestion caused by a single mass using one route. It also allowed an army to disperse for swift movement in order to concentrate at a pre-arranged point into larger groupings for an encounter with an opponent. The employment of the divisional system required careful staff planning and co-ordination of troop movements for it not to collapse into dangerous disorder. For divisions to move autonomously, the dependence on a central logistic chain of supply had to be lessened, and the reliance upon forage and plunder increased, a change which presupposed major advances in agricultural productivity. Finally, the movement of troops in this manner also presupposed improved road communications (ibid; H. Strachan 1983: 34–51).

In relation to tactical control, the flexible use of the column and the line improved the mobility and firepower of armies. Troops were trained to deploy in columns or in a defensive line for attack or defence as conditions dictated. In the second half of the eighteenth century, the firepower of the infantry, which had lessened the significance of cavalry, was now thwarted on the battlefield by the destructive power of lighter and more mobile artillery. Troops could be aided in their advance by skirmishers ahead of the main body engaged in drawing enemy fire, harrying enemy forces, sabotage and the like. Soldiers involved in such activities required a greater initiative than that possessed by the ordinary soldier trained in the drill of mechanical discipline. The use of skirmishers not just ahead of the main body but in the main body itself, and, indeed, the blurring of the boundary between soldier and skirmisher was achieved in France as a consequence of the French revolution and the development of a citizens' army (H. Strachan 1983: 25-37).

The forces released by the French revolution enabled Napoleon to implement the military innovations of the late eighteenth century in a new social and political context (W. McNeill 1983: 187-215). There were two important features of this development. First, under the Napoleonic military system, very large armies could be deployed and controlled through a flexible organization structure. Crucial in this was the divisional system, although Napoleon relied on a personalized planning system rather than developing a fully-fledged staff organization. At least in the short term, Napoleon's organization (and strategy, of course), gave him decisive military superiority. Second, Napoleon's political and military system marked a break with the ancien regime in which war and military organization were relatively insulated from the wider society. This concentration of violence and pacification of territory had been a major achievement of absolutism (M. Howard 1976: 73-41). Wars had been fought by professionals and without a wholesale conscription of the resources of society, in part for fear of causing the economic and political collapse of the ancien regime. Now war was being fought through a total mobilization of resources. This involved a major extension of the state's bureaucratic surveillance of society in respect of taxation, military conscription, policing and censorship.

However, there are important qualifications to make about this argument. As McNeill has argued, in the 1790s the successes in military recruitment owed a good deal to population growth and civilian unemployment as well as to the bureaucratic power of the state (W. McNeill 1983: 187-206; I. Woloch 1986). In addition, the limited effectiveness of the bureaucratic provision of supplies to military organization meant recourse to the corrupt contractor system of the ancien regime. Finally, a good deal of the material resources for war were gained by plunder and levies enforced on foreign populations rather than by the bureaucratic control of France itself.

Nevertheless, the administrative and military achievements of the Napoleonic system were considerable: the nationalist democratic revolution provided the political context in which population growth and the agricultural revolution allowed the state to mobilize manpower resources for military purposes in numbers not approached in previous eras. Yet the financial and administrative instruments of the state were blunted by the limitations of time and space posed by agrarian societies. It was the process of industrialization and the attendant revolution in the organization of 'force' 'time' and 'space' which allowed states to fully realize the potential of the Napoleonic military system. Following Pearton (1982) these terms are used as follows. They are interdependent strategic elements: *force* refers to the amount of destructive power that can be mobilized and deployed by a military organization. *Time* and *space* are particularly closely intertwined dimensions and concern the ease with which military units can be moved from place to place and the degree to which orders and other communications can be sent from one part of an organization to another. In short, time and space concern the limits on the capacity of an organization to subject its component units to rational control.

However, it should be said that for the first 40 years of the nineteenth century, European states for the most part attempted to re-establish the old eighteenth-century socio-political and military order, which the forces unleashed by the French revolution and tapped by Napoleon had done so much to destroy. These issues will be discussed after examining the bureaucratization of naval organizations in the period 1600–1800.

Force, Surveillance and Naval Power

The revolutions in land warfare during the period 1600–1800 were paralleled by similar developments at sea. Here too one can identify a growth in the state's capacity to mobilize force and subject it to rational discipline. Again, the focus is on three actors: the central authorities, the officers and the men. First, there was a change in the relationship between the officers and the central authorities. This involved the creation of a disciplined officers' corps out of an informal collection of temporary naval appointments and thus the emergence of a more specialized, permanent naval war machine. Second, there was a more gradual change in the relationships between officers and men: this involved the emergence of a specialized core of seamen, subjected to a disciplinary system. This legal code was relatively arbitrary. Whilst officers became more disciplined servants of the state, from the perspective of the men their discretion remained immense until the flourishing of more rational-legal systems of authority later in the nineteenth century.

From the sixteenth to the late eighteenth century, naval force assisted in the commercial expansion of the north European states. Trade increased the resources available to the state in the form of tax receipts or returns on its own commercial speculations. This provided the financial basis for the expansion of military and naval organizations. Military power provided the means for the economic penetration of other societies by private and state assisted capitalist adventurers. For western states and their capitalist economic systems power became more *global* in scope (A. Giddens 1985: 103-16; W. McNeill 1983: 147-50; P. M. Kennedy 1988: 70-99; C. M. Cipolla 1965).

This 'feedback loop' between capitalist expansion and military power meant that trade and commerce, profit, voyages of discovery, technological improvements in naval and land warfare were all interconnected. Nevertheless, throughout this period, the expense of equipping a capital intensive navy could pose the threat of bankruptcy to governments. In addition, the ships could not easily be laid off in peacetime. They had to be maintained and replaced, though many governments for short-term financial reasons failed to do so, at their later cost. It was not until the later seventeenth century that anything approaching a standing navy could be produced by the richer states of England, France, Spain and the United Provinces. Against this background, the rationalization of discipline was associated with important changes in the technology of naval warfare.

Until the fifteenth century, war at sea was largely an extension of land warfare, fought by soldiers when their mobile 'castles' were transported to close combat. With the creation of artillery, ships could fight at a distance. Sailors became fighters and the most important personnel on board. With this merger of fighting and sailing skills, naval war as a specific occupation emerged (N. Elias 1950; M. Lewis 1948: 59-99). The differentiation of naval from land warfare and commercial shipping was consolidated by a gradual improvement in techniques of command and control exercised over squadrons and fleets of ships acting in concert. This process presupposed the financial conditions that permitted large numbers of ships to be employed regularly at sea, and it occurred in the context of an intense struggle between the north European and established Mediterranean states for maritime supremacy. To ensure that the maximum amount of firepower could be directed towards an enemy, commanders of ships had to be trained to sail in a 'line of battle'. Only ships which could both withstand and inflict a heavy broadside artillery, whilst having similar (albeit limited) manoeuvrability could be part of the line of battle. Other ships, lighter in weight and firepower yet speedier and more manoeuvrable, could perform reconnaisance and related functions. Whether acting in concert or in single combat, the firepower of warships depended for its successful delivery on disciplined drills.

The co-ordination of a fleet of sailing ships required not only a considerable degree of seamanship, but also a system of communications between a commander in chief and his subordinates. Besides conferences of officers, the development of a system of flag signals was a crucial means of co-ordinating the movements of ships within telescope vision. Ships further away had to be contacted by sending a ship with verbal or, more usually, written instructions. At sea, as on land, time and space were major obstacles. Fleet commanders and central authorities had to cope with the fact that letters from London to the Mediterranean station could take from four to six weeks to arrive, whilst those from London to the Far East could take up to nine months. Mobility, and thus the pace of naval war, were limited by wind and tide. The capacity of the state to control and monitor the application of force was limited. Consequently, power was decentralized to commanders on the spot, and in turn to subordinates when out of sight of their supervisors. Nevertheless, within these limitations, by the late eighteenth century the dominant power – England – had established the basis of a global infrastructure of naval power with permanent naval station commands.

The emergence of fleet organization, an expanding knowledge of strategy and tactics, and a system of 'command, control, communication and intelligence' (or 'C3I') provided the context for the emergence of a naval officers' corps (C. Dandeker 1978; M. Lewis 1939; J. Ehrman 1953). As officers became more regularly employed, states began to pay them a retainer when not employed at sea, so facilitating their recruitment in time of war. This constituted the financial and administrative basis for the emergence of a *service* of ranks from an informal collection of posts. For example, until the second half of the seventeenth century an officer in the Royal Navy was appointed to a command for a specific occasion, and might subsequently be appointed to a more or less important command. He might be a lieutenant on one occasion, a captain on another, and then again a lieutenant. The naval 'service' was no more than a collection of these commands at a given point in time. However, the specialization of naval war and the more regular employment of fleets encouraged the emergence of a structure of *ranks* for officers. This meant that an officer once appointed to a position of lieutenant, commander or captain kept that title as a rank when he left the ship, and received an appropriate salary for so doing, until appointed to another appropriate command at sea. By the middle of the eighteenth century, the officers' corps of the Royal Navy was organized into a rank structure. Whilst promotion was by selection in the lower grades, the principle of seniority applied to the senior ranks of captain and admiral. Naval wars were now fought regularly on a large scale by salaried, uniformed (from 1747) officers of the state. They were trained in specialized skills of naval war, graded in a rank structure and governed by a body of legal regulations. The ships in which they sailed were built, maintained and supplied by a burgeoning civil bureaucracy.

However, as in the army and in branches of the civil administration, naval officers were not components of a rationally disciplined, bureaucratic structure. In England, for example, while officers were salaried, they received half-pay when not at sea. Indeed, officers were expected to be gentlemen of independent means, for reasons relating to social status, and financial considerations. Low salaries cut the cost of naval expenditure, but also lessened the dependence of officers on the state. In addition, prize money was a crucial means of remunerating officers (and men). It spurred motivation through making war a semi-private enterprise using public capital. The fruits were shared by state and officers in legally regulated proportions. Yet the pursuit of prize did not always necessarily coincide with the strategic aims of the service as defined by the central authority.

Officers commanding ships were entitled to recruit new officers for the service, a right which, while limited by the central authorities, was often abused. The training of officers was not a centrally organized system whereby a formal set of principles and techniques was inculcated into officers in a specialized educational institution. The naval college was only attended by a minority, with most being trained at sea through practical instruction. The lieutenant's examination after six years service was the only educational barrier to future promotion (C. Dandeker 1978). Whilst promotion was by selection up to the rank of post captain, the central authority did not have a monopoly of the power to promote. It shared this power with that of the senior service officers. Both parties made selections with as much view to patronage obligation as to merit. In the Royal Navy during the eighteenth century, senior officers had fought successfully to establish seniority as the basis of promotion of captains to flag rank. This was so as to insulate themselves from what they regarded as the favouritism that structured all selection decisions. With seniority as the *de facto* principle of advancement in the senior ranks, the central authority did not have the means of controlling the overall numbers, distribution and flow of personnel through the rank structure. The officers of the service, whilst employees of the state, were also a privileged semi-bureaucratic status group which had managed to establish a considerable degree of autonomy from central control.

The partial bureaucratization of the officers' corps was accompanied by related changes in the relationships between officers and men. A corps of specialist seamen was established (N. A. M. Rodger 1988: 113-204; C. Dandeker 1985). The foundations of a bureaucratically regulated career structure and disciplinary code were laid, although the discretion of commanding officers in the management of labour was immense. In navies, systems of labour recruitment and organization varied. France had established the 'Inscription Maritime', or register of seamen. In return for placing their names on a register and being obliged to serve in time of war, merchant seamen received payment from the state. This was a more bureaucratic system when compared with the more informal arrangements prevailing in England. There, the merchant interest was suspicious of any administrative control by the state over the supply of labour. In this it had the support of the country gentlemen. They lost labour to the state through forcible press-ganging of seamen by the navy at the conclusion of commercial voyages. Merchants preferred this informal, *ad hoc* arrangement as a means of preserving their interests. At the same time, they gained Royal Navy protection for merchant shipping, and the commercial advantages that accrued from successful wars. Meanwhile, the state gained a supply of seamen without the cost or inconvenience of constructing a bureaucratic organization for registration.

In any event, no state had an effective bureaucratic system of naval conscription from either merchant seamen or other civilian occupations. In England, the great mass of seamen were recruited compulsorily for service in the Royal Navy in time of war and then released again to the merchant service at the conclusion of hostilities. On the other hand, a corps of skilled seamen was retained for peacetime service either at sea or in maintaining the ships 'in mothballs'. They provided the skilled 'core' of the service and were provided with a career structure.

As in armies, the discipline of the men was secured through severe physical punishment. Officer's prerogatives were immense and only loosely regulated by a penal code and monitoring by the central authorities. Whilst there were parallels between the drills of gunnery at sea and those of eighteenth century armies, with the exception of the marines (sea soldiers), seamen were not drilled in quite as mechanical a fashion as their counterparts on land.

The state was able to recruit forcibly the least powerful elements of society to serve, and pay them wages well below market norms. On occasion, they did not pay them at all. The impressment system, which insulated the respectable from the obligation to serve meant that a significant proportion of men in service were drawn from the most disadvantaged groups in society. In conjunction with a rapid turnover of manpower through desertion and disease, this ensured that discipline would be even harsher than that prevailing in the wider society. Yet harsh discipline was often praised by 'respectable' seamen as a way of controlling the 'incorrigible'. The real complaint was the arbitrariness of discipline – or the legal right of commanding officers to act as *petty tyrants* (C. Dandeker 1985; but also compare N. A. M. Rodger 1988: 205–51; C. Lloyd 1970: 218–26; H. Baynham 1969: 53–66).

By 1800, the north European states, and particularly England, had established a semi-bureaucratic infrastructure of global naval power. It comprised extensive fleets, naval stations, an officers' corps and cadres of skilled sailors. It was accompanied by professional military forces in the rise of western power. Despite the more extensive bureaucratic regulation of society in France, it was England that developed a more effective naval power. The weakness of England's state apparatus was counterbalanced by its more democratic power structure, commercial wealth and the relative ease with which a maritime power can tax goods moving across its boundaries.

As I argued earlier, France had constructed a substantial bureaucratized army under the ancien regime. With the French revolution, it revolutionized military organization by establishing a citizens' national army and the obligation of universal military service. This involved a break with the ancien regime and an extension of the bureaucratic surveillance of society for military purposes on a scale never approached by England. However, these developments in France were surpassed by those achieved initially by Prussia in the nineteenth century. With the conjunction of the industrial and democratic revolutions, states could build far more substantial military organizations. This involved two processes: (1) a further transformation of the relationships between officers, men and the central authorities, through the creation of a more rational bureaucracy; (2) the greater penetration of society by the bureaucratic state to achieve military goals. In the early twentieth century, even England and the USA were forced to follow to some extent patterns of organization that were forged on the continent.

The Impact of the Industrial and Democratic Revolutions: The Bureaucratization of Force and the Nation-state, 1800–1914

In the nineteenth century, the bureaucratization of military organization depended on changes in the organization of taxation. The emergence of a bureaucratic system of taxation involved an insertion of the public power into society for the collection of information on tax sources and for the extraction of payments from all members of the citizen state. Of course, not only did taxation become more effective, there was also a greater pool of wealth to be tapped because of industrialization. Without this tax system, states could not have afforded the expensive instruments of modern military power nor the range of other state services that emerged with the extension of citizenship rights.

The emergence of the modern tax state involved a departure from the financial and administrative arrangements of the ancien regime. Semi-independent contractors were separated from the means of administration and transformed into servants of the bureaucratic state. As Kindleberger has argued, 'whereas in the early part of our period with the selling of offices and tax farming, private wealth holders intermediate between others and the Crown, in the nineteenth century, *the Crown* intermediated between various sets of private investors and wealth holders and took advantage of capitalist bank structures and markets to raise wealth to fund government expenditures and debt.' (C. Kindleberger 1984: 175)

The extension of the tax system was linked with the development of industrial capitalism on the one hand together with nationalism and citizenship on the other. Both removed many of the obstacles to the realization of the administrative goals of absolutist regimes. Industrial capitalism caused a major increase in productivity and this released a larger surplus for state expenditure. However, this was only a potential surplus. The state had to devise a means of collecting it. This task was made easier by the extension of market relations in modern capitalist societies. As Ardant has argued, 'it is impossible to lay hands on taxable wealth, to recognise or estimate it without a minimum of economic exchange'. . . . 'The nineteenth century offered to those states affected by the industrial revolution ever increasing possibilities of action not only because greater production affords more effective levying of taxes but also because a more developed exchange economy allows one to establish taxes with greater accuracy.' (G. Ardant 1975: 90, 186)

In the twentieth century, the organization of income tax is relatively easy to operate,

in a country in which most men [sic] live on salaries paid by enterprise, and through that link are easy to keep track of. Other taxes are levied against interest or dividends paid by corporations; interest and dividends are both easy to discover and levy duties against, the payment of which could be guaranteed by ᵗhe corporation itself. Production is sufficiently concentrated so that taxes can be levied at that stage which will be eventually passed on to the consumer. (ibid.)

Thus the vicious administrative circle of the eighteenth century in respect of taxation was replaced by a positively reinforcing one as the market and capitalist enterprise expanded the amount of liquid wealth and concentrated it in accessible collection points. Once tapped, states could use the regular provision of funds to establish additional tax, military and other adminis- trative organs to ensure the regular re-supply of such financial commitments.

Political factors enabled the state to establish its infrastructure of taxation in parallel with the military arm. The emergence of modern nationalism and the citizenship state of the nineteenth century involved a decline of legal privileges of the landed classes in respect of tax liability. The duty to provide military service as well as to pay taxes emerged as the universal obligation of citizens in the modern nation-state. National citizenship combined with the more sophisticated techniques of tax assessment and collection of the industrial age to advance the surveillance capacity of the state. The tax revolts so common in pre-modern states disappeared with the flourishing of the bureaucratic public power, although of course evasion and avoidance by individuals and corporate bodies remained.

Against this background of the industrial and democratic revolutions, the state was able to pay for more extensive military organizations and to subject them to a more thorough bureaucratization than had been possible under the ancien regime. In the nineteenth century, Prussia initiated these develop- ments in armies whilst England revolutionized naval power. In developing more effective armed forces, other states were forced to follow suit if they wished to retain or achieve first class status in the global geopolitical struggle for power. Following in the path of Britain and Prussia were France, Russia, Japan and the USA.

The industrial and democratic revolutions changed military organization in three ways: first there was a revolution in the means of destruction; second there was an increase in the mobility of force; and third there occurred a bureaucratization of command, control and communications systems; pro- ducing an increase in the surveillance capacity of armed forces (M. Pearton 1982: 19–35; C. Dandeker 1983). As before, the cases of military and naval power can be considered separately.

The industrial revolution increased dramatically the capacity of the means of destruction in terms of firepower. Between 1840 and 1900, factory production in metal working and steel industries was applied to armanents (W. McNeill 1983: 223–61; A. Giddens 1985: 222–36). The infantryman's smooth bore, muzzle loading, musket was replaced by the breech loading and relatively rapid firing rifle. This enabled him to fire with greater accuracy and range, and allowed him to lie down when loading. Concealment was increased further after 1870 with advances in explosives, particularly smokeless charges. According to Strachan, between 1840 and 1900, the range and rate of infantry rifles had increased tenfold (H. Strachan 1983: 114). Military organizations generally placed emphasis on the mass firing of rifles by infantry in the context of the full use of cover and entrenchments. The primacy of infantry (with cavalry as important auxilary forces), was itself challenged by the ever-increasing destructive power of artillery.

The increased significance of artillery was an outgrowth of the most developed metal working industries and, as always, military competition between states provided a powerful stimulus to innovation. Modern artillery and the invention of the machine gun meant that there was a relative shift to the power of the defence on the battlefield, although this was not fully recognized until the first world war.

In addition to advances in firepower, the armies of states increased in size dramatically during the same period. This was due to a combination of political and economic factors. As I argued earlier, the French revolution had provided the political condition for national mass armies. In much of Europe, particularly in France, Prussia and Austria, the restoration of the ancien regime in 1815 involved the revival of long-serving professional forces. The ruling classes feared the political consequences of arming the people. This situation remained largely intact for 40 years. Meanwhile, industrialization and the consequent rapid rise in population growth provided the material basis for an expansion in the size of armies, although the political cost of such a move was formidable (H. Strachan 1983: 90–129; W. McNeill 1983: 242–56; M. Pearton 1983: 64–76; M. Howard 1976: 94–115).

The Prussian solution to squaring this apparent circle involved a process of 'militarization' rather than 'civilianization' (H. Strachan 1983:109). The people were armed, thus increasing their participation in the state, yet autocratic political structures were retained, including the power of the officers' corps within the highest agencies of decision-making. Short service recruits were conscripted to an army manned by a professional core of officers and NCOs. Conscripts served three years: long enough to be inculcated with the values of discipline and obedience to the autocratic state. They then passed into the reserves and territorial formations, under the supervision of the army and not local civilian notables. Throughout Prussian military organization, the idea of a 'peoples' army' was subordinated to that of an army manned by the people. As I observed earlier, 'fundamental democratization' (K. Mannheim) – the participation of all the population in the state – is quite compatible with autocratic political structures. This pattern of organization was widespread on the continent though Britain, for example, did not adopt a mass conscript army throughout the nineteenth century.

The emergence of this 'European' system of militarized conscription enabled industrial states to view their military potential in terms of national population size. The realization of this military equation depended on states acquiring a detailed knowledge of the size and distribution of national populations. Thus the extension of conscription (as well as taxation) was linked closely with the spread of national census systems in the nineteenth century. As a result of these changes, 'in 1870, the North German confederation deployed against France exactly twice the number of men Napoleon had led into Russia – 1,200,000. By 1914, the German figures had again doubled, to 3,400,000 with comparable increases among her neighbours.' (M. Howard 1976: 99–100)

Yet this system could not operate without important technical and organizational innovations. Crucial here were the railways, the electric telegraph and bureaucratic staff organizations that regulated the large-scale movements of population associated with modern mass armies. With these developments, a powerful bureaucratized war machine emerged.

In the nineteenth century, the railway and electric telegraph were the new means of transport and communication on land. They became elements of an integrated communications network. In conjunction with the extension of education and literacy in the second half of the century, these conditions unified national populations across time-space in dramatic fashion. States like Prussia, France, and later Russia, lost no time in realizing the military potential of this developing infrastructure (M. Pearton 1982: 69–76; M. Howard 1961; E. A. Pratt 1915; H. Strachan 1983:121–4; W. McNeill 1983: 242–4; B. Bond 1984: 18–20).

The impact of railways was dramatic: they provided a network of communication which was far in advance of what was possible with the roads of the period. In addition, the 'pulling-power' of steam locomotion facilitated the speedier and more reliable transportation of heavier weights of both goods and people. In England, railway building occurred after the initial process of industrialization, and rail networks were not planned centrally by the state. However, the continental railways constituted the very basis of industrialization. In addition, the military organizations there were more politically influential than their English counterpart. They were quick to realize the military potential of railways in respect of war and in controlling internal disorder. In Prussia and elsewhere in continental Europe, they were able to determine the sitings of stations, routes and junctions on the basis of military and geopolitical considerations.

Railways caused a strategic revolution by increasing the size of armies and facilitating their movement and control. They increased the speed of war; military power came to be defined in terms of mobilization times, and there was a frantic search for means of reducing them in the second half of the nineteenth century.

In the 1840s and 1850s, Prussia and Austria used railways for moving troops. In 1859, 600,000 men and 129,000 horses transported from France to Italy in a sixth of the time it would have taken by horse (M. Pearton 1982: 68). Railway communications were crucial to the Prussian defeat of Austria in 1866, and the defeat of France in 1871 can be attributed, in part, to mismanagement of the French railways (M. Howard 1961). In the 1890s, the German Schlieffen plan for fighting a war on two fronts against France and Russia depended on the efficient use of railways. France was to be attacked first, as Russia, with its lower level of industrialization and railway development, had a slower mobilization speed than France. One of the reasons why the plan failed in 1914 was that, by then, Russia had developed a far more effective railway network and industrial organization, much to the consternation of German war planners. As a result, more troops had to be taken from the west to mask Russia while France was attacked.

Railways provided the technological means of realizing the equation between military power and size of the adult male population. With a rail network, the state could mobilize its resources, transport them to depots to join their professional cadres and equipment. From there, they could be transported to the war fronts. With the railway, a whole society could be mobilized for war, its armies replenished with manpower and material resources. The division between military organization and society characteristic of the eighteenth century was broken; the bureaucratic military machine extended into society itself.

The impact of railways on the mobility of armies should not be exaggerated. Strategic advances were not always matched at the tactical level (H. Strachan 1983: 123–4). Forces could in principle be deployed by rail and could be re-supplied. However, in the field away from the railheads, armies relied upon horses and feet for the movement of men and supplies, unless recourse could be had to captured rail networks. Indeed, until the process of motorization initiated by the internal combustion engine in the twentieth century, the size and destructive powers of armies quite outgrew their means of mobility. As a result, in the comparatively limited space of western Europe (when compared with the eastern front) armies were to grind to a halt in a bloody war of attrition in 1914. For all the reliance on railways in the Schlieffen plan of 1914, the timetable for the conquest of France rested on calculations of *marching* times. In addition, railways posed problems of their own. Synchronizing the arrival of men and their equipment was an immensely complicated administrative problem. The flow of men and materials to and from the front could be interrupted by shortages of double track lines or queues in either direction.

Bearing these qualifications in mind, railways did permit the creation of a much larger military machine. Its strategic movements could be determined centrally and in detail. It could also be connected with the resources of an industrial economy. The operation of this war machine depended on the development of new means of command and control. These were the electric telegraph and bureaucratic staff organizations epitomized by the German general staff.

The war machine made possible by the railways could not have operated without the surveillance network that was provided by the electric telegraph (see J. L. Kieve 1973). It emerged in the 1840s and was soon applied to military and civilian use, usually being established alongside the rail networks. Although it was a fixed land line system, it was particularly useful for co-ordinating movements of men and materials through the rail system and in connecting HQ with units in the field. As Pearton has argued, the Crimean War, 'was the first in which the commander was directed from home by means of the telegraph' (M. Pearton 1982: 58).

However, as with the railway, the telegraph provided limited means of control to the central authorities. It was used primarily for the communication of military information rather than commands, mainly because the system suffered from problems of reliability. In addition, its security could be breached by wire tapping. For these reasons, the German army realized that considerable initiative would have to remain with commanders in the field. Communication between units in the field was not easy, and this remained the case until the invention of wireless telegraphy in the early twentieth century (H. Strachan 1983: 124).

The movement of troops and supplies to their predetermined positions of deployment, the allocation of routes of advance, targets and timetables, generated a huge volume of administrative tasks. New bureaucratic staffs were established to plan the movement of trains and troops, to write instructions, communicate them through the system, and monitor the system's performance. As will be shown later (pp. 167–70), technical imperatives – the volume and complexity of administrative tasks – forced railway companies and other large business enterprises to create similar planning staffs independently of any military exigencies. However, here I want to discuss staff organizations in terms of their contribution to the operation of an industrial war machine dependent on railways. Modern military staffs are 'central military organs assisting the supreme military authority of the state . . . in determining and implementing the higher directives which are to govern military activity' (H. Irvine 1938: 162; C. Dandeker 1984).

A distinction can be drawn between staffs concerned with planning war, and thus with the operational *use* of military organization, and those which are concerned with the administration or maintenance of the instruments of war: recruitment and personnel, supply of materials, etc. These are no less important activities, and are performed within the parameters of planning directives established by the war or 'capital' staffs. This distinction between capital or planning staffs and administrative staffs is important. As will be shown later, a similar distinction can be identified in the organization structures of the larger business enterprises in the late nineteenth and early twentieth centuries.

In general terms, four distinct activities of general staffs can be identified: first, the gathering of intelligence about opponents, the terrain of likely battlefields and so on; second, the use of such information to create operational plans. This task is performed by officers who have received specialist training in war studies at an appropriate college. A third activity concerns the organization of mobilizations and manoeuvres during which war plans can be tested. The fourth staff function concerns the communication of the results and lessons of such tests to the forces and the maintenance of training standards. These four activities can be termed respectively as intelligence, operations, mobilization, inspection and training. The duty of the staff was, then, to ensure that the complex military machine operated smoothly and to provide a uniform collective military doctrine.

The novelty of the war staffs lay not in their activities as such, but rather in their performance in a complex and differentiated administrative structure: the 'brain' of military organizations became collectivized. There were two related reasons for the development of these staffs: first, as a result of the democratization and industrialization of war, the volume and complexity of administrative tasks expanded beyond the capacities of personalized forms of administration. Second, at the same time there were those in the military who were aware that in order to realize the full potential of the new technologies of war (particularly to increase the speed of mobilizations and deployments) systematic and collective planning would offer distinct military advantages to any state which advanced in this direction. The spread of the staff system in Europe and beyond, for instance to the USA and Japan, was because of the military advantages it offered in a competitive world of nation-states.

The roots of the modern staff system lay in the late eighteenth century, when the French army had established a staff that gathered information and prepared plans for a war against England. Despite its technical achievements, the French staff organization was stunted by the effects of Napoleon's personalized command system. It was Prussia that was crucial in the development of modern military staffs. While their foundations were laid between 1780 and 1830, these organizations were developed into formidable bureaucratic instruments of war in the period 1840–80 (G. Craig 1979: 31–2, 45, 62–5).

Irvine identifies three conditions that facilitated developments in the late eighteenth century (D. D. Irvine 1938): first, improvements in transportation, particularly roads, increased the mobility of armies in the field. Second, there were advances in cartographic science and technology – the telescope, spirit level and barometer. As a result, detailed accurate maps became more readily available to those interested in using such information for the preparation of military plans. Finally, as was argued earlier, there were changes in military technology and organization: the flintlock musket with socket bayonet and better field artillery had facilitated the institutionalization of the divisional system. The divisional system allowed large forces to disperse for movement and concentrate for battle, particularly in areas where good roads and an agricultural surplus were available. However, dispersal and concentration were dangerous activities. Careful planning and co-ordination were required if disorganization and attacks of superior force on isolated divisions were to be avoided. Such co-ordination was quite beyond the individual capacities of a commander in chief when large forces were in movement well beyond the reach of his personal command. It required the activities of a staff.

The introduction of the railway and electric telegraph involved a dramatic increase in the administrative tasks facing staff organizations. This was because the complexity and speed of war increased dramatically. Consequently, a military advantage accrued to that state with the fastest mobilization time and most effective war staff. Railways permitted the rapid mobilization of national manpower resources for war, and the precise co-ordination of movements through the use of timetables. With effective railways, the Prussian general staff was able to prepare comprehensive, detailed and highly reliable military plans for war.

By the end of the nineteenth century, states in the armed camp of Europe were equipped with bureaucratized military organizations co-ordinated by war staffs. During the nineteenth century, naval warfare was transformed in ways that paralleled those occurring on land. Again, this process can be considered in terms of changes in the means of destruction, the means of mobility, and the means of command and control.

Industrialization revolutionized the technology of naval war. Between 1840 and 1900, it has been estimated that more technical changes occurred than in the preceeding 600 years (E. H. Archibald 1971; O. Parkes 1966). The pace of innovation meant that, by 1914, ships were outdated within ten years of being built and were normally scrapped when aged 20. By contrast, HMS Victory was 40 years old at the time of Trafalgar in 1805 and it was still at the forefront of naval technology and was regarded as the ultimate weapon of sea war. During the nineteenth century, developments in one field of naval technology stimulated developments in related areas as the processes of military competition between states and scientific innovation reinforced each other. An example of this process was the way in which advances in armour stimulated developments in artillery (O. Parkes 1966).

The most powerful element of naval war – the battleship – was transformed. Iron and, later, steel replaced wood as building materials. Steampower replaced sails and thus broke the historic dependence of navies on wind and tide. Advances in naval artillery meant that by 1914 the larger ships could deliver many times the destructive power of their eighteenth-century forebears, at far longer ranges and with scientifically calibrated precision.

At sea, as on land, the steam engine provided the basis for an advance in the means of mobility. Journey times were cut dramatically. By 1840, it took only 14 days to cross the Atlantic compared with the six weeks often required in the age of sail. By 1873, the time had been reduced to ten days. In addition, journey times could be made the subject of precise calculation. As a result, regular and more durable systems of interaction could be built up over greater distances (E. Hobsbawm 1977: 64–87). This development was the basis for a major expansion in capitalist markets. It also had military implications: with the building of a network of coaling and supply stations the infrastructure of global naval power established in the earlier period was strengthened considerably. Force could be projected more easily than ever before whether against first class or minor powers.

As McNeill has argued, 'An amazing fact of world history is that in the nineteenth century even small detachments of troops equipped in up to date European fashion could defeat African and Asian states with ease. As steam ships and railroads supplemented animal pack trains, natural obstacles of geography and distance became increasingly trivial. European armies and navies therefore acquired the capacity to bring their resources to bear at will even in remote and previously inpenetrable places.' (W. McNeill 1983: 257)

The increased mobility and destructive capacity of naval power were linked with a tightening of the structures of command and control and the creation of bureaucratic staff organizations similar to those being established in armies. The rationalization of command and control depended on the information system established by the electric telegraph. This had extended with the rail network on land and with cable laying by steamships at sea. During the Crimean War, the British commander in chief was in contact with London by telegraph. As Hobsbawm has argued, 'from 1865 there followed a burst of cable laying which within five or six years vitually girdled the globe. By 1872, it was possible to telegraph from London to Tokyo and to Adelaide . . . such speed of communication was not merely without precedent or indeed without possible comparison; for most people in 1848 it would have been beyond imagination.' (E. Hobsbawm 1977: 76)

The telegraph permitted greater regulation of the lower echelons by the central authorities, as long as subordinate senior officers were in the proximity of naval stations and their telegraph wires. At the tactical level, communications remained quite limited; they relied on flags and flashing lights. Such techniques required units to be in visible contact with each other. Officers in command of ships on detached service retained a level of discretion that would have been familiar to their forebears in the eighteenth century. As many officers wrote later, the period of 'gunboat diplomacy' during the last decades of the nineteenth century was the final swansong of that age of independence. It ended with the return of battlefleet organizations as the main focus of naval power in the late nineteenth century and the introduction of wireless telegraphy (W/T) in the period 1897-1914 (A. Preston and J. Major 1967: 152-76; A. J. Marder 1940: 4-22).

W/T revolutionized communications because it permitted contact between central authorities and distant mobile units. Indeed, in the British case at least, the discretion of commanders in chief at sea was severely restricted in respect of naval operations. The result was a degree of administrative 'overload' as the volume of information and matters requiring decision accummulated at the admiralty (C. Barnett 1963: 107-96). For as one naval administrator had commented earlier in 1855, 'You can never have rapidity of communication without an increase in correspondence: one necessarily entails the other.' (C. Dandeker 1977: 451)

As in military organizations, the electric telegraph and steam propulsion increased the pace of naval warfare. For example, in the 1840s, a series of invasion scares (albeit exaggerated) occurred in England, because some observers felt that France's new steamships could transport an invasion force across the channel 'overnight'. At the same time, the continued specialization of the instruments of naval war made it more difficult for the state to rely on the manpower and resources of the merchant fleet to the same extent as before.

The pace and specialization of naval war ended the relatively leisurely mobilizations of the age of sail. States constructed naval war machines which, over time, became preoccupied with establishing a state of permanent war readiness. In both military and naval organizations, the distinction between war and peace became blurred when compared with conditions in the eighteenth century (M. Pearton 1982). As in the military field, the provision of manpower resources and a system of war planning were tasks quite beyond the capabilities of any single individual.

In England, a bureaucratic naval staff developed in the context of the decline of gunboat diplomacy and the increasing importance of battlefleets in the global contest for seapower (C. Dandeker 1984; A. J. Marder 1940: 4–22). Between 1890 and 1912, the administrative outline of a war staff emerged. Different components were merged into one organization with the formal establishment of the naval war staff in 1912. The naval intelligence department had developed two activities: the gathering of strategic intelligence, and the monitoring of organizational performance through arranging manoeuvres and trial mobilizations. In the 1890s, an embryo naval war college emerged. It was concerned with the strategic education of officers, and ultimately with the dissemination of a common strategic doctrine. The war college collaborated with the intelligence department in the consideration of war plans and games. In 1912, after another in a series of international crises, the cabinet discovered that despite the organizational innovations of the preceding 15 years, the professional head of the service still retained individual responsibility for providing war plans to the Prime Minister and other members of the defence sub-committee. However, he was unable to perform this task effectively: the requirements of modern war were beyond any single individual. The establishment of the war staff meant that personalized planning was supplanted by a *collective system*.

In 1914, Britain and other first class naval powers possessed a bureaucratic naval war machine structured by timetables. It could mobilize reserves with their professional cadres, deliver them to their fleets, and then to their deployments in sufficient time to avoid a pre-emptive attack by an opponent in the struggle for command of the sea. Thus the foundations of modern bureaucratized military organizations were in place by 1914. Of course, this is not to deny that important changes in the relationships between the armed forces, war and society have occurred since that time. In particular, three developments can be alluded to, briefly, as significant from the standpoint of surveillance and the development of military power.

First, advances in technology have continued to transform the means of destruction and mobility: greater firepower, faster combat units, and more precision in delivery systems. Of particular interest for the present argument is the application of modern technology to the means of command and control, or in contemporary parlance C3I (command, control, communication and intelligence). This has produced what has been termed the 'electronic battlefield': an extensive network of near instantaneous communications between central authorities and lower echelons as well as between different sub-units within military organizations (J. F. Dunnigan 1981: 250–6). Using such devices, ranging from personal radio to satellite technology, this C3I network gives senior commanders and political leaders scope for directing and monitoring military activities around the globe. This is precisely why some observers feel that in a major conflict between the superpowers, the C3I system would be a prime and vulnerable target: its electronics could be seriously damaged by one large nuclear airburst. The result would be major decentralization of authority to commanders in the field. Others have suggested that this scenario presents good grounds for doubting the possibility of the 'politically measured' application of nuclear weapons in battle, and thus the wisdom of deploying tactical nuclear weapons at all.

A second important development, which accelerated from the first world war onwards, concerns the deployment of force beneath the seas and into the air as a consequence of the invention of the submarine and aircraft. In particular, the development of airpower cut across the longstanding division between the ways of war on land and at sea, so undermining the basis for any sharp separation between the organization and strategy of armies and navies. Increasingly, military campaigns depended on co-operation between the services. The consequences for war planning and staff organization were profound, and these were particularly evident in the second world war. Joint operations required joint staffs and a proliferation of additional staff specialisms to process the higher volumes of information and administration. Perhaps the best example of this in modern history is the planning for the Allied invasion of occupied Europe in 1944 (M. Van Creveld 1977: 202–30). Indeed it can be argued that one of the reasons for the ultimate Allied success against Nazi Germany was the superiority of its joint staff organizations when compared with those of the German high command which suffered from severe centripetal or 'feudal' tendencies (H. Strachan 1983: 176–77; C. Barnett 1987: 60–2). This point can be linked with a third development which has run in an opposite direction to that relating to inter-service co-operation. While technical exigencies of modern war have demanded co-operation, this process has been punctuated by sharp conflicts of interest and rivalries between the services. The professions which operate within the bureaucratized organizations of military power are not mere passive agents of the state but groups with self-determined organizational interests. The development of new combat missions and weapon systems have implications for changes in the balance of power between services within the defence system. (Decisions on such issues affect the volume and value of jobs in different service careers and are thus the source of conflicts and fought over accordingly). In the modern era it seems that inter-service rivalries within military bureaucracies are as significant as any emergent process of co-operation (M. Edmonds 1988: 161–85; J. Connel 1986: 59–97).

Surveillance and Relations of Administrative Power in Military Organization

In the preceding discussion, the focus has been on the ways in which the industrial and democratic revolutions encouraged a bureaucratization of military power, and thus an expansion of their surveillance capacities: the former promoted the construction of a war machine in a condition of permanent vigilance; the latter linked military organizations more closely with the wider populations of modern nation-states.

The focus now shifts to the detailed implications of these changes for the relations of administrative power linking professional officers, men and the central authorities. Although the foundations of rational discipline had been laid in military organizations during the seventeenth century, it was not until the nineteenth century that all members of the armed forces became component parts of a bureaucratized war machine.

With the emergence of a modern war machine, members of the officers' corps were fully incorporated as components in a bureaucratic chain of command. Officers became members of a *'bureaucratic* profession' in the service of the state. They were professional experts successfully claiming a legitimate monopoly in the provision of a service. In addition, they had acquired autonomy in determining how the needs of their client (the state) were to be met. Although the autonomy of the military profession was guaranteed by the state, it was normally exercised within a framework set by the civil, political determination of military goals. Furthermore, the professional autonomy of individual officers was strictly delimited by a bureaucratic chain of command which assigned a range of legal competences to specific levels of authority. The experience of military officers, therefore, reflected a general trend whereby professional occupations became housed in bureaucratic organizations such as business corporations and the state itself (pp. 205-13). Officers were fully separated from the means of administration. They lost those remaining property rights in their occupation that were the

93

residues of an era when the state had relied on self-equipped and self-financing armed forces. As officers moved through their careers, they were subjected to processes of detailed evaluation and monitoring by their supervisors. The information retrieved through these processes was used to judge the technical efficiency of officers.

The emergence of the officers' corps as a bureaucratic profession involved a number of changes in the organization of their career structure. First, the central authorities monopolized the right to recruit new members of the armed services, and distributed such scarce occupational rewards on the basis of competitive examinations. This was an uneven and gradual process. In Britain, between 1830 and 1914, naval officers' rights to nominate new cadets were restricted. Then all nominees were forced to compete for scarce positions by examinations. The central authorities emerged as the sole agency to which recruits should apply in order to join the service. Recruitment became more bureaucratized and less dependent on the patronage relations between officers and potential recruits. This did *not* mean that such patronage mechanisms disappeared; they simply lost their strategic significance as the keys to occupational entry. Nor did the bureaucratization of recruitment necessarily involve a democratization of the social origins of the officers' corps. For a long time, membership of the officers' corps was confined to the upper reaches of the class structure. However, on the issue of recruitment one issue became clear: officers lost the traditional property rights in their occupation (C. Dandeker 1978; M. Janowitz 1960; M. Edmonds 1988: 20–43; C. Otley 1970, 1973).

A second aspect of officers' careers to be transformed was their training and education. Instead of being a direct result of the individual practices of commanding officers, these functions were centralized and performed in the context of formal educational institutions. The industrialization of war and the complexity of military technology promoted occupational differentiation within the military profession and a consequent proliferation of such educational establishments. The development of staff organizations in the services was linked with the formation of staff colleges for the higher education of those officers destined for the top managerial positions. With these organizational developments, a uniform military doctrine and expertise was inculcated into officers. Of course, on-the-job training under the supervision of officers in the field or at sea took place as before, but these activities took place within the detailed specifications of this centralized education system.

A third aspect of the officers' career structure to be transformed was promotion. Officers' privileges in this field were curtailed. The central authorities monopolized the right to promote and so transformed officers' rights into a highly circumscribed power of recommendation only. In addition, the basis of decisions on promotions shifted. It had always been in the self-interest of central authorities and officers to promote those who were judged technically competent. On the other hand, patronage considerations relating to contacts within and outside the service could make all the difference between successful and dismal career prospects. Again, it would be foolish to argue that such considerations disappeared. Nevertheless decisions on promotion were increasingly informed by judgements on the technical qualifications of candidates, as revealed by a professional registry. This was a store of bureaucratic information on each officer's service history, technical merits, special qualifications etc., as reported by their superiors in regular reports. In Britain during the second half of the nineteenth century, the use of such registries became more widespread and important in the determination of decisions about promotions. As I pointed out in the earlier discussion of Weber's ideas, these files were important in providing legitimacy for the monopolization of power by the central authorities in the distribution of scarce rewards. Considerations of service patronage continued to be important in such matters; but insofar as they were decisive in particular cases, they were grounded in impersonal grounds of technical merit.

A fourth change in the career structure of officers concerned the issue of retirement. The introduction of compulsory retirement was perhaps the clearest indication of the separation of officers from the means of administration (C. Dandeker 1978). In the case of the British armed services, this involved a struggle between the central authorities and senior officers for control over their commissions. Since the eighteenth century, officers had regarded their commissions more or less as private property, although actual purchase was confined to the army. Again, the enforcement of compulsory retirement for officers of every rank at a certain age, and thus the implementation of an 'up or out' system of promotion, was legitimized by grounding such decisions in technical merit.

Through these bureaucratic mechanisms, all aspects of the career structure of the military profession were controlled by the central authorities. The latter's activities addressed not only the movement of officers through their careers, but also the size and shape of the career structure itself. Under traditional arrangements, when there had been a balance of power between officers and central authorities in respect of the distribution of occupational rewards, the size and shape of an officers' corps were the aggregate results of a myriad of different patronage decisions. They were not the outcome of an explicit public policy enforced in the organization by the central authorities. By the end of the nineteenth century, such matters as the number of officers of particular specialisms in each rank, promotion rates, recruitment numbers, projected personnel requirements for the future were all determined centrally by staff organizations in the light of strategic policy and financial budgets.

The creation of a vigilant war machine also involved the establishment of a more durable and extensive career structure for the men, together with formal arrangements for the mobilization of reserves from the wider society (M. Howard 1976: 100; H. Strachan 1983: 108-9). Thus the military machine and society became more closely connected. At the same time, there was a greater intervention by the central authorities in the relationships between officers and men with the emergence of a rational-legal system of authority (C. Dandeker 1985). This system was applied to the regulation of careers and to matters of discipline, or crime and punishment. The result of these changes was an attenuation of elements of petty tyranny in the role of commanding officers and the substitution of legal process for traditional, and thus arbitrary, systems of justice.

As with the officers' corps, the creation of a modern war machine involved the crystalization of a career structure for the man and the provision of a reserve system. Under traditional arrangements, the services were more a loosely knit set of sub-systems rather than components of a co-ordinated single system. Many of the men looked to their personal relationships with their superior officers rather than to the 'service' for career advancement or employment. By the end of the nineteenth century, the manpower needs of the service, as determined by the central authorities, became the prime determinant of the careers and conditions of service of the men. Officers' large discretionary powers became curtailed as the functions of recruitment, training and promotion became bureaucratized. What was once performed within the summary authority of commanding officers was now defined by regulations and often carried out in a central educational institution.

In the field of military discipline, a similar process can be identified: intervention by the central authorities in the relationships between officers and men and the substitution of rational-legal authority for the traditional authority relations of the ancien regime. Under traditional arrangements, commanding officers had wide discretionary powers. As in the field of employment, the 'service' was more like a collection of feudal patrimonies loosely regulated by a penal code than an impersonal legal order. During the nineteenth century, the extension of rational-legal authority involved two related changes. The first was the substitution of legal process for the arbitrariness characteristic of traditional authority relations as, for example, in the organization of court martial procedure, and a specification of the code of discipline. This formal rationalization was also accompanied by a new substantive rationality. That is to say, the ideals of retraining the mind through bodily discipline or education replaced the traditional strategy of corporal punishment as a means of maintaining social order within the services (M. Foucault 1979). Imprisonment, fines and 'retraining' replaced flogging as more 'humane' methods of punishment. These disciplinary changes were connected to broader shifts in society which are examined in the following chapter (pp. 110ff.).

With these changes in the relationships between officers, men and the central authorities, officers became bureaucratic officials. Their activities were concerned increasingly with evaluating the persons under their command and reporting in detail at regular intervals to their superiors. There was an expansion in the amount of information held at the centre of the organization and of staffs to process and take decisions informed by it. The centralization of decision-making and the expansion of staff organizations reflected the extension of a detailed web of surveillance in the military machines of the modern nation-state.

The preceding analysis has shown that, in general terms, during the nineteenth century, the industrial and democratic revolutions transformed the strategic elements of force, time and space. This process involved a bureaucratization of the military organizations of nation-states and a consequent expansion of their destructive and surveillance capacities beyond the levels achieved by the armed forces of the 'old society'.

However, contrasting patterns of development can be identified amongst societies. Some of these can be discussed by drawing on the distinction between militarization and civilianization raised earlier (pp. 83-4). While the Prussian military system subsequently forced other states to adopt this prerequisite of first class military status in the modern geopolitical system, not all societies were as willing, as, say, Japan, to accept the thorough militarization of society that 'Prussianism' entailed. During the nineteenth century, both Britain and America (with the *partial* exception of the American civil war) did not adopt mass conscript armies as the military basis of the nation-state. Both relied in large part on naval power and, in the American case, a small professional army existed in a social context where the militia ideal thrived. As Wright-Mills suggested, 'in the United States, the right to bear arms was not *extended* by an arms-bearing stratum to an unarmed population: the population bore arms from the beginning . . .' (C. Wright-Mills 1956: 178-9). Although Britain and the USA were forced by geopolitical and military factors to modernize their armed forces, they sought to do so in ways which minimized the militarization of society.

Until the 1880s, the American armed forces were devoted largely to the internal pacification and consolidation of the USA as a continental nation-state. The navy was concerned with coastal defence and longer-range trade and commerce protection, rather than with establishing any claim to first class naval power. For much of this period, with the barriers of the Pacific and Atlantic, the defence of the USA was fairly secure.

Nevertheless, given that the USA was formed during the period when the industrial and democratic revolutions were transforming armed forces and societies, it is not surprising to note that some of the important foundations of a modern bureaucratic military system were laid during the period between independence and the civil war (W. Millis 1958). These included the establishment of a commanding general with supportive bureaux and the professional education of officers in formally organized settings or academies (West Point 1817; Naval Academy 1880). This was in line with broader European developments: armies sought to learn the administrative lessons posed by the larger forces of the nations and arms which had flourished between 1793 and 1815, by applying science and technology to the problems of war and military management. At the level of enlisted personnel, although there were some moves towards more humanitarian systems of punishment, the conditions of soldiers and sailors for most of the first half of the century remained not unlike those of their counterparts in Europe: for instance, in the navy, recruits included a large proportion of foreign-born seamen and a low proportion of elements drawn from the mainstream of the host society (H. D. Langley 1967).

Despite these administrative advances, there were serious deficiencies in the armed forces which parallelled those already identified in the British context. For example, while the seniority system in the US navy provided a buttress against political favouritism in the distribution of promotions, it also led to a 'clogging of the arteries' in the service. In addition, higher professional education was undeveloped, and this undermined the effectiveness of staff advice which, in any case, was hindered by bureau fragmentation in the emergent central organizations of defence. While some objected to these deficiencies, others argued that the armed forces were sufficiently equipped for their role, which, of course, excluded confrontation with first class military powers. Yet others were content to see that any incipient processes of militarization in the USA were kept in check.

This situation was transformed in the period from the 1880s to the first world war. With the final consolidation of the USA as a continental nation-state, it began to extend greater influence in the wider geopolitical system in ways which placed new demands on its armed forces. Indeed, the armed forces (as in other societies) were active participants in that process of global expansion which was stimulated by an admixture of officers' career interests, and their attempts to apply progressivist and scientific management systems in the sphere of the military; capitalist interests in defence contracts; nationalist zeal and sober geopolitical calculations (J. L. Abrahamson 1981).

As in the case of the Royal Navy (pp. 88–91), the USA built a battlefleet and the associated command and logistical apparatus on which it depended. From the organizational point of view, significant developments included the establishment of higher education systems for military officers destined for senior commands. Thus, an academic and professional context was provided for the selection and training of staff experts who manned the intelligence and other sections of an emergent staff organization in both army and navy. As was observed in the British case, so too in the USA the staff organization meant that personalized systems of influence were increasingly supplemented by 'bureaucratized policy advising' (A. R. Millet and P. Maslowski 1984: 299–300).

A significant change and precondition for the effective managerial control of the officer corps was the establishment of the principle of merit selection together with the system of individual efficiency reports on officers and compulsory retirement. These arrangements were the means of controlling the flow of officers through their careers and the ways in which those selected for advancement could be rotated through staff and line appointments as desired by the central authorities (ibid).

In respect of enlisted personnel, there were material improvements in their conditions of service, including the establishment of bureaucratized and more humanitarian systems of punishment. These changes were associated with attempts to recruit personnel more from the mainstream and 'respectable' elements of society.

The USA sought to modernize its military systems without incurring the costs of 'Germanization' or militarism. Two illustrations of the tensions associated with this objective can be alluded to. First of all, there was a conflict between those like Upton who wished to establish a Prussian style staff system and those who did not. The fragmentation in the bureaux of the central organizations of defence and the widespread suspicion of a centralized staff persists to this day. Second, as the American army expanded in the later nineteenth century, there was also a conflict between those who wanted the reserves to be organized as a component of a federal standing army, and those who wanted the national guard to be the first line of reinforcement and operating as relatively autonomous state organized units. Again, at the time the militia ideal prevailed, and the debate between it and 'Prussianism' continued into the twentieth century (ibid.: 366).

The changes in military organization discussed above were linked with *both* the industrialization of war and rise of the democratic nation-state. It is not the intention to propose a geopolitical determinism in respect of these changes. Rather, the argument is that such factors have played an important part in the expansion of the modern states' surveillance capacities in this field of military organization and in society more generally, as will be shown in the concluding section of this chapter.

Industrialization undermined the distinction between war and peace and increased the speed of warfare. It also involved an increase in the pace of technological innovation, thus expanding the complexity of war as an occupation. The pressures of industrialization and inter-state competition forced states to increase the effectiveness of their war machines and, where necessary, to subordinate the entrenched privileges of the military profession to the interests of the state.

Yet it would be misleading to view the military profession as simply a passive recipient of an identity imposed on it by a modernizing state involved in geopolitical struggles. On the contrary. The development of the modern military profession as a component in a bureaucratized war machine was, in part, the result of initatives from *within the profession itself*. These were linked with intra-professional struggles for power in the new war machines, and, by extension in the state itself. The design of professional institutions, planning for modern war, and departures from the technical and organizational ways of the eighteenth and early nineteenth centuries were all bound up with such conflicts. These were often inter-generational in nature, as well as encompassing a division between those who embraced wholeheartedly the promise of new technologies and those who were reluctant to depart from tried and tested techniques. Different groups of officers fought to take advantage of new conditions to build war machines that would serve their states better in the struggle for military power and, of course, to give themselves positions of influence within them. As I pointed out earlier, these occupational struggles are a persistent feature of modern armed services. Professionalism was then, in part, an outcome of an entrepreneural strategy of the military itself. This process of professionalization in the context of the bureaucratization of military power had parallels in their institutions, e.g. in the rise of the police and of business management (pp. 122–3; 186–92).

The rise of a modern bureaucratic war machine involved the emergence of the armed forces as a *public service* of the democratic nation-state. As was argued earlier, the administrative branches of the modern state became sectors of a public power separated from kinship and patronage commitments to status groups in the wider society and subjected to impersonal bureaucratic control. The bureaucratization of the officer corps should not be attributed solely to demands for efficiency stemming from geopolitical constraints. The birth of class society and of democratization were also involved in fracturing the webs of patronage and forging new institutions of impersonal control in the branches of the modern state. This differentiation of the public power of the modern democratic state involved a division between politics and

100

administration: political conflicts became oriented towards control of state administration as a means of policy implementation, with the bureaucracy itself becoming relatively autonomous from such disputes. Of course, this was an uneven historical process: for example, the emergence of a public bureaucracy was a far stronger development in western Europe than in the USA. In addition, in all cases, a politically centralized bureaucracy did not exclude it from engaging in the struggles with other actors in the bureaucratic politics of the modern state.

The relative insulation of the public power of the modern bureaucratic state from the conflicts amongst groups in civil society was accompanied by a process which, in a way, strengthened the links between state and that society. In so doing it added to the pressures that were promoting the growth of mechanisms of bureaucratic surveillance in military and other state organizations. Democratization involved a greater role for legislative bodies in monitoring the activities of the executive branch and its bureaucratic agencies. Parliamentary scrutiny of the policies, costs and efficiency of government added to pressures on the state to devise bureaucratic mechanisms for supervising and gathering information on its administrative subordinates. The link between democratic accountability and bureaucratic surveillance applied to both military and non-military branches of the state. As a result, officials spent a greater proportion of their time reporting on their activities to their political superiors: the representatives of the people.

The preceding argument has examined the ways in which the rise of the democratic nation-state and the industrialization of war were linked with the bureaucratization of military power and the emergence of a war machine under the control of the modern state. Due to the imperatives of modern war, the growth of bureaucratic surveillance within military institutions *extended beyond them into the wider society*. The foundations of this process were laid in the nineteenth century. During the twentieth century, there have been important changes in and additions to what can be referred to as an emerging structure of the modern security state. These require a more detailed analysis than can be offered here. However, in the concluding section, I offer an outline of the more important features of these developments.

The Infrastructure of the Security State: Some Twentieth-Century Developments

The emergence of a modern bureaucratic war machine was associated with a breakdown in the division between war and peace and a closer bond between military organization and society as the state extended its surveillance of the population for military purposes. In the nineteenth century, the bureaucratic military machine extended into society itself. The clearest indicators of this process were the provisions made for the military control of rail and other communications systems, and of the mobilization of reserves from civilian occupations in time of war. These foundations were added to during the world wars of 1914–18 and 1939–45, when the administrative precedents established by the Napoleonic system were surpassed.

Since 1945, the attenuation of conscription and the return to more professional armed forces in some western societies, and particularly the USA, has not involved the removal of arrangements for the military supervision of society in time of war or similar emergency. On the contrary: in a nuclear age, the infrastructure of the security state has been reinforced steadily. This is not to suggest that military and geopolitical considerations have been the only factors involved in the emergence of the security state. Industrial conflict and political subversion have also been important in these developments. Two senses of security are being used here: defence and social welfare. The expansion of the surveillance capacities of the modern state under the pressures of war showed how powerful this administrative machine was in successfully prosecuting large-scale administrative tasks. In the wider context of the process of democratization, many sought to apply the administrative lessons learned during war to the problems of peace (K. Middlemass 1980; R. Titmus). It is in this context that one can understand the extension of the social rights of citizenship with the emergence of the welfare state. Thus the structure of the 'security state' emerged due to external pressures of war and internal demands of democratization. These two themes can be addressed separately.

The military imperatives of the world wars in the twentieth century increased dramatically the surveillance capacities of the modern state in areas beyond the military field. The state mobilized the resources of society in ways quite unmatched before. It subjected society to detailed regulation in respect of the requisition of manpower for the armed forces, the registration and allocation of the adult population to priority sectors of the war economy, the regulation of production and distribution of goods and services, the surveillance of domestic public opinion which democratized war had made such an important weapon in the armoury of modern states (W. McNeill 1983: 307–61; M. Pearton 1982: 165–258; B. Bond 1984: 100–35, 168–200).

The first world war approximated to a total war in terms of both ends and means. In a total war the ends are irreconcilable and absolute, whilst the protagonists seek every means to achieve victory in the struggle. For most societies, the war involved a sharp break with the past in terms of the supervisory relationships between state and society. Of course this was more marked in liberal democratic societies such as the UK than in those like Germany (A. Marwick 1965: 39–43). In its emergence as a great power, the latter had been accompanied by an authoritarian state structure characterized by both extensive police powers and a developed network of population controls. These were the direct responsibility of the military bureaucracy in time of war mobilization or other emergencies (M. Kitchen 1976; G. A. Craig 1955: 217–98).

In the UK, the demands of total war became evident after a rapid conclusion to hostilities failed to materialize. Shortages in munitions and recruits for the services became apparent. As a result, the population became subject to pervasive networks of surveillance over a whole range of their activities which at the time many thought could only have been introduced in the developed police states of continental Europe.

The insatiable demand for manpower by the armed services as a consequence of trench warfare placed strains on the existing conscription organizations of the continental states (G. Hardach 1977). It also forced the UK to establish a similar system in 1916. Conscription meant the construction of a register of those fit for military service (1915) and a bureaucratic system for calling up men and dealing with anomalies such as conscientious objectors.

The shortage of men was more than matched by shortages of munitions. These problems had not been forseen by war planners, who for the most part counted on a short, decisive campaign. The imperatives of war production forced states to play a far more directive role in the organization of the economy than before. This was a particular shock for liberal England. Of course, such government intervention built on the provisions for regulation of transport and communications in time of emergency that had been made in the period 1890–1914.

The demands of the first world war meant that the principles of bureaucratic control predominated over the market mechanism in respect of a whole range of economic activities: currency regulation, imports and exports, allocation of scarce resources to priority producers of war related goods. In Britain, there was a central government which assumed powers of supervision and control far wider than those it had exercised in the nineteenth century. In 1914 the Defence of the Realm Act gave massive discretionary powers to government in respect of the prosecution of the war. These were not unlike the martial law provisions that states such as Germany already had in place. This act provided the legal umbrella under which state collectivism or 'war socialism' was constructed. State direction of the capitalist economy involved the co-ordination of an administered economy run by committees of businessmen working in conjunction with the armed forces and the trade unions in industry. This burgeoning military-industrial complex flourished in all of the great powers. However, the degree to which it was subjected to political control varied, with the USA for example, following a more self-regulating path than western Europe owing to the relative weakness of central government machinery. There is also some debate over the role of the trade unions in these structures, and specifically the extent to which their members achieved benefits from such authoritarian arrangements (A. S. Feldman 1966; W. McNeill 1983; M. Kitchen 1976; K. Middlemass 1980).

The expansion of the surveillance capacities of the state in time of war was a reflection of the breakdown of the distinction between 'military' and 'civilian': whole societies were at war, not just their armed forces. This meant that popular opinion or the morale of the home front was an important strategic resource. (M. Saunders and P. M. Taylor 1982). In this context, the military and security services extended their role of monitoring behaviour presumed to be subversive of national security. It is interesting to note how in Britain the security services often failed to distinguish between subversion by foreign powers and the political activity normally associated with the industrial conflicts between employers and trade unions. According to Andrew, in Britain by the end of the first world war, the security services were more preoccupied with domestic subversion than German espionage and persisted in exaggerating the impact of foreign subversion on domestic unrest. (C. Andrew 1985: 224–45). In any event, the extended surveillance activities of the security services in the first world war involved the interception of cable and postal communications through the censoring system, the use of reports from the police on suspicious persons, direct surveillance of the latter, and collection and analysis of data on suspects which were stored in an expanding card index.

The security service was also responsible for the implementation of the Aliens Restrictions Act, which involved the internment and monitoring of aliens in the UK. The extent of this and related work was reflected in a major expansion in the numbers of staff employed in the service. The service worked, as it still does, in close collaboration with chief constables via the special branch and with the assistance of military intelligence agencies.

The demands of the second world war imposed a further wave of state collectivism on the major powers which, as in the British case, built on and extended further the web of controls of the security state. Although some parts of the security state had been dismantled in the inter-war period, an emergency system of control had been maintained to deal with civil unrest and war contingencies. This system provided the basis for the rapid reintroduction of a 'war socialism' after 1940. The emergency organization tructure was adapted specifically for war use from 1936. According to

Jefferey and Hennessy (1983) by 1945 Britain had become a very self-disciplined nation. Almost six years of total war 'had left no citizen untouched by its rigours whether in the form of the siege economy on the home front or by military service abroad. The population was used to receiving orders and to strict regulation in the face of shared dangers.' It should be noted however that there is some dispute as to how much this 'self-discipline' may be attributed to the consent of the subordinate population or to the extensive canopy of legal powers which the government had established, drawing on the precedent of DORA (N. Stammers 1983).

The state took powers to restrict the movements and activities of the population by administrative regulation and without reference to the judicial process. This was particularly the case with regard to the control and internment of aliens, an activity which illustrated the influence of military and security chiefs on state policy and general importance of 'security' issues in government thinking. As is always the case with security problems there was a difficult distinction to be drawn between the requirements of military security and rights of freedom of expression.

In relation to industrial conscription, the 1940 legislation meant that

Bevin [was] armed with sweeping powers to order anyone to do anything he might require. . . . One of the most remarkable features of the second world war was the extent to which Britain took powers to mobilise and re-locate labour: powers greater, it has been suggested [by A. J. P. Taylor] than those taken by any other belligerent nation. (N. Stammers 1983: 162)

The advent of nuclear weapons and the partial return to professional systems of organizing the armed services has not entailed a dismantling of the security state. Rather, the security state has continued to flourish and become entrenched as the administrative basis of a society permanently ready for war in the nuclear age.

A range of security measures has been introduced to protect the networks of defence installations against penetration from unauthorized personnel. These networks include those military C3I facilities that have flourished since the advent of NATO. Arrangements have been made to facilitate a rapid and disciplined transition from peace to war in time of crisis, and the effective management of war and post-war conditions in face of subversive elements should the need arise (G. Rumble 1985). In the context of the cold war from 1948 onwards, arrangements were made in Britain for civilian defence against nuclear attack; these drew upon the administrative precedents established earlier in the century in respect of fear of the air bomber. Fear of atomic war stimulated the provision of a government emergency apparatus in which the military and police figured strongly. Again precedents from the past were used in organizing arrangements for food supply systems, health, disposal of casualties, police and security measures. By the late 1950s it seems that civil defence administration came to be regarded (by government at least) as of marginal use to the general population and of rather more significance in demonstrating the resolve of government to pursue the logic of nuclear deterrence to war should the need arise. In the 1980s, although there has been a reassertion of the importance of home defence, again, however, the emphasis has been less on protecting the population and more on the efficient prosecution of war and the management of post-war social conditions.

As Rumble argues, the specific objectives and planning assumptions of home defence in the UK during the period 1973–82 were to secure the UK against any internal threat (of subversion); mitigate the effects of conventional nuclear, biological or chemical warfare upon the population; provide alternative government machinery at all levels; enhance the basis for national recovery in the post-attack period (Rumble 1985: 159). The transition to war would involve the dispersal of key personnel to secure command and control centres; the mobilization of the UK warning and monitoring organization; the state control of all communications networks including telephones, roads, etc.; the placing of police and military personnel at all key points; the relocation of ministries to emergency positions as part of a general devolving of powers to regional commissioners (who would be government ministers) exercising full emergency powers in the 11 designated areas. In the aftermath of war such regional commissioners would work in close liaison with, if not be dominated by, the senior military officers in charge of the military regions whose geographical jurisdictions coincided with the former official areas. This process of war mobilization would also involve the suspension of parliament as a result of which the powers of regional commissioners and senior military personnel would be largely unchecked by legal process.

Four general conclusions can be made about the links between the security state and the imperatives of war and military organizations. First, the lineages of the security state can be traced to the demands of the two world wars, together with the impact of the industrial and democratic revolutions in the nineteenth century. Second, there are important discontinuities here, in that contingency planning for war has to envisage a scale of destruction and post-war chaos hardly imaginable before. In addition, the pace and urgency of a transition to war in a nuclear context is of a kind not seen before, just as 1914 was a break with the more leisurely mobilizations of the pre-industrial era.

Third, although the emergence of the security state in response to defence imperatives has been a quite general characteristic of modern industrial societies with military aspirations, in the British case it has until recently been associated with an extraordinary degree of secrecy surrounding its operations and organization. This important point cannot be pursued here, although it would appear to be connected with the monarchical legal foundations of the British state and the discretion that a substantially unwritten constitution offers to various government agencies.

Fourth, and finally, military imperatives have been responsible for the erosion of some civil liberties in respect of assembly, movement, provision of information, etc. Yet it would be foolish to ridicule the argument that any state has the duty to protect its citizens from external and internal threats to its security and liberties, in the process of which some of those liberties, particularly in an emergency, should be curtailed. These are difficult moral and political issues; the point is to recognize the military realities that have placed them on the agenda.

Although the infrastructure of the security state developed in the context of the demands of war, it had other social foundations. These lay first in efforts by the state to regulate society in time of civilian unrest and industrial conflict, and second in the application of administrative lessons learned in war to problems of citizenship in time of peace.

In Britain the emergency state organizations established during the first world war flourished in the post-war period of severe conflicts between employers and trade unions. Since that time governments of all political persuasions have maintained and enhanced such organizations in order to mitigate the impact of trades disputes on social order and to maintain essential services. In Britain after the second world war, the Labour government was aware of the significance of the emergency government apparatus during the difficult transition from war to peace. Despite the suspicions of the Labour movement, Atlee's cabinet supported and used the emergency apparatus for the management of industrial disputes in the post-war period. Conservative and Labour administrations continued to develop these arrangements during later decades, particularly from 1964 onwards. Atlee's government used the emergency organizations for crisis management in response to strikes affecting essential services, and in April 1947 the Industrial Emergencies Committee was charged with 'supervising the preparation of plans for providing and maintaining in emergency, supplies and services essential to the life of the country, and in any emergency to co-ordinate action for this purpose' (K. Jeffery and P. Hennessy 1983: 186). The role of the home office in co-ordinating the emergency system was broadened in the period 1958-65. Yet this was a period of relative tranquillity compared with the following years. The reconstructed Industrial Emergencies Committee whose powers had been extended in 1951 was made permanent in

1964, and this date marked a revival in its fortunes in face of domestic unrest, particularly in the context of the seamen's strike in 1966. During these years, there was a spurt in the growth and sophistication of the structure of the emergency organizations, especially during and after and miners' strike of 1972. The civil contingencies unit is now prepared for all sorts of emergencies. Its secretary is charged with drawing up and continually monitoring a list of vital services and industries most vulnerable to industrial action and making contingency plans for emergencies. It has the assistance of a number of regional emergency committees on which sit representatives drawn from relevant industries (though excluding trade unions) government ministries, local authorities, the police and military. During the late nineteenth and twentieth centuries, the imperatives of modern war have interacted with those of democratization in the development of the security state. The state has developed its surveillance capacities not only to prepare for and conduct war, but also to provide the social foundations of universal citizenship. In the twentieth century, war has accelerated the mutually reinforcing relationships between democratic citizenship and the bureaucratic surveillance of society by the state.

After 1945, the Labour government in Britain sought to use the instruments of state regulation and information gathering in pursuit of the implementation of citizenship rights. There were two main aspects of this development. First, the machinery of the war economy was adapted for peacetime use. Corporatist structures, including nationalized industries, were to be used to pursue economic growth and a general standard of living which was less susceptible to the cycles of boom and slump normally characteristics of the capitalist economy. Second, new state bureaucracies were established for the provision of social security and other welfare services and thus the material basis of citizenship to those unable to purchase it for themselves on the market. These developments were the culmination of earlier attempts to incorporate the Labour movement within the social structure of modern capitalism (C. Crouch 1979; K. Middlemas 1980; T. H. Marshall 1973).

The second world war provided a crucial institutional and ideological basis for the corporatist consensus of post-war western capitalism. The merits of a planned society in peace could be praised against the backcloth of the successful struggle against fascism. The emerging 'welfare-warfare' equation has provided a modern umbrella of legitimacy for the watchful corporate state in post-war capitalist societies. This has only been seriously challenged, at least at the level of ideology, since the late 1970s with the revival of liberalism or 'neo-conservatism' (R. Skidelsky 1988).

Whilst, in Britain at least, we may be experiencing something of a partial 'roll back' of the state in pursuit of a free market economy, there is little reason to suppose that governments sympathetic with such a goal would wish to weaken the organizations of the security state concerned with law and order. Indeed, there is a case for arguing that less of the first is linked with more of the second: a 'free market society' is one which requires a strong state in the field of law and order and security matters. Besides, there is evidence to suggest that the present efforts to shift British society to greater reliance on the market system of allocation are directly linked with a centralization of political and administrative power in pursuit of what are regarded as favourable conditions for an enterprise economy – e.g. in the field of education, local provision of finance for industry, etc. Furthermore, there is little evidence to suggest that notwithstanding the dissolution of the national role of trades unions in government macro-economic and social policy, the government itself is willing to dismantle wholesale the 'steering mechanisms' that it has inherited from the past. It remains to be seen how far the 'dependent state' can be dismantled in the light of the political pressures of those who wish to see it retained. What is clear is that the defence and emergency components of the security state are hardly likely to decline in significance.

4

Bureaucratic Surveillance in a 'Society of Strangers': The State and Social Control in Modern Capitalism

The Great Transformation: The Rise of Bureaucratic Surveillance

In the preceding chapter, I examined the ways in which the industrial and democratic revolutions facilitated an expansion in the surveillance capacities of the military organizations in modern nation-states. I also suggested that, although the security state developed because of military imperatives, the problem of internal social control was also a significant factor. In addition, I argued that, since the second world war, important elements of the security state have been adapted for civilian welfare purposes, that is to say, the further extension of citizenship rights. In this chapter, the concern is less with the state as a geopolitical entity and more as a means of internal control. The focus of analysis is on the relationship between capitalism and the increasing role of police surveillance rather than military power as a means of internal pacification. As I argued earlier, capitalism created both a class society and an impersonal 'society of strangers' (M. Ignatieff 1985). The mechanisms for controlling crime and other disorders inherited from the pre- and early modern periods were called into question and in consequence there was a wholesale rationalization of social relations. Although the main outline of the changes involved is largely agreed upon, the problems of why they took place and their wider social significance remain matters of controversy (M. Ignatieff 1985; S. Cohen 1985: 13–17). Together they constituted a process of the bureaucratization of social control. These changes can be defined as follows:

1 The decline of publicly inflicted corporal punishment with the emergence of a greater emphasis on imprisonment as a means of controlling and changing the behaviour of offenders. Between 1750 and 1860 there was a revolution in punishment in western societies.

2 The emergence of a range of bureaucratic organizations for the incarceration and 'reprocessing' of criminal and other deviant populations.

3 The establishment of bureaucratic organizations for the punishment of criminal offenders and treatment of other deviants was part of the emergence of a more consolidated state. It became armed with the means of penetrating society in ways quite unmatched in previous eras. For example, the 'new' uniformed police became the agent of a continuous rational discipline of society.

4 In these organizations, the exercise of supervision became the occupational basis of a range of bureaucratically controlled professions.

As I indicated earlier (pp. 1–6), those who have sought to explain this great transformation in the means of social control have drawn on different traditions of social theory. The debates between progressive and revisionist approaches to these issues can in part be reconstructed in terms of a dialogue between the industrial society thesis on the one hand, and, on the other, a range of Marxist, Foucaultian and Weberian analyses. The argument here is that an adequate account of this great transformation requires an integration of these different strands of social theory.

Discipline, Punishment and Social Order in the 'Old Society'

The emergence of the bureaucratic discipline of the urban, industrial age involved a break with the 'old society', in which social control was secured through mechanisms of 'indirect rule'. This phrase refers to a particular type of relationship between state and society. Despite structural differences between western societies in the late seventeenth and early eighteenth centuries, one similarity concerned the persisting difficulties which elites encountered in being able to rule at a distance from an administrative centre (S. Spitzer 1985).

There were a number of structural limitations on the 'presence availability' of elites (A. Giddens 1981: 39). A series of technical problems shortened considerably the radii of effective administration from the centre: for instance, systems of transportation and communications were still quite rudimentary until late in the eighteenth century. Communications difficulties were reinforced by demographic considerations. Although the size of populations in western societies in 1700 was small, this did not make them easy to control from an administrative centre. The population of each country was dispersed into numerous, small, relatively self-sufficient agricultural communities, and despite the process of commercialization, only a small proportion of the population lived in towns and cities. The limited division of labour and the demographic distribution reinforced rendencies towards the dispersal of control over the population to local areas (R. Goldstein 1983: 91–3). Furthermore, the severely limited tax base available to the state inhibited the formation of rational bureaucratic discipline even in the most absolutist of western states. 'Tax farming', corruption and thus the sub-contracting of state functions constituted obstacles to the will of the central authorities, notwithstanding the genuine advances made in central administration in the late seventeenth century (pp. 66–72).

A further limitation on the administrative penetration of society from the centre was the fact that the political aspirations of Royal Houses encountered the jealously guarded prerogatives of local power centres – agricultural landlords and city elites. The extent of state penetration depended largely on the form in which local and central powers were articulated. It will be recalled that, drawing on the examples of France, England, colonial and post-colonial America two broad patterns have been distinguished: the autocratic and liberal management of local power centres (pp. 66–72). In both patterns, central government was relatively weak from the administrative point of view. Differences between them concerned the degree to which central authorities could monitor and manipulate local power-holders, and their susceptibility to 'popular' influence. The similarity was that in neither case were subordinate populations made the objects of direct supervision by the central authorities through rational bureaucracy. Thus in both cases, the state was relatively separate from society in relation to its capacities for supervision and surveillance (A. Giddens 1981: 169–77).

In both despotic and democratic political systems until the American and French revolutions, political and administrative prerogatives, whether central or local, were formally the property of only a small minority of the population. The great mass of the people were marginal to the political community: they were not the origin of autonomous political interests, articulated at the centre and legitimized by an appropriate theory of

112

sovereignty. Insofar as the subordinate population's interests were politically articulated at all within legitimate structures, these were expressed through their connections with hierarchical systems of patron-client relations of personal obligation. Such relations were more characteristic of 'class-divided' than of the 'class' societies of modern capitalism. In the former, predominantly agricultural, societies class inequalities stemming from differential ownership of property, were not mediated by a separate market economy and so were not expressed as naked asymmetries of economic power. Rather, they were components of a deferential social order of dependence and obligation between unequals. In England, for example, this system was 'less formal and inescapable than feudal hommage, more personal and comprehensive than the contractual, employment relationships of capitalist "Cash Payment" ' (H. Perkin 1969: 49). Under these conditions, vertical status ties and loyalties tended to predominate over horizontal, trans-local class relations. The system generated 'interest politics' rather than autonomous 'class politics': the interests of politically disenfranchised majorities were expressed legitimately through the patronage of their social superiors, and illegitimately when the former mechanisms failed, through 'riotous disorder' (E. Hobsbawn 1963). The patronage system coincided with the 'separation' of states from society: that is, the state had weak supervisory powers over the population.

The patronage system meant that political and administrative prerogatives were not only diffused to the localities, but in addition were *fused* with economic and social powers. Although the class societies of modern capitalism possess central and local authorities, their peculiarity derives from the structural separation between the public authority of the state and the market economy (A. Giddens 1981: 169–81). In class-divided societies, the strength of the local landlords rested on a fusion of political, administrative, economic and social powers bestowed by the patronage system. However, like the central power, they actually had quite limited means of controlling their subject populations. In what follows the focus is on the separation of the public power of the state from society with the growth of capitalism. This involved a break with the patronage system *and* an *increase* in the surveillance capacities of the modern state. Despite the social 'cement' provided by the patronage system, the capacity of local landlords to monitor the behaviour of the population in their areas was quite limited. In class-divided societies, the market mechanism is not as dominant as it is in the class societies of modern capitalism. However, it did operate to the extent that populations such as itinerant wage labourers, traders and other 'strangers' were on the move from one jurisdiction to another. This was the case particularly in and around cities and lines of transport and communication. The development of towns, often on the administrative foundations of overlapping and competing jurisdic-

113

tions, allowed the formation of unpoliced areas. These became a haven for numerous 'criminal' activites. Similar areas existed in tracts of countryside where no particular landlord's authority penetrated (P. Rock 1985: 203-9).

The response of local and central authorities to criminal challenges to the social order – and their image of it as a deferential social order – was to supplement the structures of patronage with a variety of legal, coercive and policing instruments. In conjunction with the balance between central and local powers these comprised the system of indirect rule in the ancien regime.

The administrative structures of western European societies from 1450 to 1750 comprised a complex mixture. Some mechanisms were inherited from the feudal era, when the market impulse was of marginal significance. Others were more recent arrangements developed in response to the rupturing of the feudal social order by the process of commercialization. There were two aspects of this process: the extension of inter-societal economic relations through the generalization of commodity production; and the shift from subsistence to market exchange in the rural economy (M. R. Weisser 1979: 71).

The older administrative and disciplinary mechanisms were particularly appropriate in societies with a limited population dispersed into relatively self-sufficient agricultural communities. It should be remembered that western Europe remained a fundamentally rural society until well into the nineteenth century. For example, the informal threat of violence in master-servant relations could be most effective as a means of controlling subordinate populations. The same could be said of 'hue and cry' and parish constable systems of policing.

In this context, 'policing' meant simply the internal governance of a community, rather than the activities of a specialized state bureaucracy – its nineteenth century and modern meaning. In England, policing arrangements were supervised by magistrates sitting in petty and quarter sessions. The magistracy was one of the focal points for the dispersal of state administration to the control of local landowners. Constables were drawn by rota from the parish community or were organized through a system of paid substitutes. While effective in small, fixed communities, these arrangements were less effective when dealing with more mobile, transient populations. In any case, they often had to cope with confused or fragmented jurisdictions. The constable system was an intermittent and reactive response to specific indicents rather than being the basis of a detailed and regular supervision of a clearly defined area (P. Rock 1985: 196-7; M. R. Weisser 1979: 56).

Between 1450 and 1700, the strains put upon traditional disciplinary mechanisms increased dramatically. Commercialization and urbanization led to a flourishing of areas of illegality beyond the reach of the face-to-face controls and patronage powers of landlords in the traditional rural economy. The extension of trade, division of labour, the creation of mobile wealth and new opportunities for illegal gain in urban areas created areas of infamy and 'crime waves'. These could in no way be controlled through a simple extension of traditional disciplinary mechanisms (M. R. Weisser 1979: 89–102).

As I argued earlier, the renaissance of economic activity offered opportunities for the state to extend its administrative capacities in relation to taxation and military power. The state also supplemented traditional means of controlling crime with new arrangements. These illustrated its more intrusive role in society as an early modern state. However, the extent of this intrusion should not be exaggerated. It may be expressed in terms of a *relative* shift from a private to a criminal system, together with a greater emphasis on public corporal punishment as part of an increasingly severe penal code – e.g. in respect of the number of capital offences.

The public criminal system was mediated by absolutist conceptions of sovereignty. Torture and inquisitorial procedure implied that the very casting of suspicion on an 'offender' was itself part proof of that person's guilt. Justice was an expression of the will of the sovereign: the majority of the population were objects and not subjects in legal procedure. Interestingly, the situation was rather different in England where the absolutist impulse was tempered by the jury system (D. Hay 1978; P. Rock 1985; J. Innes 1980).

Thus absolutist sovereignty, or in England the sovereignty of the Crown in parliament, was linked with the development of a more repressive system of punishment; particularly an emphasis placed on public brutality to the bodies of offenders. Public executions and other corporal punishments were supplemented with monetary or property confiscations, banishment and imprisonment, although the latter did not attain great significance until the nineteenth century.

There were connections between increasing repression, absolutist sovereignty and the administrative weakness of the state. As Foucault and others have argued, the spectacle of public punishments was supposed to deter and terrorize those in the community who either escaped direct supervision of their activities or were tempted by criminal opportunities (M. Foucault 1979; P. Spierenburg 1984; D. Cooper 1974). The spectacular brutality visited upon the few contrasted with the liberties or tolerated illegalities of the many offenders who escaped supervision or apprehension. Yet the success of such punishments depended, in part, on the co-operation of the spectators. This was crucial in ensuring that such events did not become opportunities for the expression of popular sympathy with the condemned and thus challenges to the authority of the state. They also revealed the difficulties the latter

115

experienced in monopolizing the means of legitimate physical force and exercising direct supervision over the population within its territory (P. Spierenburg 1984: 202). Despite the development of a more intrusive state, private vengeance persisted until the nineteenth century and beyond as a significant mechanism for controlling crime (M. Ignatieff 1985: 99–100).

The weakness of the state machine meant that those who wished to control crime had to resort to other measures. States endeavoured to use financial rewards to bribe private citizens to inform on offenders; that is, they subcontracted to private agencies state functions that it was unwilling or unable to perform itself. This development was similar to those in related areas of financial and military administration (pp. 66–72).

In England during the eighteenth century, commercialization was associated with processes of criminalization and the growth of crime. That is to say, market relations in rural and urban areas produced new types of opportunity for criminal gain as well as efforts by propertied classes to redefine traditional privileges of the lower orders, e.g. those of rural labourers, as criminal offences (E. P. Thompson 1975). An increasingly savage legal code was established. In part, this was a concession to urban interests by the landed class. However, it was operated in such a way – as for example through the discretionary withdrawal of the death penality – so as to preserve the traditional order of the patronage system. There was not a dramatic rise in the number of executions; rather, there was a sharp rise in the number of offenders sentenced to transportation (M. Ignatieff 1978: 19–20). It was also in this context of commercialization, the industrial revolution, and the new forms of criminality engendered by these social processes, that suggestions for novel policing and surveillance techniques emerged (C. Emsley 1987: 18–47).

Capitalism, Class Relations and a Society of Strangers

Modern capitalism undermined the vertical connections and horizontal rivalries of the old society. Class societies are ones in which class politics become matters of the autonomous self-expression of interests rather than heteronomous issues of paternalism and patronage (S. Beer 1982: 133). The rise of class society was not simply associated with the process of urbanization; the extension of the market was just as much a rural phenomenon. In both contexts there occurred quite dramatic shifts in spatial and demographic structures. These increased the anonymity of social relations and produced a 'society of strangers' (M. Ignatieff 1985).

In this novel type of society, new webs of bureaucratic surveillance were forged. The impersonalization of social relations weakened the effectiveness of community policing and undermined the vitality of family self-help in times of trouble. In addition, particularly in urban areas, anonymity was linked with the spatial proximity of concentrations of working-class populations to the propertied and respectable. This situation generated fears about property crime and 'crime waves'.

There are well-known methodological difficulties associated with assessing the significance of apparent 'crime waves' in this or any other historical period. In the English context, however, there is strong evidence that the years 1780-1830 witnessed not simply 'more crime' in some absolute sense, but a criminalization of acts considered hitherto as legitimate. For example, one can refer to the removal of traditional rural 'perks' of labourers by the process of enclosure. Related developments can be identified in the context of the shift from out work to factory labour (S. Pollard 1963). In addition, there were new and expanding opportunities for criminal activities: the growth of a commercial society was associated with increases in the amounts of moveable and disposable goods of value. Furthermore, there appeared to be more crime because such activity had not been contained within the patronage system of the old society. Finally, there was an increased sensitivity to crime on the part of the authorities and the propertied. This was, in part, because increasingly effective policing systems were available, particularly in the urban areas, and partly because the collection of criminal statistics from 1800 onwards made crime a more visible phenomenon (W. R. Cornish 1978: 2 ; D. Jones 1982: 2-7, 117-42; V. A. C. Gatrell, B. Lenman and G. Parker 1980: 279-84; C. Emsley 1987: 18-47). Whilst debates about the nature of the 'real crime rate' in this period continue, there seems little reason to doubt the significance of the fear shown by the propertied in relation to this issue. Their fear was rooted not just in a perception of 'more crime', but also in a recognition of the emerging and politicized working classes (J. Tobias 1972: 14-21, 256-67). In this context of class relations, those concerned with social order sought to introduce new disciplinary techniques appropriate to a more anonymous age. These new techniques were forged in a novel ideological as well as socioeconomic context.

In the latter decades of the eighteenth century, there developed an ideological challenge to the system of indirect rule and discretionary terror. This challenge had three principal sources. First was the belief in rational science as a means of transforming and improving the natural and social worlds. Second was evangelical Christianity, and third was utilitarianism, particularly the Benthamite strand (M. Ignatieff 1978: 44-79; D. Phillips

117

1980; W. R. Cornish et al. 1978: 7-10). The importance of modern positive science lay in its view of the natural and social worlds as comprising observable sequences of cause and effect which were amenable to human understanding and control. From evangelicalism, as with Howard's ideas concerning the doctine of sin, salvation and conversion, came the humanitarian argument that the reform of the individual character was both possible and desirable through penitence and productive work. This process was the culmination of a successful conversion initiated by the rational art of persuasion. Criminal characters could be saved for both God and society by being transformed into moral, productive and law abiding citizens.

Utilitarianism shared with evangelicalism an emphasis on personal responsibility for one's actions and an optimistic view of the possibilities of transforming individual characters through human intervention. However, this goal was to be achieved through a rigorous programme of bodily discipline – a regime of calculated physical rewards and punishments. These were not to mark the body but to change behaviour. Such a regime of punishments presupposed a rational actor who would respond accordingly to minute changes in the calculus of pain and pleasure. This assumption was the basis of arguments in favour of imprisonment as a standardized and precise means of punishment. Such views were often associated with the belief that a calculus of pain and pleasure could only work so long as there was a certainty of being caught and subjected to its rigours should one choose to offend. Furthermore, from a utilitarian point of view, a prison regime organized on these lines would not only transform criminals into productive citizens and deter crime, it would also offer the cost benefits of a rational business enterprise.

Writers like Bentham, Romilly and Blackstone drew on Beccaria's reformist ideas, and particularly his suggestion that capital punishment was inappropriate to a more democratic age: it reflected the system of autocratic absolutism rather than an age based on the social contract. Furthermore, Beccaria realized that the moderation of the penal code and the substitution of a regime of productive labour and financial penalties for a system of spectacular terror, required a means of effective police surveillance. This would provide a basis for the certain apprehension of offenders and thus allay the fears of the law abiding about any apparent humanizing of the system of law and order.

In this context of ideological challenge to the system of indirect rule and the birth of class society, the systems of policing and punishment in western societies were transformed. Systems of indirect rule were supplanted by the rational legal authority of the modern state. The introduction of the new police and the prison were two key aspects of that process.

Policing and Bureaucratic Surveillance

The new police forces were charged with the consistent and methodical application of the criminal law. Their presence was supposed to ensure the certain apprehension of law breakers. In England, the introduction of these organizations involved a considerable extension of the surveillance capacities of the state. Like the military, the police were to be organized as professional and bureaucratized arms of the state. The formation of the new police meant that the enforcement of the law was less the function of private initiatives mediated by 'thief takers' and voluntary associations such as those concerned with the prosecution of felons, and more the direct responsibility of the state itself. The uniforms of the police indicated that they were the functionaries of the state rather than persons delegated by local communities for policing duties in the context of systems of indirect rule.

As Emsley has argued, in the eighteenth century continental states regarded absolutist France as an organizational model for policing society. However, in the conditions associated with the birth of class, it was to the uniformed police created in England that states increasingly turned as a guide for policing modern industrial societies (C. Emsley 1983; V. Bailey (ed.) 1981: 11).

In many recent discussions of the origins of the new police, attention has been focused on the impact of the industrial revolution. Emsley suggests two significant consequences have followed from this: accepting the undoubted impact of industrial capitalism on the evolution of policing, some writers have still failed to recognize the peculiarity of the English experience. As was observed earlier, it was unusual compared with most of western Europe in respect of its weak mechanisms of state surveillance, including police agencies. States like France had well-developed police structures in the seventeenth century, in which case, while the industrial revolution may have changed the character of policing it cannot be viewed as its sole root (P. Stead 1983: 2–4).

Secondly, much of the recent literature has focused on a critique of those narratives of police history which consider the arrival of the new police as evidence of the triumph of administrative rationality in the field of crime control. (e.g. C. Reith 1956; T. A. Critchley 1967). The police are viewed as servants of the neutral state, battling against criminals who have opted out of society. The politically neutral, bureaucratic, police satisfies a functional imperative of an industrialized, urbanized society, where the scale of social organization and the mobility of populations renders redundant the community controls inherited from the past.

Recent writers have drawn on Marxist social theory to question these views. They have sought to locate the emergence of the new police in the context of the crisis of social order associated with the rise of modern capitalism. It is not denied that the early nineteenth century witnessed an attenuation of personalized ties of patronage and dependence. However, this process is regarded not simply as a 'collapse of community' but as the emergence of more transparent asymmetrical power relationships between capital and labour. In this context of class power, the new police were designed not as a means of reconstructing a politically neutral state but as a force for the subordination of the new working class in capitalist society (S. Spitzer 1985: 215).

Phillips's account provides a subtle blend of Marxist and other strands of social theory (D. Phillips 1980). He locates the new police as one element of a 'new engine of power and authority' or system of law enforcement designed during the class struggles of early industrial capitalism in England. Reformist ideologies, critical of traditional systems of punishment and law enforcement, appealed particularly to the new business and propertied middle class of the urban areas. They experienced the threats and fears associated with the collapse of traditional authority relations and the expansion in the opportunities for criminal gain. The entrepreneurial middle class demanded not only improved techniques of policing but also more effective means of prosecuting and punishing offenders. Thus the construction of the new police was one aspect of the emergence of a socio-legal basis for a bourgeois society.

Phillips views the opposition to the formation of the new police not in Whiggish terms as the 'persistence of negation', but in the context of contending class forces. The industrial working classes saw the police, at least initially, largely as a new agent of repression. Liberal and radical middle-class opinion, although recognizing that the rule of law was a precondition of liberty, nonetheless were concerned that England should not imitate the despotic ways of France. They were joined by the majority of the country gentlemen with their long-standing suspicion of central government or of any governmental powers not under their own supervision. From their point of view, the continuation of the 'bloody code' and its discretionary application were necessary precisely because they were reluctant to permit the introduction of a legal mechanism which would ensure a more certain apprehension of offenders.

Because resistance to the idea of the new police was not confined to the least powerful classes, those who wished to introduce it encountered great difficulty in doing so. Peel's success in 1829 was largely due to his astute handling of the City interest (the City of London was exempted from the Act), and a careful use of data on prosecutions. The latter appeared to confirm the worst fears of those who thought they were experiencing a crime wave. There were important wider considerations too: by 1829 those in favour of the new police could mobilize supporters on the basis of fears of civil disorder and revolution. The often violent unrest in rural and urban areas could be placed with ideological effect against the backcloth of the events of 1789 in France (A. Silver 1967).

In a sense then, the foundation of the new police in England was a further concession gained by sections of the propertied middle classes from an aristocratic polity experiencing the unrest associated with the rise of market society. However, as Bailey has remarked, while Whiggish historical accounts have underestimated the impact of class conflicts on the formation of the new police, some Marxist writers have committed the reverse error – to argue a somewhat conspiratorial view of the police as a mechanism constructed by the ruling classes as part of a bureaucratic system of discipline and surveillance (V. Bailey 1981: 11). The merit of Phillips's account is that he avoids the temptation to view the dominant classes as united by some strategy of social control, and thus, by implication, the suggestion that the traditional landed class was either the tool or 'anticipator' of bourgeois class interests.

Phillips's account also discusses the impact of Benthamism on the organization of the new police. This ideology demanded a unified administrative state, run by professional experts and based on the principles of investigation, legislation, inspection and report. The police, prison, public health and other agencies were to be its various bureaucratic arms. However, in the field of police administration and more generally, this ideology had to contend with powerful forces of opposition in English society throughout the nineteenth century (H. Parris 1969: 259-71; N. Gash 1979: 45-6). Thus there were powerful 'non-bourgeois' interests which were in favour of the persistence of localism and amateur administration. In addition, governing elites acted not simply in response to middle-class pressures but according to their own pragmatic views concerning how best to secure social order in a period of dramatic social change.

These considerations accounted for the pattern of police administration in England during the nineteenth century: it was at one and the same time a break with the past and a continuation of traditional structures. The element of continuity was the persistence of localism until well into the twentieth century and the *gradual* process by which the central state intruded into local affairs. This resistance to central state power was in part a reflection of the stronger common-law tradition in England compared with the statist, Roman legal traditions of continental Europe.

Gradually, during the nineteenth century, the central state in England played a greater role in organizing the police surveillance of society. In matters of police, health and other aspects of the state supervision of society, the overall patterns of central state intervention were very similar. Each involved a succession of distinct phases. Permissive legislation was followed by compulsory legislation, which was, in turn, followed by partial state funding of official activities. In this third phase, state funding depended on the observation of minimum standards laid down by the central authority, and these standards were monitored by an 'inspectorate'. Then followed a degree of central co-ordination in procedure and policy, and finally there was a phase of rationalization in organization, through amalgamations and related measures.

Although many rural areas had a low ratio of police per head of population in the late nineteenth century, within six months of the 1856 County and Borough Police Act, 'every community in England was under police surveillance for the first time.' (C. Steedman 1984: 6) In the period 1850–80, the new police became the administrative vehicle for the implementation of legislation relating to the regulation of working-class life. They gradually became the means for implementing statutes determined centrally and in ways which by-passed local authorities.

At this point, the analysis of the emergence of the new police needs to go beyond considerations stemming from class power. Professionalism and technical factors were also of importance.

As police functions proliferated, the new police acquired a favourable occupational basis for the pursuit of a strategy of professional autonomy. One aspect of this process concerned their efforts to confine police activities to a monopolization of the business of detecting and apprehending criminal offenders (R. Reiner 1985: 59). Thus, while the new police became a rationally disciplined bureaucracy, it also acquired the capacity to exercise autonomy in the way it carried out its function of surveillance of the population on behalf of the state. Related to this strategy of professionalization in the nineteenth century was the emergence of the criminal investigation department, the application of scientific techniques to the problems of the detection, apprehension, surveillance of and storage of information about criminal areas and populations. The belief that policing could deter crime waned somewhat in the nineteenth century; thus the greater emphasis on regulation and detection of criminal populations (W. Forsythe 1988). In England during the latter decades of the nineteenth century, professionalism and the execution of duties on an increasingly nationwide basis rather than as an expression of local initiatives, enabled the police to view themselves as a national body in possession of a unique specialized role in society (R. Reiner 1985: 59).

Police professionalism should not be viewed exclusively in terms of either collective benevolence or as an instrument of the ruling class. The evidence indicates that the police were in part a self-interested occupation, able not only to achieve autonomy from the demands of dominant classes, but also to serve the interests of sections of the subject population. It is difficult to accept the 'class instrument' view of the police: members of the working class did not always view the police as agents of repressive surveillance. Indeed, certain police activities could aid working-class interests, particularly as wider sections of the population became property owners (V. Bailey 1981: 13–15). Thus the portrait of the police as a 'domestic missionary', or as a means of spreading bourgeois values amongst the lower classes seems rather overdrawn (R. D. Storch 1975, 1976).

An adequate analysis of the new police would have to link professionalism with what can be termed 'technical' considerations. The new police constituted the basis of more formal methods of exercising surveillance over more mobile and contractually organized populations. As Munkkonen has shown in relation to the USA, the spread of the new police in modern society should not be viewed as a response to class conflict in urban areas, although the police were involved *subsequently* in the suppression of disorderly subject populations. Rather, their emergence was a response to the scale of the tasks of social control posed by the process of urbanization. However, while technical considerations may necessitate the existence of new police surveillance in large-scale market societies, they do not explain the different patterns of accountability of the police to subject populations that can be observed in modern societies (E. Monkkonen 1981; C. Emsley 1983). Recently, the issue of police accountability has become an issue of public debate in Britain. This is partly because of general trends towards the nationalization of police organization and the expansion of its surveillance capacities which have occurred during the twentieth century.

Policing and Surveillance in the Twentieth Century

With the proliferation of police agencies in all industrial societies during the twentieth century, three major changes in police organization reveal the extension of bureaucratic surveillance by the state over its subject populations: first, the establishment of a national network of policing; second, advances in the techniques of command and control in respect of the disposition and operation of police units – a process which involved a tightening of the control structures within police forces; third, a major expansion in the information capacities of police organizations both in respect of knowledge about their internal operations and resources and of the behaviour of populations in the wider society.

These developments resulted in the flourishing of what Silver has termed a policed society in which 'the central power exercises potentially violent supervision over the population by bureaucratic means widely diffused throughout civil society in small and discretionary operations that are capable of rapid concentration' (A. Silver 1967: 81). In the nineteenth century, the foundations of such a society were laid; at this point in the twentieth it is a fairly imposing structure.

The establishment of a nation-wide police organization has been an uneven development. Societies have been characterized by different patterns of central-local relations. These in turn have been associated with distinct legal traditions: the Roman continental on the one hand, and the Anglo-American common-law tradition on the other (C. Emsley 1983; B. Chapman 1970: 33).

The examples of Britain and America offer significant contrasts to the continental pattern with its absolutist lineages (P. Stead 1983: 1-2). The development of the modern nation-state in Britain and the USA has not been associated with a strong national police tradition: both were characterized by localism and the fragmentation of police powers amongst different jurisdictions with weak co-ordination from the centre. Nevertheless, during the last 20 years in Britain the firm outline of a national police force has emerged.

The trend towards nationalization was stimulated by civil and industrial unrest on the one hand and the demands of war on the other. In this wider context, an 'entrepreneurial' strategy of police professionalism based on advances in policing technologies also became significant.

In the early twentieth century, a certain degree of inter-regional police co-operation had been encouraged by labour unrest, and the security demands of the First World War reinforced such links. The Police Act of 1919 laid the framework within which government initiatives to standarize and centralize police organization could be made. In the period 1919–39, labour unrest again encouraged spasmodic state intervention and the trend towards police nationalization, so that by 1939 the home office had built up a position of considerable influence in police affairs. Post-war force rationalization was accompanied by closer regional co-operation and home office co-ordination through the provision of common support services such as forensic science laboratories, supply and maintenance of communications equipment, mutual aid schemes, police training schools, and the provision of other specialist facilities such as regional crime squads and record offices, all of which have increased the capacity of the police to act as a co-ordinated force (J. L. Lambert 1986: 1–30; R. Reiner 1985: 179; S. Manwaring-White 1983: 7–19; M. Brogden 1982: 1–16; F. Gregory 1985: 33–8; D. Brewer et al. 1988: 6–46).

In the last few years, the threats to the state posed by international terrorism, labour unrest, and the increased mobility of criminals who can utilise the dense communications networks of a modern industrial state, have only served to increase inter-force co-operation and nationalization. Yet it should not be thought that this process has involved the simple insertion of the home office as the determining agency in police practices. While it has provided the organizational and financial basis for nationalization and a degree of overall supervision, the senior police officers have become the core of an autonomous police professionalism, with considerable discretion in the formulation of police policy within the state. Bureaucratization has enabled the police to become subordinate officials of the state *and* autonomous experts.

Recently, Lambert has expressed his concern at these developments in stark terms:

> the reduction in the number of forces and the trend towards regionalisation and centralisation has distanced the police from local communities and raised fears about the movement towards a national or state police force controlled from the centre and carrying out policies directed by the government of the day. (J. L. Lambert 1986: 3)

In the context of the trend towards nationalization, some writers have questioned the effectiveness of existing mechanisms of police accountability. The latter comprise home office co-ordination combined with local monitoring by police authorities and the subordination of the police to the rule of law. Local police authorities are empowered to provide finance for equipment and to review force efficiency, but not to determine police operations. Whilst some would argue that local political control of operations would constitute a shift towards democratic accountability, others suggest that such a move would undermine both police professionalism and its capacity to act as an impartial agency in society (J. Benyon 1986).

Historically, in the USA, as in Britain, the job of keeping the peace and dealing with crime and vice was left to a 'patchwork of weak instruments aided by the military at periods of peak tension until well into the nineteenth century' (J. F. Richardson 1974: 3–18). With the process of urbanization, the USA borrowed the institution of the new preventative police from Britain in order to resolve the problems of social control posed by three aspects of city life during the nineteenth century: the dramatic rise in the scale of population produced by successive wages of immigration; the conflicts associated with the divisions between capital and labour as industrial capitalism developed rapidly; and the ethnic divisions of interest which very much overshadowed

125

the axis of class when compared with the situation in European societies (P. Manning 1977: 93).

In the face of these challenges, American cities established new police forces and thus entertained the prospect of a 'policed society'. However, they did so hesitantly, as they shared with Britain a fear of encouraging a central governmental power and its potential for despotism. Indeed, the obstacles to the development of a national police force were more formidable in the USA than in Britain because the institutionalization of pluralism was accompanied by a powerful democratic sentiment on the one hand and vigorous ethnic conflicts on the other. This combination of pluralism, democracy and ethnic division produced a pattern of police-society relations in marked contrast with the British system and that prevailing on much of the European continent. The American pattern has been characterized by Silver as 'delegated vigilantism' in contrast with the legalism of Britain and what might be termed the statism of the continent (A. Silver 1967; J. F. Richardson 1974: 16). Statism meant that the police were associated with a strong division between state and society in which they were both armed with considerable means and powers of penetrating civil society, and were agents of a despotic executive power relatively insulated from the influences of the popular will. This tradition has been at the heart of French administrative development and was simply accentuated by the French revolution. Britain illustrates the pattern of legalism in which the police, at least in principle, are impersonal agents of the law of the land.

The American policeman offers a significant contrast to, while remaining part of a tradition shared with, the British case. In America, historically, the 'democratic policeman's authority was *personal* resting on closeness to the citizens and their informal expectations of his power more than on formal bureaucratic or legal standards' (W. R. Miller 1977: 20). The rise of the professional police in the USA during the latter part of the nineteenth century, thus encountered the heritage of 'anti-professionalism'. This was linked with a suspicion of despotism inherited from the age of Jackson which was not as evident in either the British or continental experience. A recent commentator has argued that 'since 1945, the police forces of the USA have remained among the most decentralised and locally based of any in the world.' (J. D. Brewer et al. 1988: 110)

As in Britain and other industrial states, the USA, despite the persistence of localism and fragmentation, has witnessed the rise of an increasingly professionalized, bureaucratic police force since the late nineteenth century. With the formation of an autonomous police organization, both more distant from and less dependent upon, the communities it polices, it has also become more reliant upon administrative and technological means of *initiating* police strategy (P. Manning 1977: 98; J. D. Brewer et al. 1988: 108–29). This process has involved a shift towards pre-emptive and 'pro-active' policing. These arguments are the subject of the following two sections.

The novelty of the new police forces established in the nineteenth century lay in the fact that they were bureaucratized preventative organizations, as was illustrated by the territorial character of their strategy and structure. As Rubinstein has argued, '[f]or the first time the entire city was to be continuously patrolled by men who were assigned specific territories and whose courses [beats], were prescribed by their superiors' (J. Rubinstein 1973: 10). However, the early new police forces faced severe problems relating to the quality of recruits and high labour turnover (C. Steedman 1984: 105–10 on Britain, W. R. Miller 1977: 25–44 on the USA). In addition, as was observed earlier, it was easier to build a bureaucratic police force in Europe than in America. Thus, Miller shows how in Britain, policemen were organized as components of a well-regulated machine. Through drill and discipline, as in the military organizations of earlier periods, the means were found of creating a sort of automatic policeman as a key element of impersonal authority. This was in contrast with the policeman in New York who 'was still but a part of the citizens, despite modifications of the force's original democratic structure' (W. Miller 1977: 40).

Notwithstanding these variations in police organization, police authorities encountered difficulties in exercising effective control over the lone policeman patrolling his beat and thus ensuring the beat was patrolled continuously. Furthermore, there were problems associated with the tasks of, on the one hand, dispersing in order to exercise territorial surveillance and, on the other, combining in the face of a larger threat or attack.

To resolve these difficulties higher police authorities resorted to a number of strategies, and, as in other fields of administration, took advantage of advances in the means of transport and communication spawned by the industrial revolution (J. Rubinstein 1973: 12–24). At first, the links between patrolling policemen and higher authority were established through regular face-to-face contacts at pre-arranged locations and times with superior officers relying on horse transport for mobility. Patrolling officers could also raise the alarm and call for assistance through the use of whistles. In the USA by the mid-nineteenth century, telegraph networks were being established which enabled police districts to be connected with headquarters directly, thus rendering unnecessary daily personal meetings between captains of districts and the police commissioner. Telegraph communication was adopted subsequently for use at lower levels of authority, in particular in connecting patrolling policemen with their station house. This was achieved through the use of call boxes, and in the 1880s, the introduction of the telephone. These technologies provided a basis for the organized dispersal and concentration of police manpower.

In the USA between 1930 and 1950, and subsequently in other industrial societies, motorization and the radio transformed the command and control systems of police organizations, as it had done already in military organization. Apart from facilitating easier access of the public to police organizations, thus causing a major expansion in police work, these technical innovations provided a means of continuous two-way communication between patrolmen and their superiors. The radio and motorization facilitated a decline in the isolation of individual policeman and thus an increase in their sense of security. On the other hand, this was at the cost of a corresponding diminution of privacy with the centralization of police organization and the greater capacity of higher authorities to exercise surveillance over their subordinates (D. Rubinstein 1973: 23).

Recently, computers have offered higher authorities even more means for the command and control of police organization. As is the case in modern business enterprises, the widespread application of computers in organizations since the 1960s has had three broad consequences for their surveillance capacities (D. Campbell 1980: 72–96).

First, computers allow for a massive increase in the information storage capacities of an organization, both in terms of numbers of items as well as cross reference and analytical capabilities. Second, they allow rapid access to this information, and thus, in principle, promote a closer approximation to real time organization functioning. This means that an organization can produce outputs in response to input demands extremely rapidly: e.g. requests from distant locations for information or for assistance, as in the rapid response times of modern technological police forces or the instantaneous transmission of information and money in modern commercial transactions. Third, through their facilitation of the storage, processing and retrieval of management information, computers allow an organization to survey its resources and commitments and to distribute them rapidly to stated priority areas.

Here, the focus is on the command and control implications of computers, i.e. the increased means offered for the surveillance and control of police organization by its chief functionaries.

As Baldwin and Kinsey have argued, computerized command and control systems are designed to assist in the best use of police resources by ensuring the fastest attendance at urgent and important incidents of the correct resource for that type of incident, and through the provision of the correct type of management information to appropriate levels of management (R. Baldwin and R. Kinsey 1982: 86–95). Such systems offer a number of

128

advantages in the prosecution of police work: they increase the control that higher authorities may exercise over the management of incidents, and in particular can prevent the 'writing off ' of incidents through the unmonitored activities of police discretion. Computers offer the means for the more efficient use of organizational resources through the systematic recording of the demands for and use of resources, and thus the capacity for forward planning. They also reduce the mass of paper work which non-computerized recording activities generate. Computerized command and control systems have provided the basis for more mobile police forces, each component being networked into higher levels of authority which can determine with precision and flexibility the pattern of their dispersal and concentration.

Computers have not only enhanced the internal command and control systems of police organizations; they also mark a high point of their surveillance capacities in respect of subject populations in the wider society. This development involves not simply the triumph of new technology, but is part of a broader shift in the social organization of policing over the last 20 years in Britain and elsewhere. The change may be expressed in terms of the rise of 'techno-policing' (S. Manwaring-White 1983), the flourishing of the strategy of professionalism, and a move from reactive or preventative policing to pro-active policing through surveillance and intelligence gathering.

In the Anglo-American context, these changes have led some writers to fear that policing is approaching continental patterns. Specifically there is a concern that instead of society policing itself through delegated yet accountable functionaries, a state organization armed with extensive means of penetrating society, yet insulated from popular accountability by professional and bureaucratic barriers, arrogates to itself the power of determining policing policy (M. Brogden 1982: 127-47).

At this point the surveillance capacities of the new police of the nineteenth century will be examined, for it is these which have served as benchmarks for many of the fears of contemporary commentators on current police organization.

In Britain, 'the role of the new police was to prevent rather than to investigate crime. Whilst investigation meant interference and the invasion of privacy, prevention . . . demanded no more than a public presence on the streets.' (R. Baldwin and R. Kinsey 1982: 9) This was in contrast with the concealed surveillance characteristic of the French system. While the new police in the USA were entrusted with more powers than their British counterparts (because of their insertion into more democratic political structures, pp. 125-7), in both societies, the formation of detective agencies of policing was delayed by the concern to prevent the rise of despotism. In Britain such agencies did not flourish until the last third of the nineteenth century. They did so as the high hope in the success of the preventative police waned in the face of the persistence of crime.

However, even in their preventative role the new police had always been expected to exercise surveillance over subject populations through their continuous, albeit public, patrols. In so doing, they were supposed to familiarize themselves with their territory and its criminal, or potentially criminal, populations. This information was largely personal in that it was fed back directly into policing the area from which it was gained.

The advance of detective, deterrent systems, involved the application of science to the detection of crime and the recording, circulation and analysis of criminal records and intelligence between police forces. These changes were associated with the gradual professionalization of police work.

During the last 30 years, the traditional balance between the preventative role of the uniformed presence and the deterrent effect of detection through the application of science in the surveillance of criminal populations has shifted towards a more pre-emptive mode of policing. This has involved the application of new technology and a more vigorous strategy of police professionalism. In Britain, this development was marked by the trend towards force rationalization, discussed earlier, together with changes in the organization of police work, as for example in the Unit Beat system (ibid.: 32–80; R. Reiner 1985: 78–82; J. L. Lambert 1986: 18–20).

The application of motorization and personal radios facilitated the introduction of the Unit Beat system in the 1960s. The system was intended to improve police-community relations, to improve police efficiency through the technologically informed use of police manpower in a time of scarce recruits, and to enhance the professional status of the police force. Thus, the area constables were supposed to be the focal point for effective police-community relations; panda cars would provide a fast effective means of handling incidents in addition to their street presence; and all would gain from higher job satisfaction and professional status. An important element of the Unit Beat system was the division of labour between the various police roles and the co-ordination provided by a collator at the sub-divisional station. He was the means of circulating information as a supplementary resource to the four policemen working an area.

The Unit Beat system did not achieve its stated objectives in that the system generated more work than it could manage: the area officers in particular faced severe pressures to obtain information which they could not meet so that in many cases an 'old hand' was taken off street patrol and used as an information source in the station in order to add to the card index. More importantly, the status of the area PC was not held in high esteem by the rank and file, with greater preference being shown for 'real' police work, i.e. in detecting and apprehending criminals through panda car work, or through attachment to the proliferating specialist police squads in other parts of the organization (R. Baldwin and R. Kinsey 1982: 30–2). The dominant emphasis became the use of information to detect crime and react quickly to incidents rather than to use information to enhance the preventative role of the uniformed police in close liaison with the communities they policed. Good policing became 'fire brigade policing'. This was defined as the application of technology and scientific professionalism to the achievement of rapid reaction times in dealing with incidents, and to the detection of crime both after the event, and through the surveillance of populations likely to commit crime (ibid.).

The rise of fire brigade policing out of the failure of the Unit Beat system involved a transformation in the role of the collator as one aspect of the emergence of a more centralized, pre-emptive pattern of police work. The sub-divisional collator became the first stage on the supply line to newly appointed intelligence officers at divisional level. Thus the local origins of the Unit Bear system were 'transformed in the interests of a more rational system of detection and investigation. . . . [T]he system became increasingly geared to the centre and away from the needs of the local policemen.' (R. Baldwin and R. Kinsey 1982: 76; S. Manwaring-White 1983: 54–90). The importance of collators grew as divisional intelligence became more important in criminal investigation. They became elements in an intelligence network supplying information not just at divisional but subsequently at force and inter-force levels. Information was now to be used as an investigative tool in relation to populations very often in excess of 200,000 persons.

This shift towards a pre-emptive pattern of policing involves a change in the relationship between police and society and specifically the way in which information about the latter is gained and used by the former. Pre-emptive policing through surveillance means that police work relies less on voluntary contributions from the public and more on the police's own autonomous investigative skills based on an infrastructure of administrative penetration of society and linked mechanisms for the collection, storage and processing of criminal records and intelligence data. One important issue concerns whether 'community policing' is simply one aspect of this development. Campbell argues that the police intelligence collators are 'new components of a nation wide information gathering system. . . . [B]etween them they have created a coordinated network of basic intelligence records.' (D. Campbell 1980: 67) Motorization, the personal radio and computers – particularly the Police National Computer (PNC) – have simultaneously provided the basis for a more rationally disciplined, near national police force, and thus the means of extending a 'net' of bureaucratic surveillance across society (ibid.: 92).

With this ongoing expansion in the surveillance capacities of police organization, some critics have suggested that the Anglo-American tradition of policing is now being transformed in a statist or authoritarian direction. To conclude this part of the discussion, one can focus on three specific features of techno or pre-emptive policing which have stimulated widespread debate (J. C. Alderson 1985; J. L. Lambert 1986; R. Baldwin and R. Kinsey 1982).

First, it has been suggested that this style of policing involves a serious rupture in the relations between police and society. There are two aspects to this problem: first, the strategy of police professionalism involves not only the development of a panoply of increasingly coercive police powers, but also their concentration, in the hands of a group of senior officers whose autonomy from public scrutiny is minimal, and is perhaps less than that of the senior officers of the armed services (M. Brogden 1982: 55). In addition, all the evidence indicates that a principal cause of police success in controlling the rate of crime is the voluntary submission of information from the public to the police. Yet it is this factor which is marginalized by pre-emptive technological strategies of police professionalism. In this context, some writers (e.g. Benyon), have proposed policies of police 'de-professionalization', or a return to greater reliance by the police on the community for information (J. Benyon 1986; Scarman 1982; R. Baldwin and R. Kinsey 1982: 94–9).

A second implication of technopolicing which has aroused concern relates to the consequences of new police powers for the liberties of the subject. Of particular concern here are powers relating to the arrest, detention and surveillance of suspects, as defined by the Police and Criminal Evidence Act of 1984. As in the late eighteenth century, the problem once again is how to balance the costs and benefits of controlling crime and the preservation of the liberties of the citizen. On occasion the full prosecution of one goal can undermine the other (J. L. Lambert 1986: 202).

A third implication of technopolicing concerns the reliance of the police on centralized stores of knowledge as a means of investigation in their work. This knowledge incorporates both official records and criminal and related intelligence data. This distinction between official records and intelligence data is of great importance. Criminal records contain information which is available to challenge in the courts. As is well known, the problem with criminal intelligence concerns the veracity of such data, based as they often are on the subjective opinions of the officers concerned. This problem of validity is exacerbated when such data are recorded systematically on card indexes or computer files where they acquire a spurious 'objectivity' which they often ill deserve. This problem is further compounded if the persons about whom such information is collected do not have the right to inspect them and to ensure that inaccurate, irrelevant or out-dated information about them is removed or clarified (ibid.: 207-14; S. Manwaring-White 1983: 60-4).

Surveillance and Deviancy Control

In the previous section, I argued that the development of bureaucratized police forces was an important component of what Cohen has referred to recently as the 'increasing involvement of the state in the business of deviancy control' (S. Cohen 1985: 13). The emergence of a policed society was accompanied by the development of the prison, asylum and other houses of rational discipline.

This second development – the development of carceral regimes – involved the substitution of private enterprise by the state in parallel with developments in policing (and earlier in military organization). The formation of these regimes also revealed a third change: the substitution of systems of discretionary terror directed at the body by a universal tariff of imprisonment concerned with reclaiming and transforming the mind of the offender. These developments were connected. The 'humanized' penal code and the ubiquity of the prison depended on the structures of surveillance provided by a policed society. For instance, the prison could only be popularized in the social context of higher levels of crime prevention and certainty of arrest which were promised by those in favour of continuous police surveillance.

Within the enclosed receptacles of the prison and asylum, inmates were subordinated to a detailed, individualized discipline. Space and time were organized to facilitate the monitoring of behaviour through the collection and evaluation of data on 'cases'. Cohen views this process in terms of a fourth 'master pattern': the rational discipline of inmates was accompanied by the generation of classificatory grids, constituting them as particular types of deviant in the map of disorders. Every inmate was located in a specific category, 'each with its own body of scientific knowledge, and its recognised and accredited experts – professionals who eventually came to acquire specialised monopolies' (S. Cohen 1985: 13).

In the old society, prisons were relatively marginal mechanisms of punishment in a disciplinary system that was structured around the principles of indirect rule and discretionary terror (M. Ignatieff 1978: 15; M. Foucault 1979: 73-103). For example, Ignatieff argues that in England before 1775, prisons were more of a place of confinement for debtors or those

133

passing through the wheels of justice than places of punishment. In the eighteenth century, there were three main types of prison: debtors' prisons, county and borough jails, and the declining bridewells. The latter had been intended as a means of transforming the indigent poor into industrious labour suitable for employment in manufactories. Discretionary, public, corporal punishment reinforced the discipline provided by traditional authority relations of patronage which, in any case, permitted a wide range of popular liberties and illegalities in what was essentially an unpoliced society.

In addition, the organization structures of prisons were influenced by the wider social context, namely that of 'old corruption'. Administrative structures and disciplinary procedures were heterogeneous. In addition, the relations between the prison and the outside world were highly permeable. Inmates were allowed access to friends and relations through the corrupt contract and fee system which constituted an important means of social and psychological support for prisoners. As Ignatieff argues, 'visitors enjoyed the run of the yards, women commonly brought their husbands meals, and debtors drank together in the prison tap room' (M. Ignatieff 1985: 188). Whilst the fee system exacerbated the heterogeneity of disciplinary practices in prisons, in that an individual prisoner's circumstances would vary with the ability to pay, it was also the case that prisoners could sustain a social order which was autonomous from custodial power.

In stark contrast with the eighteenth century, by the mid-nineteenth century prisons had become the central means of punishing crime in the wider context of the emergence of a policed society. Moreover, prison regimes were structured less in accordance with the tolerances of old corruption and more with the principles of rational bureaucratic discipline. They became 'total institutions' (E. Goffman). Relations between prisoners and the outside world were controlled rigorously through a system of high walls, constant body searches and checks so as to ensure a minimal amount of external sources of contamination, and to maximize the deterrent value for prisoners of deprivation of the liberties of the outside world. Accordingly, the degree to which prisoners' culture could be reinforced by outside sources of support was correspondingly diminished. Similarly, the traditional 'power sharing' arrangement between prisoners and custodial staff was replaced by a system of close personal surveillance, and the imposition of a rigorous routine of activities whose timetables were under the control of warders. The warders themselves were subjected to a bureaucratic discipline (matching that of the new police). Both inmate and warder wore uniforms as visible expressions of these new social relations.

In Britain, America and France by the 1840s, 'a silent routine had been imposed to stamp out the association of the confined and to wipe out a sub-culture which was held to corrupt the novice and foster criminal behaviour' (M. Ignatieff 1985: 81). Initially, the silent routine took two forms: the silent associated system under which prisoners for some of the time during the day were allowed to congregate together in workshops but were forbidden to communicate with each other; and the separate system, as adopted in Philadelphia and, later, Pentonville, under which prisoners were kept in complete cellular isolation. They were forbidden any communication or association. Proponents of both systems argued that they suppressed prison sub-culture. Through the imposition of isolation on the prisoners they were exposed to behaviour modification through bodily discipline, or their consciences were subjected to the ministrations of the prison chaplain (U. Henriques 1972).

In Britain, the excesses of the separate system, which caused hallucinations and suicides, were tempered by the addition of more associational disciplinary elements. However, it should also be noted that until 1865, there were great variations in English prisons. Disciplinary regimes ranged from solitary drudgery to productive association (W. Cornish et al. 1978: 28–34).

The difference between the role of prisons in the eighteenth and nineteenth centuries can be illustrated by Ignatieff's discussion of the Andrews case. The case involved a boy who resisted the new prison discipline, and was subjected to extremes of punishment as a result. The boy finally escaped the rigours of the system by committing suicide. Andrews was a petty offender, and

> would not have been sent to prison *at all* in the eighteenth century. Had he been apprehended or prosecuted – unlikely in itself given the state of the police – he would have been whipped or reprimanded and delivered back to his master. In the nineteenth century, he was sent to endure a new historically specific type of pain – the strait jacket, the hand crank, the hallucinations engendered by solitude – and he was sent to endure them *alone*. In the 'reformed' prison, the inmate collectivity that might have intervened to prevent his total victimisation had been broken up and silenced. The crowds of outsiders whose presence in the yards of eighteenth century institutions acted as a rough check on custodial power were all but barred by the victory of reform. (M. Ignatieff 1978: 208, my italics).

The emergence of the modern prison involved a dual process of change: an alteration in organization structures and a shift in the ways in which deviancy was conceptualized. A similar process can be identified in respect of the rise of the asylum as a bureaucratic total institution. Here was another new organization concerned with the surveillance of deviant populations. Within

135

it, rational discipline was linked with scientific knowledge. Scull argues in the English context,

> Prior to the eighteenth century . . . lunatics were not treated as a separate category or type of deviants. Rather, they were assimilated into the much larger, more amorphous class of the morally disreputable, the poor, and the indigent, a group which also included vagrants, minor criminals and the physically handicapped. . . . It was only in the eighteenth century, and then to a comparatively limited extent, that the older ways of coping with them began to be abandoned and to be replaced by a system based on isolation and incarceration. During the nineteenth century this became the dominant response to their existence, and lunacy assumed the status of a major social problem. (A. Scull 1975: 40)

The triumph of the asylum, as with the prison, marked the ascendancy of a world view in which human deviancy was construed as transformable into normality by scientifically informed disciplinary and reformatory practices.

In Victorian England, asylums emerged as state directed, funded and inspected organizations for the incarceration and treatment of the insane. This intervention by the state in the business of deviancy control, together with the emergence of the medical and psychiatric professions as occupants of strategic positions in these organizations, were matched by the apparent willingness of all sections of society to confine the afflicted in the new carceral institutions. Furthermore, despite the emergence of the asylum as a 'curative' institution, its organizational routine were characterized largely by custodial practices in the nineteenth century. As a result, inmates of up to 1,000 in the larger asylums were confronted by an impersonal, bureaucratized total institution (A. Scull 1975: 424).

As Ingleby, drawing on Foucault, argues, although the introduction of confinement of the insane occurred during the seventeenth century in absolutist France, 'it was not for another two centuries that the establishment of public asylums became standard policy in most of the west.' (D. Ingleby 1985: 146-7). The triumph of bureaucratic control in the nineteenth century was followed by that of the therapeutic state (D. Ingleby 1985. The next few paragraphs draw extensively on this work.) This comprises three components. Firstly, the primacy of the medical profession's expertise in dealing with the insane is firmly established. Asylum management and decisions about who should be incarcerated are formally entrusted to the profession. The concept of mental illness is also accepted as an appropriate formulation for all kinds of insanity – a situation characteristic of western Europe and the USA by the mid-nineteenth century. Secondly, with the base of asylum practice firmly established, medical authority is extended beyond the asylum population. This practice is reflected in a shift in discourse: the concept of mental illness is extended beyond insanity to cover social deviations regarded as not severe enough to call for incarceration. 'New categories of pathology are devised – specifically the neuroses – and new sites of intervention are established in which psychiatry can attack pathology at its very roots – family life, industry and the school system' (D. Ingleby 1985: 161). Thirdly, the development of this more extensive system of professionally directed supervisory activities is legitimized, or, *pace* Foucault, constituted in part by the flourishing of the social sciences. These formulate 'methods of surveillance and theories that extend into every nook and cranny of social life, employing techniques established as reputable within the realm of the natural sciences' (D. Ingleby 1985: 161). The power of the 'medical model' became entrenched in society. In the medical model of control, the doctor determines who is sick and what is in the best interests of the patient. Illness is regarded as a purely natural event without social meaning and without any author. The problem of affliction resides within the patient him or herself, rather than in the wider social context. As the medical model acquired generalized significance in the wider society, the asylum – the original site of its operations – became less important. Thus, as the carceral regimes of total institutions experience a relative population decline, the circuits of surveillance exert their grip over the wider population (ibid.: 160–2).

The extent of the move away from incarceration as a strategy of surveillance and social control remains a matter of debate. Before dealing with this issue, the problem of explaining why deviancy control became a focus for the growth of bureaucratic surveillance will be discussed.

The birth of the prison and asylum has been the subject of a number of revisionist discussions (S. Cohen and A. Scull 1985). As with debates on the new police, these have questioned the validity of accounts which either accept the humanitarian, progressive intentions of reformers at face value, or locate them in the context of a teleological view of the triumph of scientific reason and humanity (M. Ignatieff 1985: 75). Revisionism has also questioned those accounts which explicitly connect the prison and asylum to the functional imperatives of complex industrial societies, in which formal bureaucratic organizations supplant informal community-based mechanisms for the regulation of social life. However, as was observed in the case of the police, some revisionist authors, in drawing on Marxist theory, have not escaped from falling into a few functionalist traps of their own.

The view presented here draws on different strands in revisionist accounts: it includes a focus on the relationship between the new regimes and the demands of capitalism as an economic system together with the interests of dominant classes; the location of reformers' motives in the context of a non-reductionist account of ideology; an equally non-reductionist view of the pragmatic interests and behaviour of the state in ordering a society of strangers and in dispensing privileges, for instance to new professional occupations.

The ideological changes associated with the birth of the new prisons and asylums should not be regarded as the reflex of economic imperatives. The intentions of reformers cannot be understood in terms of the 'ventriloquist' activities of a dominant class. Of course, one cannot understand the birth of the prison and asylum outside the constraints of a capitalist economy. However, that system provided opportunities for the pursuit of professionalism as an occupational strategy and this cannot be interpreted simply in terms of the asymmetrical interests of capital and labour. In addition, such regimes, as technologies of social control, once created are useful enough to survive a transplant to other types of society, e.g. socialist ones. Finally, these new regimes had important connections with democratic sovereignty as well as with the economic constraints of capitalism.

These arguments can be defended by considering three related questions: why were these regimes introduced? How can their organizational routines and timetables be explained? In what respects and why have recent developments involved a break with the bureaucratic carceral archipelago established in the nineteenth century? The first two questions will be discussed together.

The new prisons and asylums did not simply involve new techniques of organization and surveillance; they presupposed a major restructuring of how criminality, insanity and deviance generally were conceptualized. It will be recalled that during the later eighteenth and early nineteenth century, there were three components of such an epistemic transformation: evangelical Christianity, utilitarianism and an ethos of positive scientific enquiry (pp. 117–18).

In contrast with previous views, which stressed that crime was an outcome of innate wickedness, criminality was now increasingly regarded as an environmental product amenable to social transformation. Thus the criminal was constituted as a person who could be saved and returned to society as a moral, productive citizen. In the utilitarian vision, this salvation was to be engineered through the rational discipline of behaviour – the repair of a defective mechanism through techniques of bodily discipline, isolation and surveillance. Alternatively, techniques of isolation were to be employed as a means of promoting a religious transformation of the individual: isolation would produce an experience of shame and a desire to return to society as a moral being. The differences between these ideological views were illustrated in part by the silent and separate systems respectively. As Cornish has argued, 'evangelism invoked useful work and moral instruction; utilitarianism an arduous puritanical deterrent regime of behaviour modification' (W. R. Cornish et al. 1978: 27; C. Harding et al. 1985: 143-7).

In the eighteenth century, mental disorder was in the main construed as unchained animality. This could only be controlled externally through brutal discipline; this was a mark of the afflicted's loss of contact with humanity. The modern age shared an abhorrence for insanity with the preceding period, but felt it could, with self-confidence, dismiss the cognitive validity of the insane's view of the world *and* through therapeutic intervention reinstate sanity within the afflicted individual.

Scull argues that evangelicalism and Benthamism were important sources of lunacy reform in the nineteenth century: the first as a means of changing and moralizing the individual (although to this one must add the influence of rational science); the second as an advocation of centralized professional administration. As Scull suggests,

> Benthamites and the rising class of professional administrators . . . sought radical reductions in the numbers of [autonomous, local] authorities and their subjection to central direction, to ensure the effective and efficient implementation of the policies productive of the greatest happiness of the greatest number. (A. Scull 1975: 184)

In England, by 1845,

> the insane had been sharply distinguished from other types of indigent and troublesome people, and the asylum had been officially recognized as the most suitable place for them. . . . It was, the reformers agreed, a triumph of science and humanity. (ibid.: 214)

Ignatieff takes up Foucault's suggestion that these ideas were aspects of a broader cultural and political context – one of democratic sovereignty. The ideology of the new discipline included a political theory within its visions of power and order.

> Democratic republics which represent law and order as the embodied will of all the people treat disobedient minorities more severely than monarchical societies which have no ideological commitment to the consensual attachment of their citizens. (M. Ignatieff 1985: 84, 1978: 212)

The discretionary, spectacular terror of the ancien regime was rooted not just in the administrative weakness of the state but also in a view of sovereignty as an expression of the personal will of the monarch. Democratic sovereignty has a natural affinity with the centralization of political power and the universal implementation of the will of the majority through a bureaucratic machine, as for example in the application of an impersonal legal code to all citizens equally. This Tocquevillean theme is echoed in Foucault's suggestion that in the ancien regime, power was personalized around the figure of the monarch, with the mass of the population being a relatively undifferentiated object of that power. By contrast, in modern society, power is impersonalized in the social system, applies universally to all, subjecting every individual to its rules and record-gathering activities. Impersonalization of power, then, goes hand in hand with a process of individualization (M. Foucault 1979: 193; J. O'Neill 1986).

Ignatieff seeks to integrate the insights of Tocqueville and Marx by linking the impact of democratic sovereignty with the constraints of a new class society. Thus he argues that

[t]he extension of rights within civil society had to be compensated for by the abolition of the tacit liberties enjoyed by prisoners and criminals under the ancien regime. In an unequal and increasingly divided society, this was the only way to extend liberty and fortify consent without compromising security. (M. Ignatieff 1978: 212)

In this context, Ignatieff views the emergence of professional administrative and entrepreneurial classes (the principal carriers of the ideological currents in question) as elements of a new strategy of class power. However, as Ignatieff later acknowledges, this suggestion underestimates the diversity of interests and views amongst these groups (M. Ignatieff 1985). In particular, it underplays the autonomy of professional and bureaucratic self-interest from the imperatives of capital. (As will be seen below, pp. 142–4, this issue also arises in relation to recent discussions of the asylum.)

This line of argument points to the fact that the ideological changes discussed above did not occur in a social vacuum. Yet this does not mean that they were simply the effects of socioeconomic structures. However, such a suggestion has been at the heart of some influential Marxist analyses whose roots can be traced from Rusche and Kircheimer's *Punishment and Social Structure* through to the more recent works of Melossi and Pavarini (G. Rusche and O. Kircheimer 1939; D. Melossi and M. Pavarini 1981; D. Melossi 1978).

Melossi and Pavarini's case involves four related arguments: first, under conditions of modern capitalism, the prison and factory are characterized by analogous organization structures, timetables and disciplinary systems; second, this rational discipline was originally a bourgeois invention, designed for the control of labour under conditions of class conflict and labour shortage; third, the prison and other related agencies of social control perform vital functions in modern capitalism, (i.e. over and above the intentions of their original designers); and fourth, the historical phases of modern capitalism are associated with changes in the structures of surveillance. Three changes are regarded as of particular significance: (1) within the factory, a shift from personal control to impersonal technical rationality as a mechanism for supervising the labour process (see pp. 176–92); (2) a concentration of capital with the emergence of 'organized' capitalism. This involves a greater planning of production and the introduction of administered prices, the tightening of instruments of social control outside the factory, the design of new instruments of control outside the factory, particularly in respect of propaganda, control of the media and the tighter policing of urbanized populations. In this context, the city itself rather than the prison becomes the analogue of the disciplinary structure of the factory; and (3) a shift in recent decades from secondary to primary mechanisms of surveillance. This process involves a relative decline of the prison and related organizations and an increased emphasis on other foci for the surveillance of populations, such as the school and the family, or in societies with conscription, the army.

The second and third changes identified by Melossi and Pavarini will be considered in the next section. Here the focus is on their account of the origins of the prison and the supposed connection between it and the factory.

There are a number of problems with arguments which link the prison with the imperatives of modern capitalism. On occasion, the connections between the market economy and class conflict on the one hand and the evolution of the prison and asylum on the other, are based as much on conjecture as on historical evidence. This means that either the motives of those who established these organizations are regarded as epiphenomena of economic imperatives, or that reformers and dominant classes are viewed as united, conspiratorially, in a strategy of class power. However, as Bailey has argued, to see the prison reformers as 'unified groups certain of their objectives is to neglect the diversity of viewpoints to be found in the nineteenth century' (V. Bailey 1981: 13). These would appear to be sensible criticisms; nevertheless, they should not be allowed to dictate a view of social change as a seamless web of events. This would constitute a return to the weaknesses of narrative accounts considered earlier. Ignatieff himself has commented usefully on this issue. He argues that an adequate account of the relationship between the prison and modern capitalism, in addition to rejecting an *ad hoc* narrative approach to historical events, would have to avoid two other pitfalls: a teleological view of history as the unfolding of a moral crusade; and a portrayal of the prison as an outcome of the strategy of a seemingly all-powerful ruling class (M. Ignatieff 1985: 83–101).

However, a Marxist analysis reconstructed along the lines recommended by Ignatieff would also have to question the connection which writers have drawn between the prison and the factory. Of course, it would be difficult to deny that the regimes of good order, useful work and discipline established in the new prisons were infused with the bourgeois values of an emergent capitalist society. However, as Ingatieff himself recognizes, the deprivation of a person's liberty through imprisonment is a democratic punishment as much as a capitalist one. It is hard to see how the abolition of capitalism would in any way reduce the appeal of the prison to democratic sentiments, notwithstanding any of its supposed 'failures' (M. Ignatieff 1978: 215–20). In addition, as Foucault, following Bentham himself, has stressed, the techniques of 'panopticism' were as much expressions of technical rationality as they were instruments of class power. They were very successful means of exercising surveillance by the few over many individuals. It is possible both to accept this argument and admit that in certain societies prisons are filled disproportionately by people from one class rather than another.

However, to say this is not to follow Foucault's exaggerated view that modern rational discipline takes the same form in all institutional contexts. Modern discipline is not all of a piece. As Giddens has argued,

By lumping together the surveillance of the prison with that involved in other contexts of capitalist society, and indeed in regarding the prison (panopticon) as the *exemplar* of power as discipline, Foucault produces too negative view of bourgeois freedoms and of the liberal reformist zeal they helped to inspire. (A. Giddens 1981: 172)

For Giddens, there are two important differences between the prison and the capitalist factory. First, 'the capitalist workplace is not as prisons are and as clinics and hospitals may be, total institutions.' (ibid.) Second, 'the worker is not forcibly incarcerated in the factory, but enters the gates of the workplace as "free wage labour".' (ibid.) Problems of worker resistance and the managerial control of labour are encountered in forms which are not found in prisons. Thus, the analogy drawn between prisons and factories and related Marxist or Foucaultian attempts to reveal the despotic reality behind the appearance of freedom in modern capitalism are at best overdrawn and at worst misconceived.

Some of the difficulties associated with drawing a connection between the imperatives of capitalism or class interests and the prison can also be found in the literature concerned with the emergence of the asylum. The significance of Scull's analysis is that, as in related discussions of the new police and prison, a critical stance is adopted towards Whig narratives of lunacy reform. As with Ignatieff's view of the prison, Scull locates the asylum in terms of the imperatives of capitalism and the objectives of a new strategy of class power. However, the merit of Scull's analysis is that he also focuses on professionalism as an occupational strategy of power (A. Scull 1975: 321-5, 494-562).

For Scull, the birth of the asylum was linked with the emergence of psychiatry as a profession. The strategy of professionalization was associated with the creation of insanity as a specific social and medical category together with the emergence of the central state in the activity of deviancy control. The latter process was defined by a shift away from localism, self-help and family support as the foci for the giving of help to the insane, towards bureaucratized, institutional provision.

This new society which cut across the rural–urban divide weakened the mechanisms of family assistance whilst offering opportunities for those who wished to pay for the specialist services of private mad houses. Meanwhile, the great majority had to make do with some sort of household relief. However, many of these were new wage earners: with the boom and slump cycle of the capitalist economy, they found it difficult to rely on household relief.

The rising costs of poor relief and the inconvenience caused by dislocated populations to the authorities made the institutional model of incarceration increasingly attractive on the grounds of cost and practicality. It provided an effective means of exercising surveillance over suspect populations and instilling in them appropriate work habits. The establishment of workhouses raised the question of what to do with the insane who disrupted the organizational routines of those institutions. Thus, consideration was given to disposing of such individuals within separate receptacles. In England, while magistrates played a role in securing the separation of the insane from the able-bodied poor, their reluctance to commit public money to the establishment of asylums led to the flourishing of private houses for the insane in the first half of the nineteenth century. The construction of a public asylum system with a national inspectorate was a slow development in England. As with public health and the police, there was a deep-seated resistance to the formation of a Benthamite, centralized state.

The new system of asylums, as an aspect of a stronger public power, was associated with the emergence of psychiatric and medical professions together with the substitution of the moral by the medical model of insanity. Medical expertise became the basis for the professional definition of the needs of clients. One consequence of this successful strategy of professionalization was an increase in the size of the insane population. In order to explain this development, Scull emphasizes the impact of the eager profession *and* a willing public, persuaded by the value of medical definitions of reality in respect of problems of insanity (A. Scull 1975: 593–616).

The 'eager medical profession' was successful in its occupational strategy because market society allowed it to become a provider of services in exchanges between strangers where systems of self-help and localized family provision proved ineffective. Shifts in knowledge allowed the emergent profession to accumulate expertise, legitimacy and thus leverage in selling their services. In addition, the public power of the state was crucial in disposing and guaranteeing the occupational privileges of medical and other professional status groups (cf. T. J. Johnson 1972: 51–61; M. Larson 1977: 2–18).

Scull's thesis, rather like that of Ignatieff, is connected with a broader Marxist framework of assumptions. He views the professions and other privileged groups in state and society as the 'upper classes' who, collectively, were responsible for the creation of the asylum and other carceral regimes. They had shared interests in devising cheap, effective regimes of surveillance to assist in the promotion of labour discipline and the social control of an emerging working class. In socially organizing the differentiation of the able bodied from the mentally incapable poor, they obeyed the rationality of the market and thus helped to smooth the process of capitalist development.

However, this particular argument undermines the value of what preceded it. Again, as Bailey was seen to comment earlier, it is not very helpful to view the upper classes as united in a conspiratorial strategy, let alone one which functions to secure the imperatives of capitalism. Rather, the profession had its own interests, as did the pragmatic state in reconstructing the social order of market society.

In the preceding arguments, the focus of discussion was on the emergence of the prison and asylum as expressions of the growth of bureaucratic surveillance and the power of the modern state. The nineteenth century was an age in which bureaucratic total institutions were created in response to problems of deviancy and social control in a society of strangers. However, a number of writers have argued that, with the transition from liberal to organized capitalism, the carceral regimes decline in significance. As Melossi has suggested, there has been a shift from secondary to primary circuits of surveillance. In addition, in the remaining field of secondary surveillance, there emerges a new emphasis on non-custodial techniques and the development of inter-linked systems of mass adminstration. Thus, in the more policed societies of organized capitalism, the prison and asylum are revealed as mechanisms of social control whose true place is in liberal capitalist societies. In organized capitalism, *society* itself becomes the disciplinary mechanism.

In some respects, this argument is paralleled in Foucault's discussion of surveillance and modern discipline. As was observed earlier, for Foucault the birth of the prison and asylum marked the perfection of surveillance techniques or a 'microphysics of power' developed in the seventeenth century. Once instituted in the carceral regimes of capitalist society, these techniques are increasingly dispersed to the wider society itself; the prison was simply an exemplar of what has become a disciplinary society.

As Sheridan argues,

Crime produced the prison, the prison the delinquent class; the existence of a delinquent class an excuse for the policing of the entire population. This policing led to extraction and recording of information about groups and individuals; the human sciences gained a terrain and patron; crime came to be seen as a departure from the Norm, a sickness to be understood if not cured; this provided a justification for the 'examination' of the entire population. (A. Sheridan 1980: 161–2)

Thus today, 'judges of normality are present everywhere. We are in the society of the teacher judge, the doctor judge, the educator judge, the social worker judge; it is on them that the universal reign of the narrative is based' (M. Foucault, cited in A. Sheridan 1980: 162).

For Melossi, these changes in the structures of surveillance reflect the requirements of modern capitalism. In contrast, Foucault's analysis emphasizes the demands of technical rationality and the effects of the classificatory impulses of a constantly proliferating number of expert occupations. These apparent changes need further, more detailed, analysis. It is in this context that Stanley Cohen's challenging contribution to the social theory of surveillance can be evaluated (S. Cohen 1985).

Cohen considers the question of whether the decarceration or 'destructuring' movements initiated in western societies during the 1960s should be viewed as an indication that the bureaucratic system inherited from the nineteenth century is in the process of being fundamentally transformed.

Destructuring ideologies are discussed in terms of their advocacy of four changes in the structures of surveillance and social control: first, a shift away from centralized state control towards decentralization, deformalization, and non-intervention; second, a move away from categorization, separate knowledge systems and professionalism and the classificatory impulse towards de-professionalization, de-medicalization, anti-psychiatry and forms of self-help; third, the substitution of the asylum and the prison by community care and non-custodial responses to deviance; fourth, less emphasis on positivistic science as a means of establishing causal knowledge about the mental processes of deviants in favour of, on the one hand, neo-classical and justice models which emphasize 'just' punishment for offences committed by morally responsible individuals, and, on the other, more behaviourist models which eschew explanation in favour of programmes for the control of deviancy that simply 'work' (S. Cohen 1985: 30-6).

Cohen suggests that in-so-far as any of these processes have occurred, they do not constitute a serious departure from the bureaucratic patterns laid down in the nineteenth century. For example, in the field of mental health, the partial introduction of decarceration and community control occurred largely for administrative reasons to do with the budgetary crisis of the welfare state rather than as the result of a successful intellectual critique of institutional provision. In addition, to the extent that destructuring ideas did have an impact on these changes, the new techniques of control were not proved to be either cheaper or more effective in reducing significantly the rates of recidivism than the traditional custodial regimes. More importantly, in relation to crime and delinquency, if not for mental illness, the process of decarceration or the 'death of the prison' and other custodial organizations was simply not occurring, as is evident for example from the rates of institutionalization of offenders, particularly in the UK (ibid.: 37-8, 76-86).

To the extent to which such processes of decarceration have occurred, Cohen questions whether they are more humane and less intrusive than traditional custodial based systems. The old carceral regime remains while the new techniques simply involve the state in preventative intervention in the field of deviance at an earlier stage than had been the case before.

Cohen reconstructs the historical process of prison reform as an example of what has happened to the structure of surveillance since the nineteenth century. Four historical phases are distinguished: first, control in the community (what was referred to earlier as the system of indirect rule, pp. 111-16); second, the introduction of the prison as a sequestrated and idealized model of what a community should be in a bourgeois democratic society; third, the reformation of the prison so as to decrease the differences between its disciplinary system and that of the wider society (the humanizing of prison discipline in the twentieth century); and fourth, the techniques of prison discipline are introduced into the wider society as part of the extension of a dense network of preventative surveillance. As with Foucault and Melossi, the contemporary focus of surveillance and discipline is not the prison, nor even the city, but rather the whole society (ibid.: 40-86).

Cohen's explanation of both current changes in the carceral archipelago and developments in the nineteenth century derives from a critique and synthesis of different strands of revisionist thinking in social theory. The strength of his account is that he seeks to integrate a number of arguments. These entail a non-reductionist view of reformer's ideologies, and an emphasis on the imperatives of the political economy of capitalism and class interests. He also stresses the administrative constraints of bureaucratic organizations which, for example in the field of mental health in the nineteenth century, could transform treatment into custody. Finally, Cohen wishes to focus on the self-interest of emergent professional groups.

Although Cohen's thesis tends towards an acknowledged eclecticism, it is clear that he is impressed by the impact of what has been termed here as the classificatory impulse and professionalism on current developments in the carceral archipelago. Thus, he refers to the 'seemingly inexorable process by which society keeps classifying, controlling, excluding more and more groups according to age, sex, race, behaviour, moral status, ability or psychic state' (ibid.: 267).

It seems that this process involves all members of society: drawing on Foucault and echoing Scull's views, the urge to classify is viewed as a product of the age of science and technical rationality. However, this process is also one which can be used to good advantage by groups seeking to gain professional status and the conferral of legitimacy by a willing state and public. Thus Cohen shows how the destructuring movements of the 1960s involved only a superficial dismantling of professionalism and an intrusive state in the field of deviancy and social control.

Cohen also attempts to connect current developments with strategies of class power in modern capitalism, particularly in respect of the problem of what some writers have referred to as the 'underclass'. On the basis of this view, Cohen predicts that in the future social control of deviance, what he refers to as inclusionary and exclusionary techniques will be combined in ways reminiscent of Orwell's vision in *1984*. By strategies of exclusion and inclusion, Cohen is referring to, for example, the regimes of incarceration and sequestration of the nineteenth century, and the destructuring movements of the 1960s respectively. Considerations of class power in part determine the nature of the oscillation between the two methods and their objects. Thus, it is to be expected that inclusion will be extended, but only at what is termed the 'soft' end of criminal deviance. At the 'hard' end, systems of exclusion would persist. By the soft end Cohen is referring to 'mental health, the new growth therapies, middle class thought crime, the tutelage of family life, the minor delinquent infractions' (ibid.: 232).

A second area in which inclusionary strategies of surveillance are to be

147

expected is that of public space: this will involve the extension of inclusionary work at present concerned with the surveillance of families to the wider social environment. Here Cohen is referring to the part played by surveillance objectives in the design of housing, leisure and other public spaces (ibid.: 233–5).

Meanwhile strategies of exclusionary surveillance in bureaucratic institutions will persist at the hard end of deviance. This is for two reasons: as a bargain with those at the soft end, to reassure them that the state 'means business' with those serious and incorrigible offenders; and secondly, for the Durkheimian reason that the existence of a stigmatized, sequestered group of deviants provides a basis for the celebration by society of the division between the virtuous 'us' and the evil 'them'. Of course, at the hard end of deviance and providing a disproportionate number of the inmates of such institutions are the working class (ibid.: 234–5).

The strengths of Cohen's thesis lie in its integration of a number of different strands in contemporary social theory and the way it makes sense of much of the contemporary scene: the variations in strategies of surveillance depending on the social status of the subject population; how the state is tempted to use new technologies and knowledge to construct preventative strategies against deviance; the ways in which professions seek to exploit that temptation; and finally, the ways in which the public *itself* on occasion actively seeks out control and guidance from experts in order to sustain a meaningful existence in a society of strangers. Surveillance is then, in part a product of what Fromm referred to as people's 'fear of freedom' in modern societies.

However, Cohen's work is not free of weaknesses. These stem from his argument that moves towards a socialist transformation of society would reduce radically the significance of bureaucratic surveillance in society. In this context, he argues that at present, urban design, for example adventure playgrounds and the like, is used as a means of controlling the incidence of vandalism on the part of young inhabitants of urban high-rise flats. The 'control' thinking behind such schemes is similar to that which inspires the placing of video cameras at strategic locations in the urban landscape. Cohen argues that the government should 'direct scarce resources right away from the system (of social control) and devote them to policies (family, education, community, health, fiscal, etc.) which are not justified in control terms at all' (ibid.: 264). This suggestion 'offers instead of planning for order and control the opportunity to plan for human happiness and fulfilment' (ibid.). At the same time, Cohen advocates the reversal of the processes of professionalization, and argues that the state itself should play a far less significant role in the field of deviancy and social control (ibid.: 267). By this he means that social control should be located in community institutions and that figures of authority should be far more accountable to the wishes of *local* populations.

There are a number of difficulties with these arguments. As has been argued earlier, socialist planning mechanisms would involve an increase, not a decrease, in the growth of bureaucratic surveillance; such are the consequences of planning for the 'happiness of all'. In addition, such planning systems would include coercive or 'power over' elements because there would continue to be disagreements between groups as to what such plans and priorities for human happiness should entail.

Cohen argues that the accountability of agents of surveillance to subject populations might be increased through an institutionalized separation between central and local administration of services and a diminution of the role of the state in the activities of deviancy control. However, no convincing grounds are provided in support of the view that such arrangements are more likely to flourish under socialist rather than capitalist conditions. Indeed, as Weber and Tocqueville argued the reverse seems far more likely. It was observed earlier that the strength of Cohen's analysis concerned his discussion of the relationships between surveillance, professionalization and the classificatory impulse. However, this discussion stands in an uneasy relationship with Cohen's focus on the impact of class power and political economy on the organization of surveillance. As was argued in the case of Foucault, the 'seemingly inexorable process by which society keeps classifying' and the opportunities this process provides to expert professions and the pragmatic state, all seem constituitive of modern societies. They would easily survive any social transition from capitalism to socialism.

5

Capitalism, Surveillance and the Modern Business Enterprise

The dynamics of modern western societies derive from a conjunction between the rivalries of nation-states on the one hand, and the competition amongst capitalist enterprises in the market system on the other. In each field of struggle, the organizations concerned have undergone a process of bureaucratization. Having examined the development of the military and policing powers of the modern nation-state and the ways in which the resources of capitalism provided their economic basis, the discussion now turns to the market system itself and the bureaucratization of the capitalist enterprise.

As in the past, the market system continues to be 'bigger than the nation state' (J. Hall 1983; I. Wallerstein 1979). Whatever particular governments may do in the capitalist world system, that system is defined by the mobility of capital and the ability of corporations to act independently of political control.

The core of the capitalist economic system comprises market competition amongst privately owned enterprises engaged in commodity production. Although market competition has been a constant feature of the development of the capitalist economic system, the latter has been characterized by a number of phases in the context of which the rise of the modern bureaucratic corporation can be understood. These have usually been described in terms of a shift from competitive to organized capitalism. Despite the terminological variations employed by writers on this issue, the changes involved seem clear enough. They involved shifts in the relationships between the capitalist economic system and the state, and changes in both the relations amongst enterprises within the economic system and their internal modes of administration.

Following Habermas and Offe, 'liberal capitalism' can be defined in terms of the principles of the free market and a 'facilitative' state, whereas, 'organized capitalism' involves an administered market and a 'directive' state. The difference between the two systems is indicated by the relative priority of the market and bureaucracy as mechanisms of allocation and co-ordination (J. Habermas 1976; C. Offe 1972).

Under liberal capitalism, the relationship between the rational-legal state and the market economy is a facilitative one. The 'laissez-faire' state has in the past been referred to by some writers as a weak institution, but as others have argued, this is a quite misleading view. The strength of the liberal state was revealed in its provision of the conditions of existence of capitalist economic activity in respect of social relations internal and external to the national state. Habermas identifies two facilitative activities of the state under liberal capitalism: first, the political constitution of the capitalist economic system or its conditions of operation, through the provision of systems of civil law, guarantees of property and freedom of contract. In addition, he identifies activities that protected market capitalism from 'self-destructive side effects', as in currency stabilization, the regulation of monopoly tendencies in the economy, provision of infrastructure services such as transport and communications, armed force at home and abroad; second, Habermas focuses on state provision of what he terms market complementing activities: such as the adaption of the legal system to business requirements, e.g. changes in corporate law in response to the growth of the firm.

Thus, the laissez-faire, liberal state was far from weak in its political relationship with the free market economy. On the other hand, it *was* weak in respect of its incapacity to subordinate the national economy to overall political direction and, in conjunction with other states, subordinate international exchanges to political planning other than through the facilitative processes identified above (J. Habermas 1976: 20-4).

Within this institutional context, the free market economy was based on transactions between small and medium-sized enterprises which approximated conditions of perfect competition. In addition, although liberal capitalism developed in the context of a world-trading economy, the scope of the typical enterprise's market activities was local and regional. Its operations were largely within the confines of the nation-state.

As is the case with all ideal types, that of liberal capitalism has only been approximated in any given society. More importantly, it has been an exceptional form of capitalist development, typified most strongly by England and the USA in the early and middle nineteenth century. The more normal occurrence has been capitalist development under the supervision of a more authoritarian or directive state.

Modern capitalist societies have adopted a more organized structure than

151

that characteristic of the liberal era, although, of course, this has not necessarily involved recourse to the authoritarian arrangements of the fascist regimes (J. Habermas 1976: 33-42).

Under organized capitalism, the facilitative relationships between political and economic institutions have been transformed into a more directive system. As Habermas has suggested, this shift is defined by an intensification and extension of the facilitative activities of the state and the emergence of two new forms of market-replacing activities. Here Habermas refers, firstly, to government investment in the production of commodities that market forces are unable or unwilling to provide, e.g. in research and development, training of the labour force, high-risk capital projects, or those regarded as of national importance. Secondly, Habermas focuses on how the state 'compensates for the dysfunctional consequences of an accumulation process that have elicited politically effective reactions on the part of individual capital groupings, organised labour or other organised groups' (ibid.: 54). Important examples include the provision of state expenditure on controlling the ecological impact of industry; the regulation of health and safety at work, the protection of industrial and agricultural sectors that would be eliminated by the normal processes of market competition, and a range of social expenditures in an age of universal citizenship.

Both these areas of 'market-replacing' state activities are linked with the growth of a larger public sector as a proportion of the employed work force, consumption of GNP, and in terms of the general centrality of the state in organizing the economy. Some of these resources are redistributed to the business sector, thus indicating the more collaborative arrangements between large business enterprises and the state under organized capitalism. This tendency is especially marked in the state-dependent sectors of the economy, e.g. in the defence and aerospace industries.

Within this broad institutional framework, the economic system of organized capitalism, more narrowly conceived, comprises a number of features. In turn, these provide the context for considering changes both in the relationships amongst business enterprises and in their internal modes of administration.

Following Lash and Urry, who draw on the work of Kocka, the more important features of the economic system of organized capitalism are:

1 A concentration of industrial, financial and banking capital in the capitalist economy with the rise to pre-eminence of large-scale business enterprises.
2 The growth of large business enterprises means that the co-ordination of the economic division of labour through relations of market exchange

amongst a multitude of autonomous competing enterprises has been supplanted by the bureaucratic co-ordination of tasks by managerial hierarchies within large firms.

3 The growth of large-scale business enterprises is defined not simply in terms of their assets, number of employees, plants or size of output, but also in terms of the scope of their operations. As Chandler and others have shown, in modern capitalism the activities of large corporations extend from regional and national contexts to the international arena (A. Chandler 1979).

4 With the growth of the large business enterprise, the bargaining groups within these organizations, particularly employers associations and trades unions, operate increasingly at the national level in respect of political and industrial activities.

5 The emergence of organized capitalism is associated with a process of spatial regionalization. This involves the development of industrial capitalist activities within key industrial sectors and regions, and in a few: 'centrally significant nation-states' (S. Lash and J. Urry 1987: 4). Within this economic and regional structure, extractive and manufacturing activities play the dominant role (S. Lash and J. Urry 1987: 3–4).

The shift from liberal to organized capitalism involved a major expansion in the surveillance capacities of large-scale business enterprises, which have experienced a process of bureaucratization. However, before discussing the process in more detail, some of Lash and Urry's recent arguments will be considered. In their view, the processes of bureaucratization and centralization in modern capitalism observed by Marx and Weber are now being reversed: thus their reference to the emergence of what they term 'disorganized capitalism'.

Lash and Urry point to important changes in contemporary capitalism. However, the view to be defended here is that these processes, do not constitute a major reversal of the long-term trend towards bureaucratization: there has been an increase in the surveillance capacities of large business corporations and the economic pre-eminence of such enterprises remains intact. The term 'organized capitalism' remains a useful means of characterizing the structure of modern capitalist societies, and the changes which concern Lash and Urry are perhaps best considered as processes of reorganization.

From the standpoint of economic institutions, six interrelated developments over the last decade or so are of particular significance for Lash and Urry's thesis on disorganized capitalism:

1 The larger corporations have moved to a global rather than simply

153

national or international level of operations. Taking advantage of electronic means of surveillance and techniques of transferring information, financial and other resources, such enterprises have sub-divided their operations and located them in different countries depending on product markets, labour costs and so on. Modern large corporations can control these dispersed operational units because electronic techniques of surveillance break through the space-time limitations of communications systems based on word of mouth, handwriting and the printed word.

In addition, the dispersal of operations has been linked with a process of product diversification. The identity of large firms can no longer be understood in terms of a single product or product range. Tobacco companies become involved in media industries and so on. Global companies cut across both product markets and the boundaries of nation-states with their dispersed operations (J. Scott 1985:13-14).

2 With this growth of the global corporation, there has been a corresponding decline in both the capacity of the nation-state to regulate corporate activities, and a weakening of the international political mechanisms for the control of the international capitalist economic system.

3 There has been a decline in the centrality of extractive and manufacturing industries and an increase in the significance of the service sector of the economy. At the same time, the remaining extractive and manufacturing capacity is increasingly deployed in Third World or newly developing countries instead of in mature capitalist centres. Consequently, the regional concentration and fixity of the past, both within particular societies and between them is giving way to spatial dispersal.

4 The dispersal of economic activities in part reflects the expansion in the number of societies experiencing capitalist development: thus capitalism is no longer confined to a 'few centrally significant nation-states'.

5 The emergence of global corporate activities is linked with a decline in corporatist arrangements amongst capital, labour and the state. The focus of capital has shifted away from industrial negotiations within the political arena of the nation-state. At the same time, the dispersal and complexity of the economic division of labour means that the more important sectors of the labour movement are hardly in a position to provide an effective collaborative structure for the collective discipline of the *national* work force. Organized labour is less in a position to provide what capital is in any case less interested in receiving.

6 Within the economic division of labour, there has been a relative decline in production for mass markets in favour of the provision of customized goods for more specific market niches. Large firms at the leading edge of modern capitalism have encountered the challenge of Third World produc-

tion for mass markets. In response to this, these enterprises have relied on new machine tool and electronics industries to stay ahead of the competition. They have sought to provide better quality, customized goods for the more individualistic and discriminating markets created by the 'postmodernist' currents of the contemporary age. For example, machine tools are produced for multi-purpose use in more craft-oriented plants rather than for long runs of uniform products. Under these conditions, independent, small and craft-based enterprises can flourish, as indeed can the subsidiaries of large firms. These subsidiaries can exercise a new discretion in their activities, reflecting a looser or 'weaker' structure of control than that characteristic of large firms in the era of mass production.

Within this context, the average size of plants has decreased. This has allowed the flourishing of more flexible work practices, for example, craft group work, instead of the more regimented bureaucratic structures so characteristic of mass production systems such as the traditional production lines of the motor industry.

These are important changes in the economic structure of modern capitalism. However, it is misleading to conceptualize them in terms of a process of disorganization. Three grounds can be adduced in support of this view. First, on more than one occasion, Lash and Urry indicate that the term 'disorganized' is either misleading or inappropriate and suggest the alternative term 'restructuration' (S. Lash and J. Urry 1988: 8).

Second, although a wide range of social, economic and political changes are grouped under the term 'disorganized capitalism', the most important purpose it serves for Lash and Urry is to reveal a set of developments that reverse the processes of bureaucratization and centralization identified by Marx and Weber. However, as they themselves argue in relation to the first and last changes outlined immediately above:

> Although . . . one important feature of modern disorganised capitalism has been a tendency both for average plant size to decline and for some increases in the number of small enterprises, this does not mean that large enterprises are decreasingly significant for the overall development of western capitalism. (S. Lash and J. Urry 1988: 88)

Large firms remain pre-eminent. New customized production runs are far from being the preserve of small independent businesses. It is true that subsidiaries of large companies caught up in these new technological and market changes have acquired more autonomy in their operations. However, as will be shown later, this administrative development is an extension of

155

fairly long standing *bureaucratic* structures which increasingly hinge on a division between strategic and tactical control. Subsidiary concerns can pursue autonomous operations within overall strategic plans formulated at head office, and within strict financial and budgetary controls. Indeed, this bureaucratically restricted discretion presupposes the extension of precisely those electronic means of surveillance which Lash and Urry rightly argue are distinctive features of contemporary capitalism.

It is also the case that with the relative shift away from mass production, enterprises can have recourse to the more flexible work practices in smaller plants for their labour forces. But, so far, this does not seem to constitute a reversal of the bureaucratization of the control of labour which has occured since the nineteenth century. The heritage of systematic or scientific management may be being supplemented but it is hardly being discarded on a major scale. At least in respect of economic institutions then, bureaucratization hardly seems to be a process in reverse.

Attention can now be turned to the question of how the emergence of these bureaucratic hierarchies, and thus the growth of surveillance in business organizations, can be understood.

The Modern Corporation and the Problem of Surveillance

As Hannah has argued, while large corporations existed before the industrial revolution (for example, the large overseas trading companies of western Europe during the eighteenth century), the process of industrialization 'radically transformed the nature of capitalist enterprise and created an economy in which factory concerns employing hundreds (and in some cases thousands), of workers became the representative form of business unit' (L. Hannah 1976: 8).

In the context of the transition from liberal to organized capitalism, the growth of surveillance within business enterprise involved what I have termed earlier as a shift from personal to bureaucratic control (pp. 41–3). The process of bureaucratization encompasses three principal actors: the central authorities or directors of the enterprise, the direct labour force, and the emergent managerial or bureaucratic class. In addition, it is important not to conflate discussions of the bureaucratization of relations between central authorities and management on one hand, and between management and the labour force on the other. In particular, I want to show that the idea that the activities of management are in the main concerned with the control of labour should be rejected. Furthermore, in analysing the process of bureaucratization, it should be noted that, as with military organizations, the focus should be on both the internal and external dynamics of the enterprise.

Accounts of the part played by bureaucratic surveillance in the capitalist enterprise draw on three stands of social theory. The industrial society thesis views bureaucratization as a response to technical imperatives flowing from the size and complexity of administrative tasks associated with the application of modern technology to production. Bureaucratic hierarchies and the concentration of knowledge and decision-making in the upper reaches of management are analysed in terms of mechanical or biological analogies, as for instance in Galbraith's analysis of the 'technostructure' of modern organizations (J. K. Galbraith 1967).

In contrast, for Marxism, the place of bureaucratic surveillance in the capitalist enterprise is explained in terms of the imperatives of capital accummulation rather than as a rational response to technical exigencies. Specialist bureaucratic work has no technical or functional *raison d'être* in its own right. Thus, writers like Clawson fail to grasp the specificity of managerial work in respect of its contribution to organizational strategy planning and co-ordination (D. Clawson 1980).

In contrast again, what has been termed the neo-Machiavellian perspective highlights an important error in Marxist interpretations or bureaucracy. This is to conflate the two dimensions of bureaucracy that were distinguished above and thus to suppose that the genesis of modern management is contingent upon imperatives relating to the control of labour under conditions of capitalist production.

Writers in this tradition stress the technical necessity of specialized bureaucratic work in large complex organizations. However, the activities of officials cannot be presumed to represent consensual values and interests nor the imperatives of capital, but rather self-determined organization interests. Perhaps the clearest example of this view is provided by James Burnham (J. Burnham 1962; M. Djilas 1957).

Edwards discusses the development of the modern firm and a range of different enterprises in contemporary capitalist society in terms of a typology of personal, technical and bureaucratic control. Technical and bureaucratic administration are both structural rather than personal forms of control:

Bureaucratic control like technical control differs from simple forms of control in that it grows out of the formal structure of the firm rather than simply emanating from personal relationships between workers and bosses. But while technical control is embedded in physical and technological aspects of production and is built into the design of machines and industrial architecture of plant, bureaucratic control is embedded in the social and organizational structure of the firm and is built into job categories, work rules, promotion practices, discipline, wage scales, definitions of responsibility and the like. Bureaucratic control establishes the impersonal force of company rules or company policy as the basis for control. (R. Edwards 1979: 131)

For Edwards, a transition from technical to bureaucratic control offers distinct advantages to an employer. With technical control, the labour force acquires powerful bargaining positions through its capacity to disrupt the technologically interdependent aspects of the production process. Under bureaucratic control, the employer gains greater means of monitoring labour and undermining its resistance to managerial directives. However, under both these forms of structural control, the power of administrative intermediaries within the firm, particularly sub-contractors, or independent shop foremen, is reduced considerably through the construction of a more bureaucratic system of command.

These administrative developments have been promoted by the increasing scale of capitalist enterprises on the one hand, and the challenge of organized labour on the other. Technical and bureaucratic control constitute 'two halves of the story of the managerial revolution in the twentieth century' (ibid.: 132).

Bureaucratization is not construed as a simply, unilinear process. Edwards also links variations in structures of control with different types of enterprise and labour market in contemporary capitalism.

There are two main difficulties with Edwards's approach. First, he does not distinguish adequately between the processes of management and the management of labour. As a result he exaggerates the impact of conflicts between capital and labour on the rise of bureaucratic surveillance within the firm. Changes in the regulation of the labour process had other causes, particularly those relating to problems of monitoring the external environment of the firm and planning future products.

Second, Edwards, like Clawson, develops a quite misleading view of bureaucratic control as a twentieth-century development and fails to understand that it is a far deeper and more long-term historical process. As I argued earlier, disciplinary developments in military organizations of the seventeenth century provide clear evidence that the adoption of bureaucratic administration in industrial enterprises of the late nineteenth and twentieth centuries involved the application and development of innovations discovered long before in other institutional contexts.

Michael Useem has discussed the development of the modern firm, particularly in the USA, in terms of three phases. These are defined as family, managerial and institutional capitalism (M. Useem 1984: 4). The mid-nineteenth century is identified as an era of family capitalism. Individual entrepreneurs managed their own firms as extensions of themselves. The pursuit of collective interests was an outcome of personal connections and alliances between members of the great business families. This is understood in terms of the dominance of the upper-class principle.

Useem argues that from the late nineteenth to the mid-twentieth century, family capitalism gave way to managerialism and corporate rule. This was a historic transformation of the firm from 'an extension of the founding family to a distinct entity with an internal logic entirely of its own' (ibid.: 176). The managerial revolution is accompanied by the emergence of a corporate principle as a basis for the organization and selection of the business elite. This is the era of the 'organization man' committed to the pursuit of the corporation's interests.

In the USA since the 1970s, Useem detects the development of institutional capitalism and a class-wide principle as a basis for the organization of the business elite. Senior executives focus less on the interests of single corporations and more on wider inter-corporate interests. Other writers have suggested that the development of 'institutional capitalism' in the USA can be traced back to the 1920s and 1930s. What Useem refers to as managerialism was an interregnum between family and institutional capitalism which, in the USA during the 1920s, was associated with the dominance of investment bankers who engineered large-scale amalgamations (I am indebted to John Scott for this point.)

The inner circle rests on an economic infrastructure constituted by the concentration of the economy and an emergent network of interlocking directorates: 'The central dynamic of these interlocks lies in efforts by large companies to achieve an optimal 'business scan' of contemporary corporate practices and the 'general business environment' (ibid.: 45). External relations are then a crucial determinant of the emergence of the 'inner circle' (M. Zeitlin 1974).

The merit of Useem's analysis is that he analyses the development of bureaucratization with a clear recognition that management and the management of labour are quite distinct social processes. In addition, Useem shows the relevance of both internal and external dynamics of business organizations in respect of the development of bureaucratic surveillance.

Useem's view of the rise of the 'visible hand' of management draws on Chandler's work. Chandler discusses the growth of the firm in the USA in the following terms:

159

Modern business enterprise took the place of market mechanisms in coordinating the activities of the economy and allocating its resources. In many sectors of the economy the visible hand of management replaced what Adam Smith referred to as the invisible hand of market forces. The market remained the generator of demand for goods and services, but modern business enterprise took over the functions of coordinating flows of goods through existing processes of production and distribution, and of allocating funds and personnel for future production and distribution. As modern business enterprise acquired functions hitherto carried out by the market, it became the most powerful institution in the American economy and its managers the most influential group of economic decisionmakers. The rise of modern business enterprise in the United States, therefore, brought with it managerial capitalism. (A. Chandler 1977: 1)

Thus, large bureaucratic firms performed activities that were once carried out by a multitude of smaller, personalized enterprises connected by relations of market exchange. The emergence of the visible hand entailed an extension of the boundaries of the firm and a bureaucratization of the social relations within it.

As with Useem, in his discussion of the shift from personal to bureaucratic control, Chandler distinguishes clearly between the two dimensions of bureaucratization and focuses on both the internal and external dynamics of business enterprises. In addition, he stresses that bureaucratization was promoted largely by the size and complexity of administrative tasks and market imperatives rather than by conflicts between capital and labour.

Chandler shows how the growth in the size of firms and the application of capital and energy intensive production systems were linked with the emergence of a managerial class together with a range of novel administrative techniques such as the differentiation of line and staff functions and the divisional system. In the twentieth century, the bureaucratization of management has also involved the specialization of strategic planning as a distinct administrative function no longer performed by a single individual. This process was similar to that which had already occurred in military organizations: bureaucratization meant that the warrior and entrepreneurial hero were supplanted by a corporate bureaucratic machine. Chandler goes on to examine the bureaucratization of relations between management and labour. In particular, he focuses on the emergence of scientific management and the displacement of autonomous intermediaries in the labour process by a bureaucratic system of command.

Drawing on Chandler, the emergence of bureaucratic surveillance in the capitalist enterprise can be presented schematically as in figure 5.1.

In the following discussion, the two aspects of bureaucratization are linked with the external and internal exigencies of business enterprises. In turn, these are located in the broader context of the shift from liberal to organized capitalism. The starting point for this analysis is the emergence of the managerial class and related innovations in the field of organizational surveillance as firms grew in size and complexity.

Surveillance and the Development of Modern Management

As Pollard and Hannah have argued, large-scale economic enterprise and management techniques have a long history. However, there is a sense in which the genesis of management in the factory enterprises of modern industrial capitalism was a distinctly new development. This was because of a conjunction of social forces which hitherto had remained relatively separate: 'the concentration of ownership of the workplace, the means of work, source of power and raw material in one and the same hand. This combination was only exceptionally met with before the eighteenth century' (S. Pollard 1968: 18).

Furthermore, during this period, business enterprises faced a novel environment: the widening capitalist market. They were providing goods and services for a mass rather than a narrow range of consumer wants. In addition, the discipline of formally-free labour was one of the central administrative problems of these organizations. One of the most important features of these business enterprises was that they were characterized by relatively 'simple' forms of control. The clearest example of this was that of the personal enterprise.

The personal enterprise is typically a small-scale single unit organization owned and managed by an entrepreneur perhaps with the assistance of family members. However, as in Britain during the early nineteenth century, personal enterprises constituted only one of a range of non-bureaucratic organizational forms which included others based on the delegation of administrative functions to autonomous intermediaries – either foremen or internal contractors (C. Littler 1982: 123–4).

Although enterprises with simple forms of control have not disappeared from contemporary capitalism, they no longer constitute the lynchpin of the

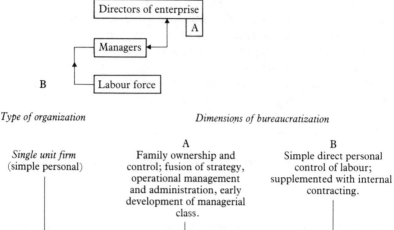

Type of organization	Dimensions of bureaucratization	
	A	B
Single unit firm (simple personal)	Family ownership and control; fusion of strategy, operational management and administration, early development of managerial class.	Simple direct personal control of labour; supplemented with internal contracting.
Multi-unit firm *with national operations* (entrepreneurial) (rise of 'managerial' firm)	Development of managerial hierarchy; line and staff mechanisms. Centralized functional administrative structure. Problems of administrative overload; disruption of strategy and structure. Scientific control of management.	Hierarchical close surveillance through managerial control, scientific management, bureaucratic technical control of production.
National and multi-national *enterprise of large scale*	Differentiation of strategy and operational administration. Centralization of strategy and financial control; delegation of operations to autonomous divisions. Accountancy and budgetary mechanisms of managerial surveillance.	Bureaucratization of social and psychological context of work: personnel management, human relations and the construction of bureaucratic careers for sectors of labour.

FIGURE 5.1 Modern business enterprise and the growth of bureaucratic surveillance

economy as was the case in Britain and the USA during the first half of the nineteenth century.

Within personal enterprises, mechanisms of control were unsophisticated; the personal authority of the entrepreneur constituted the primary means of administration; he carried out in person activities which in larger modern enterprises are normally performed by a variety of specialized officials or departments.

In his discussion of the emergence of a managerial class, Pollard deliberately excludes the issue of organizational strategy and concentrates on the contribution of the new managers to organization tactics. The former was for some time and particularly in Britain, a personalized function of the entrepreneur. As will be shown later, it was in the period after 1900 that organizational strategy became a focus for the bureaucratization of management.

In most of the personal enterprises in Britain during the late eighteenth century, employers distrusted managers because of fears concerning fraud and disloyalty. They were therefore reluctant to employ them. However, the forces of market demand promoted an increase in the size of business enterprise and a decline in the effectiveness of personal control. Brewing, coal, metallurgical and associated engineering enterprises, together with the cotton mills, pioneered the formation of a managerial class. However, firms encountered a shortage of management skills and these had to be discovered on an *ad hoc* basis unless they were fortunate enough to recruit ex-military officers used to 'controlling a large staff and executing detailed large scale plans' (S. Pollard 1968: 160).

With the growth in the scale of the early industrial enterprises, owners sought to devise more effective ways of exercising financial control over their managerial subordinates and of determining rates of return on the very large amounts of capital employed. A number of developments in accounting enhanced the rationality of organizational decision-making and provided important techniques of exercising impersonal surveillance over subordinates.

As Pollard argues, employers in the new factories in Britain could draw on accounting techniques already developed in a range of older, well-established enterprises. However, the new industrial firms generated quite new problems from an accounting point of view: their scale of operations; the quantity of fixed capital employed – which posed difficulties concerning the value and depreciation of such investments as well as that of any technological innovations introduced or countenanced; and the problems facing any single employer in checking and controlling the operations of a complex enterprise.

In the early nineteenth century, there were four main developments in accounting procedures that enhanced significantly the surveillance powers of employers in the new factories:

First, the adoption of regular, periodic returns instead of ad hoc reports or a journal type of book keeping. This development in effect 'forced the natural rhythm of work into a strait jacket of comparable sections of time'.

Second, such accounting reports were used in the detection of errors or fraudulent behaviour on the part of managers or workers.

Third, firms developed more sophisticated approaches to partial costing in respect of the comparative evaluation of different units or departments.

Fourth, more effective means were devised for estimating the total costs and profitability of the enterprise as a whole. This was a particularly difficult task given the scale of fixed capital that was often being employed. (S. Pollard 1968: 252)

However, these developments did not constitute that radical a break with the past. A number of problems remained unresolved for some time to come. Despite the existence of extensive accounting precedents, there was still a relative absence of a tradition and knowledge of accounting in the industrial field. In addition, there was also a limited supply of accountants available for employment in the new enterprises (as there was of managers generally). Finally, industrial accountants found it extremely difficult to deal with the main new factor in the business enterprise: the large amounts of fixed capital. To some extent, employers were able to avoid the potentially serious financial consequences of ineffective accounting procedures during the early phase of the industrial revolution because there was a substantially higher rate of profit and 'a larger margin for inefficient pricing and planning compared with after 1870' (S. Pollard 1968: 285-6).

Thus, 'it was only precisely at the point at which serious competition set in or at which profit margins for other reasons were depressed, eg., in a general industrial crisis, that firms began to calculate their costs more seriously and exactly' (ibid.). Although accounting practices emerged as administrative tools of employers for monitoring the behaviour of their subordinates, evaluating profitability, and guaging where and when to introduce techno-logical innovations, the flourishing of such techniques into a more exact science was a phenomenon of the late nineteenth and twentieth centuries. During that period, western capitalist economies became dominated by large-scale business enterprises equipped with bureaucratized managerial hierar-chies. These administrative developments expressed a shift in the balance between market and bureaucracy as principles for the allocation of resources

THE MODERN BUSINESS ENTERPRISE

and the co-ordination of production and distribution of goods and services. A decisive reason for the advance of bureaucratic surveillance within the enterprise was that, under certain conditions, the visible hand was technically superior to the market as a means of co-ordinating the economic division of labour. This point requires more detailed consideration. Chandler defines large bureaucratized firms as organizations owning and operating a number of units with an administrative system based on a many layered bureaucratic hierarchy. Under certain conditions, these are far more effective means of providing consumers with goods and services than those provided by a system of market transactions amongst a multitude of smaller independent firms. As Daems has suggested, bureaucracy also has technical advantages over intermediate forms of co-ordination such as federation or cartel arrangements under which negotiation and legislative procedures replace market mechanisms and administrative direction (A. D. Chandler and H. Daems 1980: 4–5).

Daems argues that large firms developed in sectors where it was possible for them to use marketing techniques such as advertising and branding, together with the provision of after-sales services, such as consumer credit, in order to influence the level and stability of consumer demand. These techniques were established in the context of efficient transport and communications on the one hand, and on the other, the existence of geographically dense, large-scale markets such as the large urban areas of modern industrial societies (H. Daems 1980: 203–21).

This influence over consumers allowed firms to schedule the volume of production in conjunction with accurate estimates of demand. The scheduling of production was linked with efforts to achieve economies of scale, as well as to overcome the problems of dealing with high volumes of perishable products. Technology and new sources of energy were applied to the organization of flow times. The provision of new products by research and development was particularly effective when such activities were integrated with production and marketing functions, as was the case, for example with the auto industry.

Under certain conditions then, bureaucratic hierarchy and the internalization of market relations within the administrative structure of the large firm had decisive advantages over either market or federation as mechanisms of co-ordination. Indeed, Chandler implies that the visible hand of salaried managers has such a decisive technical advantage over the market that capitalism should in the long run abolish itself! However, as Hannah has argued, Chandler's view needs some qualification (L. Hannah 1980). There are conditions when meeting the demands of consumers with supplies of goods and services through a sequence of market transactions amongst

165

smaller, independent producers can be very effective. This is particularly the case when such enterprises are involved in highly competitive relations with each other; where the transmission of accurate information about market conditions is easy and where transport and communications generally favour the rapidity of market transactions.

Hannah points to the highly effective market system which was distinctive of British capitalism in the nineteenth century, particularly when compared with developments on the European continent. There, societies were 'obliged to substitute hierarchical co-ordination by industrial banks, by the state or by large scale enterprises in order to economise on scarce co-ordinating talent' (A. Chandler and H. Daems 1980: 64). While Hannah admits that the undoubted advantages of bureaucratic hierarchy led Britain to adopt large-scale business enterprise, he is also careful to point out the disadvantages which can flow from this system. Three in particular stand out: the inflexibility associated with over-centralized management structures, which can both cause discontent amongst managers and undermine organizational performance; dissatisfaction amongst the workforce deriving from their experience of remote sources of authority in impersonal bureaucratic organizations; and thirdly, the problems flowing from a lack of balance between bureaucracy and market in the production and distribution of resources in capitalist societies. Here Hannah is making an important point: if capitalist economies veer too much towards the visible hand of bureaucratic hierarchy, (and even here Chandler warns of the dangers stemming from the bureaucratic determination of consumer wants), then all the well-known disadvantages of socialist planning systems would emerge. With these qualifications then, the technical advantages of the visible hand of bureaucracy have played a decisive part in the rise of modern corporations as houses of rational discipline.

The USA provided a pioneering example of a society that exploited thoroughly mass consumer markets through the means of large-scale bureaucratic enterprise. There were variations amongst societies in respect of the association between type of industry and the growth of large-scale enterprise. There were also similarities such as the predominance of large firms in most sectors of metal making in the USA, Germany, France and Britain. There were also important variations in the timing of the transition to the predominance of large-scale enterprises in different societies and in the institutional form in which that growth was expressed.

Chandler and Daems identify four such institutional variations: the bureaucratic corporation in the USA; the cartel in Germany, the holding company in Britain, the system of financial holding and group ties in France (A. Chandler and H. Daems 1980: 4-5; see also J. Scott 1985: 116-59).

The USA was a pioneer in terms of the speed and scale of the growth of large corporations. This was in part a reflection of its permissive state and the creation of a huge continental market by the revolution in the means of transport and communication. These large firms were impersonal rather than and familial in their ownership structure. Their managers co-ordinated and allocated resources to operating units through a bureaucratic chain of command. In the USA then, bureaucratic development was the result of three stages: from personal enterprise, to entrepreneurial forms in which owners hired managerial assistants but remained in control of strategic decisions; to impersonal managerial firms in which managers themselves control strategic as well as tactical decisions (M. Useem 1984: 175–80).

In contrast with impersonal corporations, holding companies are not bureaucratically disciplined organizations but corporations designed specifically for the purpose of holding stock in other companies. The controls operating in such concerns are legal and financial rather than administrative. Unless a bureaucratic hierarchy is created, a holding company is little more than a federation of operating subsidiaries with overall decisions being negotiated through informal agreements amongst the units. In Britain, the growth of large firms was expressed typically through mergers and holding company arrangements. In some respects the latter were deployed by employers as defensive strategies in response to foreign competition (J. Scott 1985: 134–5).

Cartels are formal federations of legally independent enterprises in which decisions about pricing policy, production and investment are reached through legislative procedures rather than by bureaucratic direction. In the late nineteenth century Germany reacted to foreign competition by employing this tactic. In contrast, France saw firms develop through group holdings. There, group participants relied on the credit or profit of more successful members and were co-ordinated through an interlocking group of families rather than by a single dynasty as was more usually the case in Britain.

Despite these institutional variations, by the end of the Second World War, in all three European societies, as in the USA, managerial capitalism prevailed. The bureaucratized large firm occupied the strategic position of economic power. As enterprises grew larger in scale and complexity, administrative imperatives forced employers to devise managerial innovations in respect of co-ordinating and controlling their firms. Again, as before, employers faced two inter-connected problems: first, controlling the activities of their direct labour force through a managerial hierarchy; second, ensuring that the managerial hierarchy itself complied with, as well as assisted in the formulation of the organization's policies. Here the focus is on the second issue. It can be explored by discussing the ways in which the railroad companies of the USA, during the nineteenth century, pioneered new organizational forms for the command and control of large complex enterprises. These innovations constituted major advances in the surveillance capacities of the capitalist firm. In addition, technical conditions relating to the volume and complexity of decisions associated with providing high outputs to mass markets were crucial in ensuring that bureaucracy was successful in the world of industry. It revealed there the competitive advantages already demonstrated in military and related fields.

In was not surprising that railroads performed such an innovatory role in the field of corporate management. As was argued earlier, together with the electric telegraph and the steamship, they provided a communications infrastructure on the basis of which occurred dramatic increases in the speed and volume of the movement of goods and passengers. They provided the means of extending and increasing the density of markets. They connected larger markets with employers of capital who, by taking advantage of modern technology and energy sources, could build large enterprises to supply them with a high volume of goods and services. At the same time, as large enterprises in their own right, the railroads provided great administrative challenges to those responsible for operating them (A. Chandler 1977; 1965).

On the new American railroads of the 1850s and the great reorganized systems of the 1880s the problems of administration were unprecedented in the history of business. In the 1850s the railroad's employees could number 40,000 while in the later period, as was the case in the Pennsylvania road, this number approached 50,000, and in both cases large sums of capital investment were involved.

Administrative problems arose in relation to providing safe and efficient service in a large organization, the units of which were greatly dispersed, and thus where face to face systems of command and control were ineffective. The size and complexity of administrative tasks, owing to the spatial distribution of units and the sheer variety of tasks involved in operating a railroad, were far greater than those characteristic of existing mill, canal or steamship enterprises.

The administrative problems of the railroads also varied over time in that before the onset of the depression in 1870, the principal strategic problem for the roads was construction and growth of new lines and facilities (and thus the appraisal of the cost effectiveness of projected new investments). After 1870, there was a constant search for new traffic to use existing facilities (as the rail system approached maturity), together with attempts to cope with the challenge of competition. The latter problem was resolved in part through the process of consolidation or merger. In any event, it is striking that during both phases, the development of managerial innovations related more to the administrative imperatives stemming from the size and complexity of administrative tasks than to the control problems attendant upon the division between capital and labour in these enterprises.

In response to these administrative challenges, the railroads devised a number of managerial innovations. Each concerned the development of a bureaucratic hierarchy for the command and control of a large complex organization. Five such innovations were of particular importance. First, there was a differentiation of management functions and specifically the separation of operations from finance and accounting. Second, an effective bureaucratic hierarchy was created for controlling the operations of the railroads. Third, a traffic department was established. This allowed a group of senior executives to concentrate on issues of strategic planning in the organization. This was a very modern invention because it involved an acknowledgement of the importance of organizational planning and the fact that under modern conditions this is best performed by a collective agency rather than an individual. Fourth, the establishment of cost accounting and a range of statistical instruments for gathering and processing information about organizational performance made possible the 'control through statistics that has become an essential hallmark of modern corporate administration' (A. Chandler 1965: 99–100). Fifth, in some railroads, decentralized systems of administration or divisional systems were established. As in the case of the military, this system facilitated the effective co-ordination of large-scale organizations without producing the attendant problems of unwieldiness or administrative 'overload' (ibid.: 99–105). As part of this administrative development, line and staff arrangements were elaborated and defined. These arrangements can be discussed in more detail. The typical form in which the bureaucratic hierarchy of the railroad companies emerged was that of the centralized functional organization: the chief officers of the enterprise co-ordinated it through the establishment of functional departments (for example, operations, finance and acounting; or as in other enterprises, technical, production, sales and marketing) each headed by a senior official reporting to the general superintendent. Executive authority was transmitted down one of the lines of authority and communication, usually the one concerned with the organizations principal activity, in this case operations. The basic idea of the centralized functional system can be expressed diagrammatically as in figure 5.2.

This type of organization structure could accommodate considerable growth. Thus, with business expansion, each department manager could simply add an appropriate number of junior managers, or increase the span of control of existing staff. It proved to be (and still is) a highly resilient structure, notwithstanding the persisting tensions between, on the one hand,

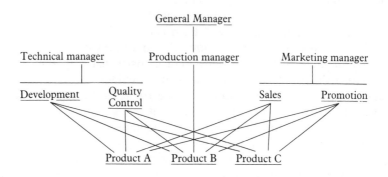

FIGURE 5.2 A functionally organized enterprise with a diverse product range (adapted and modified from J. Child, *Organizations*, 1977: 76)

the advantages of co-ordination through bureaucratic hierarchy, and, on the other, the barriers to communication attendant upon the development of a multi-levelled structure of bureaucratic authority. Attempts to reduce the latter problems by limiting the number of such levels can simply make co-ordination more difficult by introducing unwieldy spans of control (J. Scott 1985: 162, 158; J. Child 1977: 75–8; A. Chandler 1977: 425; L. Urwick 1951; 1953; 1949).

Despite such difficulties, functional departments could grow to a considerable size with no serious loss of control. However, the conditions under which this can occur successfully are an organization's concern with a narrow product range, selling in a single market, and stability in market and technological conditions. Such conditions facilitate the routinization of administration and communications and thus reduce the sources of friction in a centralized functional system.

Nevertheless, a growth in the volume of business can place such a system under considerable strain, as was the case with the larger railroad companies which were formed through merger, purchase or the process of new construction in the 1880s and 1890s. All the administrative problems of the earlier phase simply became magnified on a larger scale.

These difficulties resulted in the further definition of the duties of officials in the large functional offices. They also stimulated further efforts to establish detailed cost analyses and methods of gathering information about organizational performance. However, the inexorable growth in the volume and complexity of administrative tasks meant that senior company officials became so preoccupied with routine administration that strategic issues became marginal concerns. This could be an extremely costly development for an enterprise, given the competitive environment in which it operated as railroads fought for scarce traffic to use facilities with high fixed costs.

Some of the more progressive railroads sought to overcome these difficulties associated with the centralized functional system by employing divisional structures (A. Chandler 1965: 99–106). The idea of the divisional system can be expressed diagrammatically as in figure 5.3.

Following Williamson, five features of the divisional system can be identified:

1 Responsibility for operating decisions is assigned to essentially self-contained operating divisions or quasi-firms.
2 The elite staff attached to the general office performs both advisory and auditing functions. These have the effect of securing greater control over the behaviour of the operating divisions.
3 The general office is concerned primarily with strategic decisions involving planning, appraisal and control, including the allocation of resources among the (competing) operating divisions.
4 The separation of the general office from routine operations provides executives who work there with the 'psychological commitment to be concerned with the overall performance of the organisation rather than becoming absorbed in the affairs of the functional parts' (K. Williamson 1971: 343–88).
5 'The resulting structure displays both rationality and synergy – the whole is greater, ie., more effective and more efficient than the sum of the parts.' (ibid.)

Crucial in this decentralized system is the overall co-ordination provided by the general office with the assistance of planning staffs. The relations between the general office and the operating divisions usually encompassed three components: monitoring performance and ensuring corrective action if targets were not reached, and control through the provision of funds; planning, that is to say, the transmission to divisions of overall strategic plans designed by specialist staffs; the provision of specialist services such as transport, communications, legal personnel so as to facilitate inter-divisional co-operation, and to derive the cost benefits from such shared services (ibid.: 362–3).

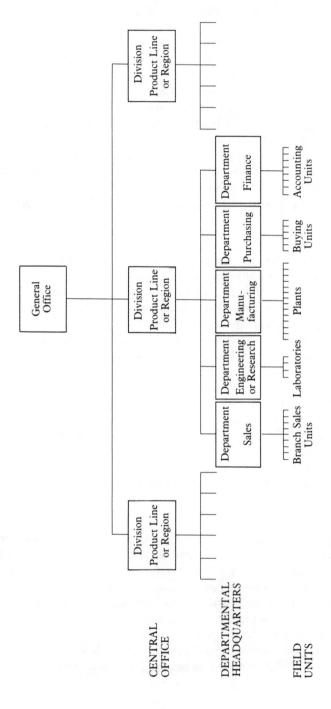

FIGURE 5.3 The basic divisional system of management (from A. Chandler 1962:11)

The more progressive railroad companies began to divide their large systems into regional units, each the size of an ordinary railroad. The general manager of a particular unit was given wide authority and responsibility for its own operations and profitability. Other than the central provision of common services such as telegraph management, freight and ticket services and wood, the general office also housed executives concerned with strategy and co-ordination. Thus a potentially unwieldy large-scale organization became a more flexible and effective structure through a decentralized system of operations within the context of central long-term planning and appraisal (A. Chandler 1965: 104–8). Without effective financial control and related information gathering and processing, such a divisional system would veer towards a structure similar to a holding company, which, as was argued earlier, is not a 'system' as such but more a collection of independent systems. The divisional system constituted a major advance in the surveillance capacities of the modern business enterprise because it combined the advantages of centralization and unity with those of decentralization. It was taken up by a variety of large industrial corporations after the First World War, particularly in the context of their growth through product and/or market diversification. In the industrial field, the pioneer was General Motors of the USA. Other corporations, e.g., Ford (GM's main competitor), were forced to follow suit or discovered the system independently (K. Williamson 1971; Hannah 1976; J. Child 1977).

During the twentieth century, large business enterprises used the divisional system even more effectively than the railroads to decentralize operations while still retaining financial control and strategic co-ordination. This achievement depended on important advances in the technologies of information gathering, processing and presentation. In part, these innovations were introduced by increasingly professionalized management specialists, particularly in the areas of finance and accounting. They provided occupational conditions under which divisional systems could be designed and operated. As will be evident, the parallels with military developments discussed earlier are striking.

Hannah has argued that 'the telephone, perhaps the most important new instrument to become widely available to management, provided a means of rapid communication between departments or between geographically dispersed branches, and this facilitated managerial control' (L. Hannah 1976: 86). Further technical advances considerably cheapened and improved the quality of telephone conversations. There was also a major increase in the development and use of office machinery, which before the First World War had been little used in British business organization. Between the wars, there was an increasingly widespread use of typewriters, duplicators, accounting

173

machines and the like. These machines increased the rapidity and cheapened the processes of information gathering, processing and presentation. Hollerith machines, for instance, could process accounting material very rapidly and they facilitated significant improvements in the collection and diffusion of information in the larger companies. Such machines had been developed in the USA during the period 1890–1930: they had been used in the US census and were subsequently adopted widely in both the areas of business enterprise and state bureaucracies. From such developments as these, computerized techniques flourished in the period after the Second World War. These technical developments eased the command and control problems in large organizations. Indeed, Hannah cites with approval Powers-Samas who had argued in 1930 that without the 'mechanisation of office accounting, the rapid growth of business and the formation of large consolidations would have been difficult if not impossible.' (L. Hannah 1976: 86).

These advances in information technologies were crucial in facilitating the application of divisional systems in the large business enterprises of the twentieth century. These administrative innovations were aspects of a wider development: the emergence of scientific or systematic management.

Broadly speaking there were two aspects of this process: the application of scientific techniques to employers relations with their managers; and their application to the rest of the labour force. The application of scientific management to management itself was not simply a response to the increasing size of organizations but also to changes in market conditions. The automobile industry in the USA was a case in point (A. Chandler 1964).

In the early twentieth century, like other large industrial corporations, General Motors was not simply a much bigger organization than the typical enterprise of the mid-nineteenth century; it also did far more than simply manufacture goods: 'By 1900, many of the nation's most important industries were dominated by a few large enterprises that did their own purchasing, often controlled their own raw materials and carried on their own wholesaling (and in some cases retailing)' (ibid.: 10). As had been the case with the railroads, there were two main stages of development: one of growth and a search for funds to finance further increases in production, followed by one of consolidation and competition for consumers to purchase existing levels of output. This was the specific context in which General Motors introduced the divisional system; instead of the paramount problem being production for a rapidly expanding market, the chief concern was marketing products for a market of limited volume; of finding market niches through product differentiation, of capturing customers from the competition, of ensuring that those who replaced their cars purchased one from General Motors. These problems highlighted the significance of strategic planning in respect of solving marketing problems in a highly competitive environment and one in which the severe pressures of high fixed costs were never far away.

General Motors devised a divisional system and a range of appraisal and information gathering techniques as means of co-ordination to be used by top management and its planning staffs. As with the more progressive railroads of the late nineteenth century, the basic idea was that 'the operating units, ie., trucks, parts, accessories . . . were to retain their full autonomy. Their managers were to control their own production, marketing, purchasing and engineering' (ibid.: 15). A general office was created, manned by general executives who assumed responsibility for overall co-ordination, control and strategic planning. These general executives included the president, operating and financial vice-presidents and the group executives who had overall control over groups of divisions.

The divisional system defined the lines of authority, co-ordination and communication between general executives, staff officials and division managers. It also provided an effective system of information gathering and evaluation for monitoring the performance of autonomous divisions and for the transmission of overall corporate strategy. Auditing was used as an informed basis for the advance consideration of proposed programmes, evaluation of current operational performance, and for the ex-post monitoring of oddities or patterns of organizational failure.

Thus General Motors under DuPont and Sloan became a more 'intelligent' corporation through its heightened surveillance capacities. It worked successfully at 'developing a mass of statistical information to flow through the carefully specified channels . . .' so as to 'provide the general staff and operating officers with a clear and continuous picture of the performance of the many divisions and the corporation as a whole' (ibid.:151).

Increasingly, this information and the action taken on it came to depend on the corporation's annual forecast of the market. The forecast was an indication of how General Motors devised techniques of information gathering to monitor not only the firm's behaviour but also the consumers of its products. Surveillance of consumer behaviour in a highly competitive market was used to re-orient organizational strategy in order to increase demand for the corporation's goods and to stabilize consumer loyalties. It is in this context that one can understand the introduction of a product range and a number of other related innovations. Equipped with line and staff systems of planning and co-ordination, modern business enterprises could reap many of the technical advantages that such systems had offered in the field of military organization. Similarly, the competition of the market place spurred firms to adopt these administrative systems just as states were forced to follow the precedent established by Prussia in the field of military planning.

Whether large companies have deployed product or area-based divisional systems or mixed organization structures, they have all sought to co-ordinate flows within the enterprise in as cost effective manner as possible. In this context (to return to the issues posed by Lash and Urry) they have attempted to derive maximum advantage from two features of the global division of labour in modern capitalism: first, the integrated world economy and its efficient circuits for the movement of capital, goods and services; and second, the existence of national differences in the costs of production, consumer tastes, exchange rates and so on. Thus, in the motor industry, large firms now seek to take advantage of producing components in diverse locations whilst assembling and distributing in others. These practices can then be changed as conditions change.

Such activities are associated with a large volume of administrative decisions and information. As Williamson has argued, the divisional system has allowed very large corporations to process this information and produce decisions in such a way as to challenge Schumpeter's expectation that the development of bureaucratized capitalist enterprises would swamp business dynamism with bureaucratic lethargy. The divisional system has given flexibility to the visible hand of bureaucratic surveillance in modern management (K. Williamson 1971: 387–8).

Surveillance and the Managerial Control of Labour

As I argued earlier, the rise of bureaucratic surveillance in the modern business enterprise encompassed two social processes: on the one hand, the bureaucratization of the emergent relations between management and the central authorities; and on the other, the bureaucratization of the managerial control of labour. The discussion now shifts to the second of these processes. Again, it is linked with the shift away from systems of simple or personal control characteristic of enterprises during the early stage of industrial capitalist development, particularly in the cases of Britain and the USA.

It will be recalled that in the personal enterprises operating during the industrial revolution in England, there was a minimal development of specialist occupations both in the fields of management and the control of the labour process. Nevertheless from the standpoint of surveillance and the managerial control of labour, the new industrial factories achieved major advances when they are compared with earlier systems of outwork in western Europe.

These putting-out systems were appropriate forms of organization for small-scale production linked with large-scale markets (S. Pollard 1968: 51). For example, in the textile industry from the sixteenth to the eighteenth centuries, merchant capitalists had provided raw materials and means of production to cottage industry labour, having already extricated themselves from the restrictive labour practices of the craft guilds based in traditional urban centres. These entrepreneurs, with their journeymen assistants, then collected the finished product and deposited fresh raw materials at regular intervals.

From the point of view of the entrepreneur, there were serious difficulties with this labour system. In an age of limited transport and communications, the dispersal of the labour force meant it was insulated from close surveillance by the merchant capitalist. The labour force had considerable autonomy in organizing the routines of work. Furthermore, because of the proximity of work practices to the traditional agricultural rhythm of labour, workers tended to labour irregularly, with alternate periods of intense labour and rest. Production volumes, quality and profit margins could fall far short of what the capitalist required at particular times. These difficulties increased when the market demand for the finished product increased.

Of course, the merchant capitalists were not completely powerless. For example, when, due to technical reasons, the supply of yarn increased, they pressed for corresponding increases in production from weavers by imposing wage cuts. However, other merchant capitalists attempted to move beyond the constraints of the old labour system. They sought to extend and develop further the administrative practices that had already been established in other sectors of their enterprises.

Indeed, in respect of the textile industry, Dickson argues there were four reasons for the introduction of the factory system and thus a new form of labour discipline. First, employers sought to control and market the total production of weavers in order to minimize embezzlement. Second, by controlling the timetable of the working day the employer could maximize the input of work through the imposition of tight labour discipline and speeding the pace or flow of the production process. Third, by placing workers under one roof it made it easier for the employer to adopt and modify technological inventions in ways which would benefit profit-making and minimize labour resistance to the employer's prerogatives in the workplace. Fourth, the factory system would transform the relations of autonomy and dependence between employer and workers: as Marx pointed out, the new system would make the role of the employer indispensable in the production process and, overall, tighten the structure of power and discipline at work (D. Dickson 1974: 71–83).

The introduction of factory discipline involved a process of struggle in respect of both recruiting the labour force and of subjecting it to a type of discipline which differed markedly from that which production workers had become familiar with and attached to. As Pollard argues, 'in many respects, the rational and methodical management of labour was the central management problem in the industrial revolution requiring the fiercest wrench from the past' (S. Pollard 1968: 189). In part, this was due to the problems associated with the discipline of formally-free labour in the context of the competitive provision of goods for sale on the market. Although the theory and practice of labour discipline had evolved already in military and other organizations, there were novel problems in the age of modern capitalism. In relation to labour recruitment, employers encountered two particular difficulties. These were, first, the aversion of workers to entering new factory enterprises, with their novel rules and disciplinary systems; and second, a shortage of reliable and sufficiently skilled labour.

As Weber, Thompson and others have noted, workers were for the most part non-accumulative, non-acquisitive and accustomed to work for subsistence rather than for an incentive based, 'rational' maximization of income. They had to be made responsive to cash stimuli and disciplined to react appropriately to them, particularly as many workers were reluctant to enter establishments whose architecture resembled that of the new workhouses. (S. Pollard 1963; 1968: 189–244; D. Brown and M. Harrisson 1978; E. P. Thompson 1967).

Once the labour force was recruited, employers encountered a range of difficulties relating to training and discipline. Early factories were involved in training workers in traditional occupational skills, new skills created by new trades or traditional ones transformed by the division of labour – particularly in the field of engineering. In addition, there was an increase in training activities as a response to the growing requirements for literacy and thus the ability to absorb formal book learning.

Besides the issue of skill, what employers required of their workers in the new factories was 'regularity and steady intensity instead of irregular spurts of work; accuracy and standardisation in place of individual design and care of equipment and material in place of pride in one's tools. None of this came easily to the new work force' (S. Pollard 1968: 213). Some owners sought to use the symbols and practices of the old order – feasts, holidays and paternalism or personal solidarity in order to generate the loyalty of workers to the enterprise. Others innovated in the field of impersonal, bureaucratic discipline. They sought to break down the traditional impulses of their workforce and introduced time thrift and enforced asceticism, as for instance, through the mechanism of fines for bad time keeping.

Disciplinary rules could be enforced through threats of dismissal, fines, and even on occasion, corporal punishment, particularly for younger workers. Some employers also introduced payment by results as a means of inculcating the new work discipline and undermining the 'dogma of subsistence'. These payment schemes 'formed one of the most significant developments in the field of labour management in the Industrial revolution' (ibid.: 223–41).

The scale of the problems involved in imposing a new discipline on workers in the factories was often quite beyond the managerial abilities of employers in these personal enterprises. As a result, they employed managerial assistants. In many cases these were internal or sub-contractors. In effect, employers solved their labour management problems by giving them to someone else to solve and paying them a fee.

Sub-contracting was widespread in the early forms of industrial organization. As Littler has suggested, 'in general the internal contractor system and decentralised modes of control provided an historical solution to the contradictions between increasing size of firms and simple entrepreneurial control' (C. Littler 1983: 127). In addition, the practice of sub-contracting was connected with the fact that the new factories incorporated existing occupational skills (and autonomies). Thus, most early factories exercised what Marx referred to as a formal rather than a real subordination of labour to detailed surveillance.

A range of functions could be delegated to sub-contractors, depending upon the nature of the employer and the industry: the purchasing of raw materials, the hiring and firing of labour together with related personnel functions such as pay, discipline, training and so on; planning and executing the nature and flow of production, and the costing of activities within the enterprise.

Writers such as Littler and Pollard argue that sub-contracting alleviated the tensions in the command and control systems of the enterprise in a number of ways (C. Littler 1983; S. Pollard 1968: 55–63). It provided an employer with a flexible organization structure able to cope with shifts in the market demand for goods without imposing the high overhead costs attendant upon the provision of a large central office. Thus, it spread capital risks, and, in some respects, diminished them through transferring cost calculations to others, thereby providing a form of substitute accounting. It provided financial incentives and paths of upward social mobility for key groups of workers thus assisting in promoting the social solidarity of the enterprise. It also provided a means of by-passing the problem that some employers simply did not possess the requisite skills for organizing the

179

production process. Finally it gave employers effective mechanisms for the allocation of production tasks and the provision of work discipline. However, as these functions were controlled by autonomous intermediaries, it was they not the employer who had detailed knowledge and control over what went on in the enterprise. Consequently, contractors acquired considerable managerial problems of their own in their performance of these delegated functions.

The foremen and sub-contractors provided alternative means of exercising intermediary control within the enterprise. Although the latter were not direct employees, their administrative functions were similar to those performed by foremen. One important difference between foremen and sub-contractors concerned their autonomy in the determination of production costs. As Nelson has argued in the American context, 'whereas the contractor determined the manufacturer's direct labour and materials costs when he agreed to produce a given product for a specific amount, the foreman only promised to keep costs low' (D. Nelson 1975: 40). To some extent then, in relying on sub-contractors, the employer could put an exact price on the discretion that had been delegated within the enterprise. In addition, the system meant that employers themselves had less to do in organizing the supervision of workers than others who sought to exercise more direct forms of control as for example in the case of the Springfield Armoury in the 1820s. There, detailed accounting methods had been established to control the quality of and payment for goods produced through piecework. This process of accounting and discipline involved time consuming and onerous duties (K. Hoskin and R. H. Macve 1986).

On the other hand, although the system of sub-contracting relieved the employer of such administrative tasks, he was denied detailed knowledge of the work tasks and labour practices that could serve as a means of determining *exactly* what the price of the delegation of functions actually represented. As Chandler shows, employers knew relatively little about the precise costs of labour and materials used in the contracted departments. (A. Chandler 1977: 271–4). Nor did they have the means for detailed supervision of the flow of goods and materials from one department to another. Indeed, even in the case of direct administrative control found at Springfield, as Hoskin and Macve have shown, the employer did not know in detail what workers did in producing items under piece rate schemes (K. Hoskin and R. H. Macve 1986: 7). It was not until the period after 1880 that a more complete system of labour surveillance was constructed as part of the diplacement of intermediary forms of social control within the enterprise.

It is generally accepted that the sub-contractor was a means of resolving the administrative problems attendant upon the expansion of the firm beyond the organizational capacities of personal and familial structures of control.

However, the exact role of the sub-contractor in the labour process has stimulated further debate. These discussions are significant because they relate to the problem of explaining the demise of intermediary forms of control with the flourishing of scientific management as a means of organizing the labour process; an issue taken up in the next section.

Littler has usefully distinguished three types of internal contracting in his analysis of British and American developments. These he terms 'familial control', where skilled workers employ children and other family members, 'craft control', where master craftsmen were responsible for recruitment, and the team of largely unskilled labourers organized by a gang boss (C. Littler 1982: 124-5). Littler argues that it is misleading to equate the practices of sub-contracting with craft control. The autonomy of such contractors was not necessarily rooted in craft knowledge but grounded in more mundane powers of access to sources of labour in the market. He also suggests that whilst internal contracting could be a mechanism for the preservation of craft skills, it could also be associated with attempts to 'deskill' the labour force. Littler provides grounds for scepticism in relation to any historical model of the development of the business enterprise as entailing a unilinear process of de-skilling as presented by Braverman in his analysis of the shift from the formal to the real subordination of capital (H. Braverman 1974). Leaving aside the issue of the mechanisms of this transformation, the process was at the very least an uneven one.

Other writers, like Holbrook-Jones, follow Foster in suggesting that sub-contracting was a mode of labour discipline organized through a process of incorporation (M. Holbrook-Jones 1974; J. Foster 1974). For example the English cotton spinners constituted an industrial elite in the factory hierarchy and mediated the authority of the employer – and more broadly the capitalist class hegemony over the wider community – by playing the role of privileged industrial policeman.

On the other hand, writers like Clawson, drawing on American data, have argued that sub-contractors were less privileged non-commissioned officers providing organizational conditions for effective capitalist production, and more anticipators of socialist organization structures (D. Clawson 1980). Clawson suggests that internal contractors were present in technically advanced sectors of the US economy in the late nineteenth century, particularly those using and producing interchangeable parts that depended on precision engineering machinery. Clawson argues that contractors played an important role in introducing technological innovations and providing organizational conditions that stimulated increases in productivity. They had an incentive to do so because, once a rate was set for the work, their own cut of the proceeds would increase should productivity be up, at least in the short term. In addition, these technical achievements occurred despite the fact that the contractors were not disciplined components in a highly bureaucratized chain of command. If Clawson is correct, the limitations of sub-contracting from the stand- point of employers concerned not any obstacles they provided to technical progress, but the fact that they could direct into their own and their workers' hands profits which under a regime of closer surveillance could be channelled into those of the employers themselves.

In the later nineteenth century, sub-contractors were displaced by a further bureaucratization of the enterprise. This was part of a broader process of the emergence of scientific management in respect of the control of both officials and labour. The bureaucratization of the managerial control of labour was linked with the increased scale and complexity of firms together with the interplay between market demands and new technologies (A. Chandler 1977: 277ff.). It is in this context that Clawson and Braverman's claims, that scientific management was an expression of the demands of capital rather than an indicator of the importance of technical exigencies, can be evaluated.

With the formation of large industrial enterprises during the period 1880–1930, first in the USA and then in western Europe, techniques of scientific or systematic management were applied not just to the relations between the central authorities and subordinate managers but also to the managerial control of labour itself. Bureaucratic management supplanted the personal and patronage-like autonomies of intermediary forms of control within the 'foreman's empire'.

In this discussion, the focus is on, first, the nature of the changes associated with scientific management and, second, the historical variations in these changes, together with consideration of alternative explanations of why they occurred. Finally, in the last section, the argument turns to some wider implications of scientific management for the organization of work in modern capitalism.

Most writers agree that from the point of view of the managerial control of labour three components of scientific management stand out: (1) the construction of more effective cost accounting techniques for the control and evaluation of labour processes and the payment of the workforce; (2) the integration of such techniques with detailed production control systems;

(3) the construction of central staffs for the planning and monitoring of production and the operation of a range of new information gathering and distribution systems (S. Wood and J. Kelly 1982; C. Littler 1982a: 175–7). The emergence of such staffs was connected with wider changes in the occupational division of labour: the relationships between employers, under-

managers, first-line supervisors and workers were supplanted by a functinally organized managerial hierarchy connected to the planning staffs through supportive clerical occupations. This bureaucratic system by-passed and undermined the traditional prerogatives of the foremen and contractors (C. Littler 1982a: 52–5).

It will be recalled that there had been advances in accounting as a means of exercising managerial control and evaluating organizational performance in the early industrial factories. However, until late in the nineteenth century these were still relatively primitive. In many factories, they were aspects of a broader pattern of *ad hoc* and informal administrative practices. As was noted earlier, the surveillance system, constructed as part of a structure of direct control at the Springfield Armoury in the early nineteenth century fell considerably short of a rational bureaucratic system of labour discipline (pp. 179–80). It served as a means of qualilty control, of limiting fraud by workers, as a check on attendance by the workforce, and as a means of determining payment for piecework. However, it failed to construct work study techniques for the detailed monitoring of labour performance. As will become clear, it was in this latter area that scientific management made significant advances. As Hoskin and Macve have argued, scientific management produced means of discipline and accounting operating in a 'reciprocal pattern of reinforcement' on both people and objects (K. Hoskin and R. H. Macve 1986: 7).

In the USA from the 1880s, the progressive enterprises devoted considerable energy to the development of more systematic accounting practices. They produced much more detailed and precise statements of costs. These could be used in the determination of the selling price of products together with monitoring the performance of the firm and the units within it. More precise cost controls within the enterprise were secured through the use of job cards and time clocks which enabled it to allocate prime costs to particular jobs. Such cards also provided a basis on which to control the inventories of the enterprise.

For Nelson, by 1910, 'prime cost accounting had reached its twentieth century form.' (D. Nelson 1975: 50) Moreover, he argues that such advances in cost techniques assisted in the bureaucratic consolidation of horizontal and vertical integration within the larger firms. In a related argument, Chandler also suggests that by this time 'the internal statistical data needed to control the flow of materials through several processes of production within a single industrial establishment had been fully defined' (A. Chandler 1977: 277–8).

Nelson and Chandler argue that even more important, in an era of increasingly high costs, was the development of more sophisticated techniques for the determination and allocation of overhead costs to specific work tasks. As a result it was possible to determine overhead costs to fluctuations in the flows of materials through the firm as, for example, in the calculation of the costs of the idle time of machines. Later important developments also occurred in the processes of internal auditing and in the calculation of depreciation (D. Nelson 1975: 50-8; A. Chandler 1977: 277-8).

These complex processes of cost calculation were associated with the imposition of a detailed control over each stage of production and each task performed with the enterprise. As a result, the informal and discretionary powers of intermediaries were undermined. This was achieved through the development of a more detailed division of labour or a fragmentation of work tasks, and a bureaucratic specification of work practices. These changes meant that employers could reduce the skill requirements and job learning times of some positions and/or lessen the need for skilled workers by separating out auxiliary work processes and making them the responsibility of less skilled workers. In addition, flow speeds increased and were made subject to central control through the introduction of more sophisticated machinery and the mechanization of processes whereby materials and semi-finished goods were moved from one stage of production to the next. Some details of these changes in the American context can be considered here.

Nelson identifies the emergence of more complex and detailed production planning systems in the USA during the period 1880-1914 (D. Nelson 1975: 50-79). He argues that in the 1880s most production plans involved the use of a card or ticket system. The engineering or production office on the receipt of an order, would transmit instructions to foremen and workers requesting information on work tasks and costs associated with the job concerned. These systems became more complex and detailed with both costs and production data being recorded on the same card. In 1882, Towne had published details of the first production control system: when the office received an order, it notified the foremen and required estimation of job completion data. By 1900, such production control systems had gone far beyond Towne's scheme and 'included specification of parts needed and necessary operations' control over movements of parts and materials and methods of recording the direct costs of operations and the allocation of costs to specific jobs' (ibid.: 51).

Machinery was used for decreasing production flow times and as part of a tightening in the overall control of the labour process. These innovations involved a greater use of energy and capital by the enterprise and both factors added to the weight of fixed costs and the volume and complexity of administrative tasks.

For Chandler it was in 'the production of the automobile, the most complex product to be made in high volume in the metal working industries, that the new technology was most fully applied' (A. Chandler 1977: 280;

1964: 17–40). A central feature of mass production systems was the introduction of expensive specialized machinery. On the basis of scientific analysis of workers' movements during particular operations, machinery was built to perform the same operations and semi-skilled workers were employed to tend them. Yet this whole process presupposed the operations of other highly skilled workers in the automobile industry – experimental workers, machinists and pattern makers – involved in the design construction and maintenance of machinery. As Ford himself put it 'skilled workers did not produce automobiles, they made it easier for other workers to produce them.' (A. Chandler 1964: 38)

The integration of production control and cost systems together with the development of specialized machinery for manufacturing operations and the movement of materials through the plant were associated with other changes. These involved a transformation in the occupational division of labour and the circuits for gathering and distributing information and instructions. This entailed the establishment of central planning staffs with supportive clerical positions. These occupational changes expressed the divorce between planning and doing achieved in the larger enterprises. They also illustrated the fact that any advantages associated with the detailed division of labour could be secured not only through the mechanization of production flows but also through extensive managerial co-ordination.

Uniform operating procedures were planned and monitored from an office of central staffs which stood at the apex of a functionally differentiated labour management system. F. W. Taylor's functional supervisory system was a clear illustration of this aspect of scientific management (C. Littler 1982: 50–4).

Chandler documents how in American metal-working industries of the 1880s managerial failures in ensuring that foremen and workers had either the time or interest to complete cost and work procedure slips encouraged management to employ specialist clerks and time keepers as the first 'staff employees' to control costs and co-ordinate production (A. Chandler 1977: 276–80). Such staffs were used by Taylor in the scientific determination of costs and the time necessary for specific tasks and in displacing the role of autonomous intermediaries in this process. The emerging planning department came to administer the factory as a whole with its clerical hierarchy and functionally organized labour management system.

Taylor's idea of a functional supervisory system was influential. However, many enterprises discovered that while its strength lay in specialization of different aspects of labour management, its weakness concerned the problem of co-ordination. This was because responsibility for production flow and getting the work done was too diffuse. As a result, Taylor's scheme was modified by many enterprises through the development of line and staff mechanisms. These involved the activities of generalist foremen who were on a line of authority running from the president of the enterprise and the works' manager. The functions of the planning department were attached to the plant manager's staff. The plant manager, with this staff assistance, took overall responsibility for getting the work done (A. Chandler 1977: 277–80). The line and staff system of labour management paralleled the changes associated with the bureaucratization of the enterprise as a whole. It became typical in mass production industries using complex technologies during the period after the First World War.

One other aspect of the planning department's activities concerned the co-ordination and monitoring of complex, incentive-based payment systems (C. Littler 1982a: 54–66). Most large enterprises developed extensive wages departments from which all workers received their pay. This was in contrast with the earlier common practice of paying workers by transferring a lump sum to internal contractors. This change constituted a bureaucratization of the payment function. The process went hand in hand with a continual monitoring of job times and thus rate setting by the planning department.

The integration of time study with payment systems involved the emergence of a more complete system of surveillance over labour. The undermining of the power of internal contractors exposed the work force to closer surveillance by management, reducing their invisibility in respect of norms of output, work procedures and the like. It was the process of scientific rate setting that appeared to be the most threatening aspect of scientific management from the point of view of labour. Indeed, it can be argued that the importance of Taylor in the development of new forms of labour discipline lay in his role of popularizing ideas of scientific management and in adding to its repertoire the technique of 'scientific' time study as a basis for rate setting.

As Littler has argued, although scientific management was associated with a bureaucratization of the control of labour, it envisaged a 'minimum interaction' between the enterprise and the workforce (ibid.: 61–3). This relationship was understood in terms of specificity rather than diffuseness. In addition, there was little development of career progression for the great mass of workers. Thus, in its concern for the bureaucratic regulation of rational, income-maximizing workers, scientific management celebrated the virtues of formally-free labour strictly defined. Some developments in a rather different direction will be considered briefly after dealing with the issue of why scientific management techniques were applied to the control of labour in the period 1880–1930.

In the previous discussion, the argument has been that the rise of scientific

186

management concerned both the organization of officials and the managerial control of labour. Accordingly, any attempt to explain its rise exclusively in terms of the relations between capital and labour must be viewed as at best one sided. The present argument emphasizes three lines of enquiry: the problems of capitalist organization at a particular phase in its development; technical imperatives relating to the volume and complexity of administrative tasks; and the intervention of professional occupations in their struggle for organizational power in the large corporations of modern capitalism. With these arguments one can address the problem of historical variations in the emergence of scientific management in different capitalist societies.

Braverman views scientific management in terms of the transformation of knowledge in the labour process from a set of traditional rules and practices into formalized scientific procedures; the strict division of labour between planning and doing; and the pre-planning of the detailed division of labour through the bureaucratic specification and monitoring of work tasks (H. Braverman 1974; T. Elger 1982; C. Littler and G. Salaman 1982). The dynamic of bureaucracy and technology is the effect of a strategy of managerial control by capital against labour and involved a further tightening of the surveillance networks established by the early industrial factories. The process is defined in terms of a shift from the formal to the real subordination of labour, with Braverman adding a fourth historical phase to the schema presented by Marx: (1) simple co-operation; (2) division of labour in manufacture; (3) extension of machines in the process of production.

Braverman situates the phase of automation in the context of the depression in American capitalism during the 1870s. This economic climate provided employers in the larger enterprises with the problem of financial losses caused by expensive plants remaining idle due to lack of demand. Employers sought to reduce the costs of production through cheapening labour. As was observed earlier in the case of Ford, this ambition was achieved through the introduction of specialized machinery and the attendance of less skilled machine minders. Such innovations had the advantages of lessening the demand for labour, cheapening the costs of those who were employed and increasing the velocity of throughput. As a result, the relative rate of extraction of surplus value could be increased. The price paid for such increases in productivity was the craft, skill and autonomy of the working class. Without the demands of capitalist property relations, similar productivity achievements could have been produced through a democratization of the workplace, defined in this context as a de-differentiation of the relationship between planning and doing.

Again, implied in this and other Marxist discussions of these issues is a problematic assumption: that with the advent of a compliant labour force,

187

managerial problems largely disappear, at least to a scale that would make bureaucracy redundant. Yet, as has been argued earlier, there is little evidence for this suggestion. On the contrary, the administrative price to be paid for a planned workers' state would be very high indeed: the visible hand of bureaucracy would (and does) increase not decrease. The riposte to this argument is, of course, to spell out the virtues of a 'decentralized' economy; but this would be to re-introduce capitalist mechanisms once more and/or to forgo the economic advantages that are often associated with large-scale production.

Clawson has presented arguments similar to those of Braverman (D. Clawson 1980). It will be recalled that Clawson suggests that the system of internal contracting was, in some respects, a proto-socialist one. By this he means that it is misleading to suppose that the output achieved by modern mass production systems was incompatible with the continuing role of autonomous intermediaries in the labour process. On the contrary, major productivity advances were achieved under such arrangements. This leads Clawson to conclude that the rise of scientific management was not a rational basis for mass production as such, but rather a means of diverting profits from the hands of internal contractors and the labour force to those of capital; a process stimulated by the squeeze on profits attendant upon economic depression.

At the same time, employers were concerned not simply with the financial power of internal contractors, but also by their social status as significant independent actors within the enterprise. They were not disciplined components of the managerial hierarchy. Their demise was, then, in part associated with the creation of an acceptable social hierarchy in the capitalist economic order: this development thus constituted an organizational and ideological riposte to the possibility of workers' control revealed by the functions performed by the internal contractors.

Littler's work elaborates on Marxist accounts but also draws on alternative theoretical perspectives. He too situates the rise of scientific management in America and Europe in the context of economic depression (C. Littler 1982a: 162–78). In this context, like Clawson, Littler points to the social and financial significance of the internal contractor to the employer's authority within the enterprise. He also emphasizes how the contractor's control of labour recruitment made employers concerned that in addition to their inability to monitor costs in detail, they could not prevent the admission of political agitators to the enterprise. Littler's analysis also poses the question of why the USA was a more vigorous pioneer of scientific management than western Europe, and particularly Britain. He regards three factors as being of particular importance.

First, despite the waves of immigration to the USA and the apparent abundance of labour, industrial enterprises encountered shortages of reliable skilled workers (see also J. Ellis 1986). This encouraged employers to use a combination of specialized machinery and less skilled labour. In contrast, with a low wage economy, Britain could cheapen the cost of production through wage cuts. This point raises a broader issue: some present-day enterprises may take the view that it is more profitable to organize production or other processes in a society offering low wages, or resort to price fixing and subsidies from the state rather than design a labour process based on scientific management and sophisticated technology. As Salaman and Littler have suggested, in their critique of Braverman, for capitalist enterprises, the priority is not bureaucratic control as such but the adoption of strategies and forms of control that offer the best return in particular circumstances (C. Littler and G. Salaman 1982: 264–5).

A second factor relevant to the emergence of scientific management in the USA was that with a, relatively speaking, higher wage economy, it possessed a large market for the products of consumer goods industries. This consideration was crucial in the rapid expansion of industrial enterprises which succeeded in integrating marketing, production, distribution and purchasing. As a result, in the USA, early attention was given to the professional application of science and engineering skills to the problems of production and marketing. As Lash and Urry have suggested, the influence of industrial engineers was connected with the wider impact of progressivist ideologies and national efficiency movements. (S. Lash and J. Urry 1988: 67–83; J. Scott 1985: 169–70; A. Chandler 1977: 300–25).

A third factor discussed by Littler concerns the significance of financial institutions in the expansion and operation of the large industrial enterprises during the period 1880–1920. This meant that accounting and financial controls were applied more systematically in these enterprises than in many of their European counterparts (C. Littler 1982a: 176–8).

One of the strengths of Littler's analysis is the willingness to broaden his perspective to include reference to technical imperatives. In relation to the British context he argues that scientific management emerged in the form of a more bureaucratized supervisory system. This supplanted administrative systems based on 'sweating' which had led to a deterioration in the social relations between contractors and their workforce. Yet Littler is careful to argue that these changes were linked not just with class struggles in the workplace but also with technical problems of command and control in the metal-working industries of the 1890s. There, managers grappled with the difficulties attendant upon the employment of specialized machinery and a new division of labour. These technological difficulties were also encountered in similar enterprises in the USA and they persisted in the Soviet Union after the socialization of the means of production (C. Littler 1982a: 176-8).

The importance of Nelson's analysis is that he shows the impact of strategies of professionalism in the development of scientific management. In the context of the technical problems of large complex organizations, professional engineers and accountants were an important source of criticism of the *ad hoc* practices of US management, particularly in the field of cost control. The activities of these new professions were not always welcome: 'systematic management was often introduced in the course of power struggles between the younger and older members of the management group or as part of a larger reform programme after the younger men had taken over.' (D. Nelson 1975: 75).

In his own accounts of the rise of scientific management, Chandler also documents the impact of such intra-managerial struggles for power. This argument relates to a broader view that the process of management involves as many difficulties in respect of controlling subordinate officials as it does in relation to the rest of the labour force. Indeed, these administrative difficulties have more to do with the generic features of bureaucratic organizations than with the peculiarities of capitalist enterprises (A. Chandler 1977: 266-70).

Chandler's analysis is couched in terms of the imperatives of market and technical constraints. Like other writers, he locates the rise of American scientific management in the context of economic depression. Employers sought to control and reduce costs in their capital-intensive enterprises. In increasing further the visible hand of management, they added to the volume and complexity of administrative work. This process provided an additional impetus for further managerial innovations.

It would be unwise to dismiss the impact of struggles between capital and labour on the evolution of bureaucratic surveillance within the modern business enterprise. However the argument here has been that Marxist analysis has paid insufficient attention to the organizational and technical constraints of large-scale and scientifically organized production. On the other hand, one of the weaknesses of arguments which stress the impact of technological imperatives in industrial capitalist organizations on the rise of scientific management is a failure to identify the roots of this development in non-economic contexts. These include military and educational institutions. (cf. K. Hoskin and R. Macve 1986; M. Foucault 1979) But to say this is to restate one of Weber's key insights: the rational discipline of the modern enterprise is merely one example of broader institutional trends – the separation of people from the means of administration and the rationalization of culture.

Scientific management established a bureaucratic system of labour discipline which remains at the core of modern capitalism. As was suggested earlier, although scientific management involved a bureaucratization of work, it envisaged a minimal and specific relationship between the enterprise and the workforce. However, this strategy did not resolve the problems associated with the managerial control of labour such as shortage of skills, quality control and industrial conflict. In response to such difficulties, managers turned to the social and psychological context of the labour process, one which was soon colonized by a new set of professional personnel experts (D. Nelson 1975: 109–48).

It is in this context that one important aspect of the bureaucratization of labour management can be considered: the development of careers for selected groups within the workforce. This provides an opportunity to return to Edward's analysis of bureaucracy and the labour process.

It will be recalled that Edwards identifies three broad phases in the development of the labour process: personal, technical and bureaucratic control. He suggests that through systems of technical control, the nature of work flows and procedures are determined by the layout of machinery and factory architecture. Because of the opportunities these systems provide for labour to disrupt production (and to cause severe financial losses because of the capital-intensive plant) some employers turn to bureaucratic control.

What Edwards means by bureaucratic control is the creation by employers of an internal labour market in the enterprise through the formation of a career structure for selected (usually skilled) sectors of the workforce. This involves an extension of privileges once monopolized by the managerial hierarchy.

For Edwards, bureaucratic control, so defined, is a twentieth-century phenomenon and typically adopted by 'core' corporations. These tend to be more profitable than other firms and thus more able to devote the resources required to develop career structures for their workforces. Also, they occupy more secure positions in the market than their competitors and can engage in long-term strategic planning. Finally, these enterprises are in a position to introduce bureaucratic control because union organizations are too weak to resist. Once adopted these career systems provide a means for generating stronger commitments to the enterprise on the part of the workforce, and as a result higher quality production can be expected (D. M. Gordon et al. 1982).

There is a good deal of evidence in support of this line of argument: the uneven development of internal labour markets and workers' careers in enterprises are connected in part with the relative power of trade unions in different societies. In the past, companies have found it easier to introduce such systems in the USA and Japan than in the UK.

However, there are difficulties with Edwards's thesis. First, it is important to note that in the field of industrial organization, shifts from personal to bureaucratic control can occur without any intermediary phase of technical control (F. McKenna 1980). Second, Edwards uses an overly restrictive definition of bureaucracy and fails to situate it in an appropriate historical and social context. As Braverman noted, the innovations associated with 'technical control' – i.e. scientific management and modern technology – were themselves aspects of the process of bureaucratization. Furthermore, these developments were established on the foundations of rational bureaucratic discipline laid down in the early industrial factories. Finally, Edwards gives the misleading impression that even accepting his narrow definition of bureaucracy, it was a technique invented by employers as a way of resolving labour problems in industrial capitalist enterprises. Yet all the evidence indicates that, on the contrary, employers were simply adopting and modifying principles which had been learnt by those in similar positions of responsibility in the military organizations of an earlier period.

6

Conclusion: Capitalism, Surveillance and Modernity

In this concluding chapter, I pursue three related objectives. First, the major themes underlying the preceding discussion of surveillance are restated briefly. Second, their implications for contemporary social analysis are discussed. This involves a critique of three traditions of modern social theory and their accounts of the relationships between surveillance and the rise of modernity. Third, and finally, the discussion turns to the prospects of modern societies in what is clearly an 'age of surveillance' and to issues requiring far more detailed analysis than can be offered here. In that context, three such issues are regarded as central: (a) the relationships between knowledge and power in bureaucratic organizations; (b) the connections between democratic citizenship and surveillance; and (c) the links between war, military power and bureaucratic surveillance in modern societies.

Bureaucracy and the Growth of Surveillance in Modern Societies

Drawing on Anthony Giddens's recent work, modernity has been defined in terms of four institutional features: first, the capitalist economic system of commodity production centred on the business enterprise and the class relations between capital and labour. This organization is both a bureaucratic system for administering the internal operations of the firm and a means of monitoring and managing its external relations with other organizations. Second, the technologies and organizational structures of industrialism which have both altered dramatically the relations between human societies and the

193

natural world and the space-time barriers to social interaction. Third, the nation-state as the predominant organizational framework for modern societies. Like the business enterprise, the nation-state is a Janus-faced organization: it is at one and the same time an internally pacified 'citizenship state' and, externally, a geopolitical and military actor in a world of competing nation-states. Fourth, the growth of bureaucratic surveillance as the basis of systems of administrative power in modern societies, particularly in the strategic organizations of the nation-state and capitalist business enterprise.

The development of surveillance in these key organizations of modern societies has been charted by drawing on the notion of surveillance capacity. This involved two related arguments. The first of these concerned the identification of general criteria for measuring the surveillance capacities of organizations. Bearing in mind that surveillance systems were defined in terms of processes of information gathering and supervision, these criteria can be summarized as follows:

1 The size of the files held in the administrative system.
2 The degree to which those files are centralized.
3 The speed of information flow from one administrative point in the system to another.
4 The number of points of contact between the surveillance system and subject populations, and thus the degree to which the details of their lives are transparent to bureaucratic scrutiny.

The second argument relating to surveillance capacities concerned a broad typology of surveillance systems in terms of which the growth of bureaucratic surveillance in modern capitalist societies can be understood. This typology was based on two cross-cutting axes: first, the contrast between personalized and bureaucratic administration (whether surveillance is performed with or without recourse to permanent, rationally disciplined officials and thus with or without fine-grained administrative nets). Second, a contrast was drawn between autocratic and liberal systems of interest representation (or the ways in which the claims of subject populations do or do not have a substantial impact on the policies pursued by the ruling authorities).

The growth of surveillance in modern societies has been understood in terms of a shift from personal and patronage forms of indirect control to direct control through bureaucratic systems of administrative power. The broad institutional contrasts between capitalist and state socialist societies were high-lighted by the ideal typical distinction between rational-legal, public bureaucracy and bureaucratic dictatorship. It should be stressed that to argue this was neither to exaggerate the contrasts between the administrative systems of these two types of society nor to underestimate the differences between capitalist societies in respect of the degree to which subject populations have effective access to information about them gathered by central authorities and controls over the uses to which this information can be put. In addition, it should be noted that these issues of administrative power are not simply matters concerning the dyadic relationships between ruling authorities and subject populations, but hinge on the triangle of power relations connecting central authorities, intermediate officials and subject populations. Thus, as Max Weber pointed out in relation to his own society, there are circumstances in which both ruling authorities and subject populations are placed in positions of dependence on a powerful and inpenetrable bureaucracy. Indeed, there are grounds for believing that the difficulties which central authorities encounter in subordinating bureaucracies to their will are exacerbated when subject populations themselves have little in the way of effective mechanisms for supervising those who administer their lives. As I suggested in the introductory discussion, this point provides one of the means of contrasting the systems of administrative power of capitalist and socialist societies. It is a point that is very much appreciated by those who, like Gorbachev in the Soviet Union, wish to reform the bureaucratic institutions of state socialism. This particular issue will be returned to later when the relationship between democracy and surveillance and the prospects of modern societies are discussed.

In the analysis of surveillance presented in this book, the focus of attention has been on the development of modern capitalist societies. These are based on an institutional differentiation between the public authority of the modern nation-state and the private enterprise economy. Particular emphasis has been placed on the fact that the modern state and business enterprise are Janus-faced organizations, or on the fact that their activities are focused on both the internal exigencies of managing a system of administrative control over subject populations and the problems attendant upon monitoring and managing external relations with other organizations. This theme has been central in providing a framework in terms of which the growth of bureaucratic surveillance in modern societies can be explained.

The modern nation-state and capitalist business enterprise are the pre-eminent 'power containers' of the modern era. They provide the organizational focus of three historically emergent sectors of modern societies in which the expansion of bureaucratic surveillance can be observed. First, the external relations of nation-states and the organization of military power; second, the internal policing and pacification of subject populations within the boundaries of nation-states; third, the administrative organization of the capitalist business enterprise both in respect of its internal management and its scan of the external environment. (To be precise, one could refer to four institutional sectors. However, for reasons of convenience the internal and external administrative fields of the business enterprise have been analysed together.)

Both the nation-state and business enterprise depend upon the 'visible hand' of bureaucratic surveillance for their survival. In characterizing the growth of the surveillance capacities of these organizations, a number of relatively distinct social processes need to be delineated. Each of these encompasses shifts in the relations connecting central authorities, subject populations and intermediate officials in systems of administrative power. Four such processes can be identified:

1 A shift from personal to impersonal control and the increasing significance of formal-legal regulations as the basis on which rule is exercised and legitimated within organizations. Bureaucratic surveillance rests on the enactment, enforcement and monitoring of compliance with legal orders and rules. This whole process can be referred to as one of formal-legal rationalization.

2 A shift from the personal and indirect exercise of supervisory and disciplinary powers, (as, for instance, in systems of sub-contracting characteristic of early industrial capitalist enterprises and the analogous administrative practices to be found in the military and financial structures of eighteenth-century European states), to systems of bureaucratic discipline. In the latter, the instruments of administrative power and the uses to which they are put are under the direct control of the central authorities. In this context, of decisive importance is the removal from intermediary officials of proprietary rights in the means of administration, as for instance in the imposition of compulsory retirement, the monopolization of powers of promotion and other means of regulating the passage of officials through their bureaucratic careers.

It will be recalled that this shift from indirect, personalized and patronage forms of control to systems of bureaucratic discipline is not understood here as involving a simple process of the concentration of administrative power. Rather, in the broader context of the growth in the scale and complexity of the operations of organizations, it normally involved a centralization of strategic power and a decentralization of specified authority (or tactical powers) to operating divisions or agencies. Their discretionary behaviour was monitored in terms of criteria (e.g. targets of various kinds) determined by the central authorities. Overall, these changes can be referred to as the emergence of a disciplinary hierarchy.

3 The development of increasingly elaborate and intensive systems of collecting, storing and processing information about the internal and external conditions of organizations. From the long-term point of view, of significance here are the successive invention and application of handwritten records, the mechanization of recordkeeping through the typewriter and the more recent shift from electro-mechanical to electronic systems of information. Following Pearton, this whole process can be referred to as one of the increasing knowledgeability of organizations (M. Pearton 1982).

4 Modern bureaucratic organizations comprise not simply managerial hierarchies of specified legal competences but also an occupational division of labour amongst experts. With the increasing significance of formalized and science-based information systems, the occupational structure of organizations is subjected to processes of professionalization. Within and around the disciplinary hierarchies of the modern nation-state and business enterprise, occupational groups can use their potential knowledge and expertise not only in co-operative relations with others in the division of labour but also as levers in the competition for scarce resources and organizational privileges. This entails twin strategies of controlling client groups and ensuring that rights to exercise such control are not given up to outsiders or competitors. As was apparent in the earlier detailed discussion of the development of policing, military power and the application of systematic or scientific management in the modern business enterprise, professionalized expertise can become the basis of occupational self-interest. Thus, it is a mistake to assume that professionalism is simply an exercise in the 'service of power' i.e., of the central authorities, or one of altruism in respect of a client or subject population. Here, professionalization is understood as one of the constituent elements of the process of bureaucratization or the growth of bureaucratic surveillance. However, there are serious issues raised by this assertion which will be discussed later. It can be noted here that although Weber was mistaken to collapse the distinction between professionalism and bureaucratic authority, similar mistakes can be identified in those analyses of the connections linking bureaucracy, professional expertise and power in modern societies which have drawn more heavily either on Marxism or the theory of industrial society.

The outcome of these four linked processes of change has been that modern societies are now in large part under fairly dense networks of surveillance. The main argument defended here has been that in order to explain how and why this has come to be so, bureaucracy should be linked with but not reduced to the three other institutional features of modernity identified earlier. In turn, this involves a synthesis of disparate strands of social theory and an incorporation of Machiavellian ideas.

Surveillance and Modernity: Competing Accounts in Social Theory

An adequate account of the relationships between bureaucratic surveillance and modern society has to start with a critique of the two predominant paradigms of contemporary sociology: the theory of industrial society and Marxism. These two traditions of social theory have placed the logic of industrialism and the class struggles between capital and labour centred on the business enterprise as the strategic institutional mechanisms of change in modern societies. As Giddens has suggested, they have tended to push surveillance and military power to the margins of contemporary social theory, or regard these phenomena as moulded by economic and technological forces.

It is not that Marxism and the theory of industrial society provide no accounts of surveillance and military power but rather that the accounts that are provided are reductionist in character. On the one hand, military power is viewed as contingent on forms of economic scarcity and destined to wither away with the process of modernization – either in the form of the capitalist world market or a socialist federation of industrial states. On the other hand, surveillance, as a means of domination or administrative power over other people, is viewed as a transitory phase of human history. With the maturation of modern societies, the administrative co-ordination of social life will be performed either by a technocratic elite acting to suplement the operations of the market in pursuit of the common interest, or by socialist planners establishing a framework of regulations within which many administrative functions will in any case have been devolved to local subject populations in the form of direct democracy. In both scenarios, the abolition of economic scarcity, albeit by different means, heralds the end of fundamental human conflicts and the beginning of an era of the administration of people over things rather than over other people. Thus both Comte and Marx have provided the intellectual basis for alternative utopias in the development of modern sociology.

As Giddens has emphasized, at the heart of these two interpretations of the nature of modern societies lie teleological conceptions of social change: the dialectic of class struggle on the one hand and the logic of scientific and technological progress on the other. The possibility that war between states and asymmetrical relations of administrative power together with conflicts amongst rulers, officials and subject populations are not contingent upon economic scarcity or economic class division, but are independent elements in the structuring of human societies is underplayed.

In analysing the relationships between surveillance and modernity, the arguments defended here have sought to incorporate what have been termed neo-Machiavellian ideas such as those of Weber, Mosca and Hintze into a broader synthesis. These writers not only focused on the state as a 'war-like entity' (A. Giddens 1985: 26); in addition they were reluctant to consider the relations between rulers and ruled exclusively in economic terms. They preferred to regard struggles for power within societies and the division of modern humanity into competing and potentially warring nation-states as inevitable. Furthermore, it should be noted that these writers stressed that warfare has played a central part in the expansion of the surveillance capacities and the very identity of the modern nation-state. This particular theme stands in sharp contrast with the arguments of liberal writers such as Bendix and Marshall who with their 'internalist' bias or neglect of the military and geopolitical dimensions preferred to regard it as 'a political community within which citizenship rights may be realised not as a bearer of military power within a world of other nation states' (A. Giddens 1985: 29).

It should be stressed that although Machiavellian ideas, particularly in the nineteenth century were often linked with evolutionary, social Darwinist, models of history, there was nothing inevitable about this connection. Indeed Weber and Mosca, for instance, were sceptical of the claim that history could be viewed in terms of some teleological schema according to which, with the west in the vanguard, humanity was advancing towards a terminus of peaceful global industrialism. In their writings, one can detect an alternative conception of history as fundamentally a reversible social process: different societies make advances or regressions from one type to another in different periods of time. This is because, in the absence of any internal process of 'unfolding', contingencies relating to actors' choices under bounded conditions can be decisive for the nature of historical outcomes. This is the methodological context in which Weber's famous discussion of the battle of Marathon and his argument about the role of charisma in social change, together with Mosca's remarks about the accidents of war should be viewed (M. Weber 1949: 159–72; G. Mosca 1939: 163–4).

For reasons which are not altogether clear (although the collapse of the intellectual vigour of Marxist theory must rank as one of them) a number of writers have sought to re-establish the importance of Machiavellian ideas as the basis for interpreting the nature and prospects of modern societies. This is not to deny the important criticisms that have also been levelled at this strand of social theory, for example, in respect of its pessimistic view of the inevitability of war in social life and the impossibility of real democracy in face of the 'iron law of oligarchy'.

In the context of recent British sociology, the writings of Hall, Mann and

Giddens provide clear indications that the traditional debate between the theory of industrial society and Marxism in respect of the nature of modern societies has now been broadened to include a positive critique of Machiavellian traditions of social theory (A. Giddens 1985; J. Hall 1986; M. Mann 1987; 1988). As will be fairly evident, the overall account of surveillance defended here has drawn in substantial respects on the ideas of Anthony Giddens, whose own work, particularly in recent years, has involved a critical appreciation of Machiavellian themes (pp. 29–36).

It should be stressed that the account of surveillance presented here does not depend upon an uncritical assertion of the validity of Machiavellian social theory but rather on an integration of the three strands of social theory. What this argument means is that surveillance is linked with the other institutional features of modernity but not reduced to them. In this context, the connections that have been drawn between surveillance and capitalism, industrialism and the nation-state can be restated schematically after which a number of issues arising out of this analysis will be taken up in more detail.

Modern societies are capitalist societies; that is to say, they are characterized by the centrality of commodity production, distribution and exchange in privately owned business enterprises operating in market economies. In turn, the latter are relatively insulated from political control by either individual or combinations of nation-states. Undoubtedly, the economic dynamics of the capitalist system have played an important part in the growth of bureaucratic surveillance both within modern business enterprises and in the other institutional sectors of contemporary societies. Indeed, there are three distinct ways in which the influence of capitalism on the expansion of surveillance has been significant. First of all, the wealth released by the capitalist market system provided the financial means by which specialized officials could be employed on a permanent basis to administer organizations. They were not required themselves to produce their own means of subsistence; they could purchase these through spending their salaries on the market. As Weber suggested with regard to military, financial and business administration, the capitalist market and the imposition of bureaucratic discipline in organizations are as intimnately connected as are systems of payment in kind and administrative structures of indirect rule.

Second, and this is the central claim of Marxist analysis, the expansion of bureaucratic surveillance within the capitalist workplace is in large part the outcome of two aspects of the class relations between capital and labour: first, the competition between enterprises for relative market share and return on capital invested; and second, struggles between managers of enterprises and the workforce for control over output and the organization of the labour process. Again, it is difficult to see how the bureaucratization of modern business enterprises can be understood adequately without reference to these dynamics of class power.

Third, the capitalist economic system, and thus the primacy of market relations, created class societies. These are simultaneously arenas for the contestation of class power and impersonal societies of strangers. As I argued earlier, (pp. 3–6) in most Marxist accounts, strategic priority is accorded to the first characteristic while, in contrast, for those who draw on the theory of industrial society it is the second which is regarded as of primary importance. In corroding the effectiveness of patronage and community-based mechanisms of social control and surveillance, modern capitalism provided the conditions for a reconstruction of the social order and the introduction of new bureaucratic systems of discipline beyond the factory. Here too, it would be unwise to deny the significance of class struggles within a more impersonal society as important factors in the emergence of systems of bureaucratic policing of subject populations which are so distinctive of modern societies. However, it is a serious mistake to analyse the problem of surveillance solely from the economic standpoint of class interest and the imperatives of capital accummulation. The connections between surveillance and the other institutional features of modernity are just as significant.

In this context, an emphasis has been placed on the part played by industrialism in the growth of bureaucratic surveillance in modern societies. It is interesting to note that it is just this theme (concerning the impact of scientific knowledge and technique) that Marxist analysis wishes to question as an ideological obfuscation of the real relations of capitalism.

Giddens has usefully defined industrialism in terms of four attributes:

1 'The use of inanimate sources of material power in either production or processes affecting the circulation of commodities' (A. Giddens 1985: 137–9), as in the application of water, coal/steam and electricity to production and distribution.
2 The mechanization of processes of production and distribution through the introduction of machinery.
3 The centrality of manufacturing i.e., non-agricultural production in the economic system (to which should be added the mechanization of 'agri-business' itself and its close integration with other sectors of the economy).
4 The focusing of mechanized production and distribution on the 'centralized workplace' (ibid).

Within the context of the capitalist economic system, these technical and organizational features of industrialism provided business entrepreneurs with an extremely effective means of responding to growing market opportunities for their products. Industrialism provided the technological basis for the expansion of the surveillance capacities of both the business enterprise and the organizations of the nation-state. This was what Weber meant when he spoke of the technical superiority of bureaucracy over other administrative systems in managing large-scale complex tasks. In the overall position defended in this book, two arguments concerning the impact of industrialism on surveillance have been of particular importance: first, the ways in which industrialism undermined the barriers of time and space to social interaction – as with the introduction of the steamship, railway and electric telegraph in the nineteenth century. Innovations such as these facilitated the detailed administrative control of subject populations and the construction of systems of administrative power which were both more durable and extensive than those characteristic of non-industrial civilizations. In the nineteenth and twentieth centuries, the clearest illustrations of these developments were the concentration and disciplining of formally-free labour in business enterprises on the one hand and, on the other, the mobilization and deployment of national citizenries in the mass military organizations of the nation-state.

The second way in which industrialism affected the surveillance capacities of organizations concerned its impact on processes of information gathering, storage, processing, retrieval and their application to administrative decision-making. In regard to policing, military and business sectors of society, this development involved a dramatic expansion in what was referred to earlier as the knowledgeability of organizations.

One of the most important sources of the growth of bureaucratic surveillance in modern societies has been the emergence of the modern nation-state. At the same time, one of the major errors of modern social theory has been to underestimate this factor or collapse it into the logic of industrialism or the dynamics of class struggle. In this context, two related developments have been of particular importance for the arguments defended here: first, the ways in which warfare and military competition amongst states have been linked with the bureaucratization of military power and of substantial sectors of civilian society in pursuit of military related objectives; second, the significance of processes of bureaucratization concerned with the internal pacification and 'policing' of subject populations in the broader context of the industrial revolution and the development of the democratized citizenship state. Here it is important to recall that bureaucratization was not simply an outcome of strategies of control on the part of the central authorities, but also an expression of popular demands for citizenship rights. The external and internal exigencies of the nation-state as a distinct 'power container' whilst connected with processes of capitalist development and industrialization cannot be regarded as reflections of them.

Surveillance and Bureaucracy in Contemporary Social Theory: Emergent Problems and the Prospects of Modern Societies

A number of problems arise out of the attempt to analyse the place of bureaucratic surveillance in modern societies by integrating these disparate strands of social theory. These can be identified by reviewing briefly the difficulties associated with each of the three traditions of social theory with which this book has been concerned.

Although the impact of capitalism on the growth of bureaucratic surveillance in modern societies has been substantial, the basic flaw of Marxist theory is its tendency to exaggerate the centrality of class conflict in this process. It tends to view 'top-down' hierarchies in systems of administrative power as derivative of capitalist relations of production.

It will be recalled that the theory of industrial society provides a contrasting perspective: authoritative relations of command and control are functional requirements of any social system and these take the form of technocratic bureaucracies in the industrial age. This line of argument has two principal components: first, a claim that the links between technocratic bureaucracy and social co-ordination are established through homeostatic processes of system adjustment. This suggestion means that a social teleology tends to displace any focus on the struggles for power amongst actors in organizations and society generally. This was evident for example in 'Whiggish' accounts of the genesis of modern policing and related discussions of the bureaucratization of modern business enterprise. Second, bureaucratic co-ordination of organizations is understood in terms of the performance of tasks for collective interests rather than as an exercise of power over subject populations. Basic sectional divisions of interest are quite marginal concerns for this tradition of social theory.

As I have documented in some detail, there are difficulties with both these claims. Nevertheless, the theory of industrial society is right to stress the technical advantages of bureaucratic administration and to show that bureaucracy need not always be associated with the exercise of power over subject populations. Furthermore, in modern societies, the evidence suggests that systems of bureaucratic surveillance can be expected to outlast any fundamental alteration in capitalist property relations. Put another way, no matter how much the technical and organizational attributes of industrialism can be shown to have been originally the products of the capitalist enterprise system, they are relatively autonomous from it: they can be adapted for use in quite different institutional contexts, as the experiences of state socialist societies in the twentieth century illustrate.

It is important to note that this view of the connections between bureaucratic surveillance and industrialism can be harnessed to another strand of social theory. In this context, bureaucracy is regarded as a highly effective means of exercising surveillance over subject populations in industrial societies but the struggle for power in the organizations of modern society cannot be reduced to those of class struggle. Perhaps the clearest illustration of this line of argument is Weber's focus on the geopolitical dynamics of the modern state. Indeed, he regarded the bureaucratic organizations of the modern nation-state in many respects as the epitome of the distinctive administrative features of modern societies. This accounts for the 'militaristic' emphasis that can be discerned in Weber's ideal type of bureaucracy. Of course, as was the case with Foucault, this bleak view of bureaucracy as a regimented fusion of discipline and knowledge was not simply the effect of an empirical focus on state organizations but also an expression of his conception of social life as an eternal struggle for power.

It is this approach which has played an important part in the analysis of surveillance defended here together with the associated critique of the models of power and surveillance offered by the other two traditions of social theory. However, as I suggested earlier, there are also two particular difficulties with this Machiavellian line of argument. The first of these concerns an unwarranted exaggeration of the oligarchical tendencies inherent in bureaucratic organizations. The second relates to problems in coping with the considerable empirical variety of administrative regimes which can be found within the rational bureaucratic type; that is to say in terms of the respective powers and rights of central authorities, administrative staffs and subject populations.

In drawing on the strengths and seeking to avoid the pitfalls of these disparate strands of social theory, the analysis defended here poses a number of issues which have relevance for how one views the prospects of modern societies in an age of surveillance. Three of these are of particular importance: (1) the relationships between knowledge and power in bureaucratic organizations; (2) the connections between democratic citizenship and surveillance; (3) the links between military power and surveillance.

As a preface to this part of the discussion, it should be noted that one of the implications of the non-reductionist account of the links between surveillance and modernity defended in this book is a 'decentred' view of power. There are two dimensions to this: first, across the 'horizontal' axis of societies with a fairly extensive division of labour and particularly in modern capitalist societies, lie distinct and autonomous hierarchies of power. Of course, the precise nature of the relations of autonomy and dependence amongst these hierarchies is a matter of empirical analysis. However, in general terms, the conditions of relative autonomy are rooted in the differentiation of the means of economic production and the political means of administration and violence, with each focused on the distinct organizations of the capitalist enterprise and the modern nation-state. In each case, the division of labour between occupations concerned with the internal and external management of systems of administrative power provides further conditions for the generation of autonomies and distinct interests; as, for example, in the autonomy of military and foreign affairs from class power; the distinct interests of armed force and police agencies; or of competing managerial hierarchies within the capitalist business enterprise. The general orienting idea here is that there seems little point in seeking to identify some *fons et origo* of power.

The second dimension of a decentred view of power is a vertical one: that is to say, organizations are viewed here in terms of occupationally differentiated hierarchies, the core of which comprises the emergent triangle of relations connecting the central authorities, bureaucratic staffs and subject populations in systems of administrative power. It is an error to regard any of these participants as either passive instruments or all-powerful agents, no matter how 'totalitarian' the system of rule. The processes of bureaucratization undergone by these hierarchies of power have not been viewed here as expressions of the dynamics of class conflict, the logic of industrialism or some generalized logic of disciplinary power. There is something in each of these claims, but each in turn has to be questioned in pursuit of a more adequate account. This becomes evident when one considers the three emergent issues indicated above. The first of these concerns the varying relationships between knowledge and discipline in bureaucratic organizations and the independent impact of strategies of professionalism on the expansion of their surveillance capacities.

Knowledge, power and discipline in modern societies

It will be recalled that in Weber's and Foucault's theories of surveillance, the principles of knowledge and discipline (or professional expertise and bureaucratic authority) were not regarded as independent variables but as twin expressions of the overall rationalization of power and technique in modern societies. Thus, for instance, in Weber's case, the separation of officials from the means of administration and the worker from the means of production were viewed as two different phases of the same overall process. Bureaucratization involved a 'funnelling up' of knowledge in organizations and a routinization of action through the imposition of bureaucratic rules and administrative systems for the monitoring of organizational behaviour. The divorce between conception and execution and the organization of the work of the majority in terms of a detailed division of labour with a corresponding 'parcelling out of the soul' was, then, a generalized tendency of modern industrial societies; knowledge was subordinated to discipline and both were expressions of rationalization. The rationality of bureaucratic discipline was an outcome of the technical superiority of this type of administrative system as an implement in the eternal struggle for power in social life.

Of course, very similar ideas have been present in Marxist discussions, except that the separation between conception and execution as a result of the process of bureaucratization is regarded as a product of capitalist relations of production, and specifically the shift from competitive to monopoly capitalism. The organization of knowledge is viewed as an expression of capitalist discipline not of the imperatives of organizations in an age of rational technology. Writers inspired by Braverman's thesis have continued to use this perspective in studying the nature and prospects of work in modern societies (R. Edwards 1979; D. Clawson 1980).

In contrast again, those who draw on the theory of industrial society, and especially the works of Durkheim and Parsons tend to regard some of the hopes of Marxist writers concerning the future enrichment of work after the abolition of capitalism as incipient trends in all industrial societies. This is because of the logic of industrialism. Thus, although bureaucratic discipline is a functional requirement of all complex industrial societies, with the continuing advance of modern technology it is increasingly subordinated to expertise and professional knowledge. As Brante has argued recently, it is suggested that the technical intelligentsia or 'technostructure' (J. K. Galbraith 1967) comprising scientists, bureaucrats, engineers, computer experts and other professional groups constitute 'a new administrative apparatus occupying key positions . . . [S]ociety could not function without them. In contrast to the old bureaucracy, their positions do not rest on legal authority but on argument, reason and knowledge' (T. Brante 1988: 123). Writers in this tradition do not deny that modern societies are characterized increasingly by bureaucratized organizations, particularly those of the state and corporate business. Rather, as Johnson has argued, the claim is that within modern organizations professional expertise and ideals of altruistic service will reduce the more coercive and impersonal features of bureaucracy. At a more general level, it is supposed that professional occupations based on scientific and technical expertise will provide the basis for both further technical advance and economic growth together with social harmony. Thus, an admittedly hierarchical and organized society will be one based on levels of knowledge and competence and able to steer a middle path between the extremes of egotistical liberal capitalism and the collectivist tyranny of socialism (T. Johnson 1976: 36–40).

While these writers accept that there will continue to be a separation between conception and execution in the occupational division of labour, this is not regarded in terms of a sharp dichotomy between a minority and a majority but rather in terms of a series of gradations of relative knowledge in relation to which all become increasingly more skilled. In addition, a crucial theme in this account of knowledge and power in an age of surveillance is the link with the functional theory of stratification: knowledge serves not egotistical self-interest, nor the interests of the capitalist class but rather the general interest in the context of the imperatives of industrialism.

Although the account of the relationships between surveillance and modernity defended here has drawn in large part on Weber's theory of bureaucracy, this has not entailed a rejection of the other strands of social theory. Current work on the issue of knowledge and discipline shows the merits of continuing to seek ways of integrating the three traditions distinguished in this book. While it is plain that modern organizations have undergone the four related processes of bureaucratization identified earlier, there are important variations in the ways in which knowledge and discipline can be combined. Neither these nor the co-operative and conflictual relations amongst various occupations in organizations can be understood exclusively in terms of class relations, the logic of industrialism or the rationalization of power.

These general issues can be illustrated briefly as follows: the recent application of computerized information technologies to the capitalist workplace has been regarded by many of those who have drawn on Braverman's ideas as yet a further extension of the divorce between conception and execution attendant upon the introduction of scientific management (R. Crompton and S. Reid 1982). Others have drawn more optimistic scenarios or, more cautiously, have suggested that the impact of such technologies may well vary substantially according to the type of industry. As Rowe has suggested usefully,

The key point is that the optimists (ie those who draw on the theory of industrial society CD) strongly emphasise the difference between manufacturing and process production, arguing that the latter provides more highly skilled work and that as automation gathers pace and manufacturing plants turn to continuous flow production, so the deskilling aspects of factory work will evaporate. The pessimists on the other hand (largely Marxist scholars CD) do not expect the production line to disappear overnight and even when and if it does they question whether process production in a capitalist society necessarily provides fulfilling, non-alienating work. (C. Rowe 1986: 67-8)

Rowe concludes that the future is 'open' in that the quality of work in organizations and thus the amount of discretion given to participants in organizations will depend upon the strategies of capital and national governments as well as on the strength of unions. Although the future is 'open', market pressures and continuing technical innovations in respect of improvements in the 'throughput' of business enterprises will surely mean that concessions in the areas of participation and job enrichment will be within the framework of bureaucratized systems. It is also difficult to see how any mass demands for high quality goods with high productivity could be met in state socialist societies without recourse to similar arrangements. Thus one should be wary of attributing the persistence of bureaucracy to the logic of capital, and recognize that, as was argued earlier, there is something of value in the claim that there is a 'logic of industrialism' (C. Kerr et al. 1973).

In this context, it seems clear that an underlying and persistent pattern of work in modern business enterprises will be a dualistic one: on the one hand, a bureaucratized managerial hierarchy with specified areas of discretion and organized in terms of careers; and on the other, a fairly regimented and routinized series of tasks structured according to the principles of scientific management and with wage labour contracted on a basis which excludes it from organizational careers. However, as was noted earlier, an interesting contemporary development is the extension of organizational careers to non-managerial sections of the workforce (pp. 191-2). The following argument derives from the recent work of David Ashton (D. Ashton et al.: 1989). The context in which this development is occurring comprises a series of changes in the structure of modern capitalism. Contemporary capitalist production and distribution takes place in a global system. This means that multinational corporations operate in a more unpredictable environment than that provided by the framework of a single nation-state. In this environment, Japanese enterprises have achieved a competitive edge over other firms based in large part on gains in productivity deriving from a dualistic organization of labour: this comprises a permanent, relatively privileged, core and a more casual workforce which, together with sub-contracting, provides a flexible system for adjusting to shifting market demands. In the manufacturing sector, productivity gains are also dependent on the displacement of skilled manual labour by high technology machinery and on a range of 'knowledge' workers required for the planning of production.

Similar dualistic strategies for organizing labour can be identified in the burgeoning service sector of economies, as for instance in large-scale fast food and hotel chains. Here can be found a core of permanent career-oriented employees together with a pool of casual workers employed when and where necessary.

These changes associated with the polarization of the workforce have not left managerial functions untouched. As some commentators have suggested, a question arising from this model of the polarization of work processes between functions of conception and execution concerns the future of office work and the changing position of professional and managerial labour in bureaucratized organizations.

Some evidence suggests that a good deal of office work will be pushed below this line of polarization. Again, computerized information systems have provided the technological basis for a further rationalization of office work. Recently, this has been conceptualized in terms of a shift from the industrial to the electronic office. Rowe, drawing on the work of Guiliano and Downing, focuses on two processes of change: the introduction of technologies and work practices which improve existing operations, for example, the replacement of typewriters by word processors; and those which eliminate administrative functions, so cutting costs and increasing the speed of operations, (as say the displacement of some secretarial operations by desktop technologies used directly by key managers). He discusses the impact of these processes on occupations located on both sides of the division between conception and execution (what he refers to as 'knowledge' and 'information' workers respectively) (C. Rowe 1986: 69–89). While Rowe identifies continuing processes of polarization in the area of information work, such as the division between word processing pools and secretaries attached to managers, he is wary of technological reductionism and points to the ways in which the occupations concerned can actively resist attempts to routinize their existence. This seems good advice, as does the scepticism offered in regard to claims that the electronic office will entail a democratic, participatory system of labour. Such rosy images of the future seem to underplay the structural context of managerial power in large enterprises and confuse the increased speed of administrative operations with an equalization of power amongst participants in organizations. A similar error has characterized some discussions of the organization of managerial labour in modern bureaucratic organizations.

Perhaps the clearest indication of the ways in which the present argument has drawn on Weber's theory of bureaucracy is that professionalization is understood as a component part of the broader process of bureaucratization. Industrial or 'post-industrial' societies may rely more and more on professional expertise or knowledge workers but any suggestion that we are witnessing the decline of bureaucracy should be viewed with as much scepticism as should claims concerning the trend towards 'disorganized capitalism'. Just such a claim in relation to bureaucracy has been made by those who have applied the theory of industrial society to interpret the impact of new information technologies on the nature of management. Some have suggested that these technologies are leading to the spread of more flexible management structures. In this context, Rowe's discussion of Toffler's claims is instructive.

Toffler suggests that the technological demands of advanced industrial societies require the decline of bureaucratic structures and thus of Whyte's organization man and the rise of 'ad hocracy' in its place. By this argument Toffler means that three features of bureaucratic organization are becoming increasingly outdated: the permanence of organizational structures; the relative fixity of ranks of authority; and the functional specificity of tasks in the division of labour. Managers will be expected to work in environments where organizational routines are subject to frequent change; where their positions in successive work groups will not be determined strictly by general organizational ranking; and where they will be expected to be competent in a range of different skills. These new features are referred to as transience, mobility and flexibility (C. Rowe 1986: 96–8).

It is clear that this view of the prospects of managerial work in modern bureaucratic organizations involves a reassertion of the theory of industrial society and its account of the relationship between knowledge and discipline: the demands of modern technology mean that the vertical structure of bureaucratic discipline will be converted into a horizontal collegiate system of co-operation amongst teams of professional experts.

Toffler's claims are exaggerated, yet they do point to important changes; namely the dramatic increases in the speed of information flow in organizations and the creation of a variety of task and project groups which cut across the vertical structures of modern organizations. However, such changes should not be viewed in terms of a decline in the significance of the vertical principle of bureaucratic organization. As Rowe points out, and as was pointed out in the earlier discussion of the concentration of strategic power and the decentralization of tactical decisions in many modern business enterprises,

[i]t should not be thought that a decentralised structure implies a weak centre; it is simply an alternative mechanism for maintaining control, only it operates on terms laid down by the centre and is still control. It is maintained not by centralising decisions towards the top, but by setting clearly prescribed tasks, rules and procedures within which people can operate. This less visible form of power sets limits on what subordinates might do, and provides a kind of freedom of manoeuvre within bounds; but it is still bureaucratic control. (C. Rowe 1986: 100)

Quite so; as in the case of office work, the middle management level of knowledge workers may well be subject to processes of rationalization and polarization as top managers seek to use new technical means to make their enterprises more effective.

Thus, arguments concerning the long-term attenuation of bureaucratic discipline in the face of technical expertise are not without weaknesses. The same can be said for the related view that professional expertise serves consensual or 'power to' interests of the wider organization or society. These weaknesses have been addressed by writers who have drawn on Max Weber's social theory in interpreting the connections between knowledge and discipline in modern bureaucratic organizations.

As Brante has suggested recently, writers such as Parkin and Johnson have analysed the genesis and operation of professional expertise in terms of the idea of social closure, that is, attempts to establish occupational privileges through the monopolization of market opportunities (T. Brante 1988: 127). In modern industrial societies, strategies of social closure rest on three bases: property, political qualifications (such as party membership in state socialist societies) and educational credentials. The latter are linked with conditions of technicality and indeterminacy in the relations between producers and consumers of services in the market and thus the relations of autonomy and dependence which can arise between them. With the right 'mix' of technicality and indeterminacy (that is, sufficient technicality or routinization of tasks as a basis for the generation of occupational expertise and solidarity on the one hand, and sufficient indeterminacy to create conditions of mystique and dependence of client on the expert on the other) enclosed niches of professional occupations can be established (H. James and B. Pelloile 1970). These can serve as a basis for privilege in terms of income, social status and power in respect of controlling the way in which a service is produced and supplied and the way in which it is consumed by the client group. Professionalism provides a powerful opportunity to regulate and gather information about clients' lives.

Writers in the Weberian tradition accept that in generating conditions of technicality and indeterminacy, modern industrialism establishes relations of autonomy and dependence between expert and client. However, rather than assuming that professional expertise is harnessed to the pursuit of collective goals (those of the client group and the wider society as a whole) attention is focused on the ways in which expertise is linked with occupational self-interest and the processes whereby professional occupations mobilize wider class and state power to that end. Not surprisingly this Machiavellian style of theorizing is referred to by Brante as a 'cynical' approach (T. Brante 1988: 126-7).

This line of argument is associated with a number of other claims: first, doubt is shed on the view that, with the logic of industrialism, all members of modern societies become more skilled. It is not denied that literacy and basic skills are important features of modern industrial societies, but the view of social hierarchies as comprising fine gradations of knowledge is substituted by one of experts and non-experts. This involves a *rapprochement* with Braverman's ideas although on a different theoretical basis. Second, writers such as Illich, McKeown, and Cohen have charted the ways in which strategies of professional exclusion have been associated with the growth of the surveillance capacities of the organizations to which such experts are attached or become attached (I. Illich 1975; T. McKeown 1979; S. Cohen 1985). Third, similar studies have analysed professional occupations in terms of careerism and the struggle for power rather than in terms of the disinterested pursuit of truth and service characteristic of some (what are considered to be 'naive') approaches. Fourth, most of these writers accept that, with the growth of modern societies, professionalism is increasingly subordinated to bureaucratic discipline. For example, Johnson has shown how the conditions for the autonomy of associations of predominantly 'solo' professional experts were generated by the markets of competitive industrial capitalism. Emergent professional occupations could loosen their dependence on forms of aristocratic patronage by exploiting the opportunities provided by the individualized mass clientele of market society. However, with the shift from competitive to organized capitalism and the spread of democratic citizenship, professional occupations became increasingly subordinated to bureaucratic discipline by being housed in the organizations of big business and the modern state. Thus, professionalism has been supplanted by heteronomous control from capitalist enterprise and the state, where the client once more asserts control, or forms of mediation where, for instance, the state determines the terms and conditions of the relations between profession and client (T. Johnson 1972; 1976).

Although, in general terms, professionalism has been subordinated to bureaucratic control, it is important to recognize the variations in this process and to recognize the sectional struggles for power involved. Some occupations can retain an associational form and exploit market opportunities on that basis; others are structured along the lines of professional bureaucracies such as many universities and hospitals; yet others are bureaucratic professions such as the police and armed forces. Furthermore, professions such as medicine and social work vary in status in part as a consequence of whether they were housed by the state or capitalist enterprise *ab initio*.

To conclude this part of the argument, the valid element of Weber's social theory is the contention that, in modern societies, professional expertise has become subordinated to bureaucratic discipline. However, the variations in this process indicated briefly above need to be noted. In addition, professional occupations have played an independent part in the expansion of the surveillance of populations and thus of the surveillance capacities of the organizations in which they become incorporated. They should not be seen as the servant of 'society' or of capital.

Johnson's later writings on the professions can be viewed in terms of a shift from Weberian to Marxist theory. The conditions of professional power and privilege are regarded less as arising from the potentialities of knowledge and technique characteristic of industrialism and more as a consequence of the position of the professions in capitalist relations of production. Drawing on Carchedi, Johnson has argued that the degree to which professions are resistant or not to processes of routinization and thus being pushed below the line of polarization is dependent on whether they perform functions of conception and execution for capital (and not for the logic of industrialism). As Saks has argued, this seems a somewhat restricted view of the issue and it is doubtful whether this attempt to collapse industrialism as one aspect of modernity into another, that of capitalism, is any more successful that those of Clawson and others considered elsewhere (pp. 187–92) (M. Saks 1983). The view taken here is that strategies of professionalization are not created by capitalist relations of production but are generic features of industrial societies. Industrialism creates conditions of technicality and indeterminacy which provide the basis for strategies of professional exclusion and power. Although such strategies depend upon the mobilization of state approval, they also depend upon the willingness of subject populations to look for expert help in an age of science and what I termed earlier as the 'classificatory impulse' (p. 149). It is difficult to see how the abolition of capitalism would alter these basic features of modernity. Moreover, professionalism will normally be performed in the context of bureaucratized organization structures.

Democracy, citizenship and surveillance

A further set of issues arises out of the non-reductionist analysis of bureaucratic surveillance and modernity defended here; these concern the links between democracy, citizenship and surveillance.

Modern societies are democratized nation-states. Following Tocqueville and Weber, the process of democratization can be defined in general terms as the progressive equalization of social conditions. Bearing in mind the need to avoid unilinear and teleological conceptions of the changes involved, this process can be understood as the generation of sets of citizenship rights in the various institutional sectors of modern societies: viz., formal equality before the law as an expression of the impersonal, public power of the state; civil rights of association and freedom of speech; the extension of the universal and equally weighted franchise; freedom to own and sell property and enter into contracts with employers; provision of social rights in the form of various state guaranteed claims to minimum standards of living.

As Anthony Giddens has suggested, in modern capitalist societies these rights can be viewed as clustering in particular institutional sectors: legal and civil rights are focused on the relations between citizens and the policing authorities of the modern nation-state. Political rights are generated in the context of relations between government and electorate. Economic rights hinge on the relations between capital and labour focused on the business enterprise but these have to be set within the legislative framework of the nation-state which normally guarantees a level of social rights (A. Giddens 1985: 201–21; see also J. Barbalet 1988: 1–43).

Three qualifications need to be made to this characterization. First of all, it is important to bear in mind the different ways in which modern societies have institutionalized citizenship rights and thus the equalization of social conditions they express. There are important differences amongst the national citizenship states of the capitalist type particularly with regard to (a) whether the development of industrial capitalism and a modern state are linked with a liberalization of political and civil rights; (b) the relative provision of formal and substantive equality and thus the salience of guaranteed social rights and redistributionist strategies pursued by the state in its dealings with the capitalist economy. In general terms, the first issue encompasses the division between liberal and authoritarian states; the second that between liberal and social democratic states although these divisions can of course overlap.

The second point of qualification is that although there is an important distinction to be drawn between the regimes of capitalist and state socialist societies, there is a sense in which all of these systems are 'democratized'. There are two aspects of this characterization: first, systems of rule are legitimated through symbols of popular sovereignty or the 'will of the people' (particularly in the political sphere but also in other areas). Second, the population is actively involved in decisions. Of course, this involvement can be one of a dragooned mass or an autonomous citizenry (C. Wright-Mills 1956: 298–324). As Bendix has observed, this was the point of Mannheim's concept of fundamental democratization (R. Bendix 1969: 76).

The third point of qualification is that, as Tocqueville suggested, processes of democratization and the desires for equality which inspire them cut across the institutional features of modernity and cannot be reduced to any one of them. For example, whilst political democracy was linked with the development of industrial capitalism in England, in the USA it prefaced this economic development. Tocqueville himself appeared to go as far as regarding the triumph of industrial capitalism in the west as merely one aspect of the general process of democratization or the equalization of social conditions (R. Aron 1968: 182–232). The view taken here is that, in the era of modernity, the nation-state as a police and military power is also a democratized organization; it houses a process which percolates throughout society in the conditions of industrialism whether organized on capitalist or socialist lines.

It will be recalled that in the arguments defended here, the growth of bureaucratic surveillance in modern societies has been conceptualized in terms of two broad and contrasting patterns: the rational-legal public bureaucracy of liberal democratic capitalism and the bureaucratic dictatorship characteristic of right and left autocratic democracies or totalitarian systems. As I indicated earlier, social democracy can be viewed as an attempt to avoid the institutional extremes of both right and left authoritarianism on the one hand and individualistic capitalism (with its minimalist state and preoccupation with formal equality) on the other.

From the standpoint of bureaucracy and surveillance, the major institutional points of contrast amongst these systems concern: (a) The effective enforcement of a code of correct behaviour on bureaucratic officials by the central authorities. This means ensuring that such officials apply an impersonal code to particular cases and that the possibilities for arbitrary behaviour are minimized; (b) The establishment of effective mechanisms of accountability of the bureaucracy to the subject populations. As I pointed out earlier, it is difficult to maintain either (a) or (b) without the other; (c) The significance of the separation of powers within society and thus the provision of limits on the aggrandisement of power. This involves three areas: within

215

the organization of the nation-state; between the state and society (i.e. the maintenance of a private sphere beyond state power); and within society itself, i.e. the proliferation of associations and interest groups. Of importance in this context is the relative priority of market and state bureaucracy as a mode of social co-ordination.

It is clear that both the forms and extent of bureaucratization vary in different types of both capitalist and state socialist societies. Here the focus is specifically on the impact of democratic citizenship. In this analysis, it is important to examine the relationships between citizenship and bureaucratic surveillance from each side, and secondly, to focus on both the features of those relations which are generic to modern societies and those which are specific to capitalism or socialism.

It should be recalled that the prior growth of bureaucratic surveillance in modern societies, particularly in respect of the state as a military and policing agency, provided important preconditions for the generalization of citizenship rights. The concentration of political authority and the consolidation of the state as an administrative unit was associated in large part with the pursuit of power through war and the mobilization of the resources of capitalism for this purpose. These developments constituted the material basis for the extension of citizenship rights in that the allocation of bundles of equal rights presupposed their prior concentration in an agency above society and able to enforce its rules over the community. One of the most important illustrations of this point concerns the ways in which absolutism in western Europe was crucial in generating the institutional and ideological preconditions of the state as a public power.

To reverse the equation, the forces released by the French revolution have provided important stimuli to the processes of bureaucratization. As Tocqueville and Weber observed, in the context of modern societies, the pursuit of equality presupposes an extension of bureaucratic systems of surveillance (M. Weber 1970: 224-8). There are a number of aspects to this argument. First of all, given the technical impossibility of direct democracy in modern nation-states, the characteristic feature of bureaucracy, the 'abstract regularity of the execution of authority', is peculiarly suited to the pursuit of 'equality before the law in the personal and functional sense'. It is also appropriate in an age in which there is a 'horror of privilege and the principled rejection of doing business from case to case' (ibid.: 224). As Weber also suggested, attempts to ensure that administrative functions are not monopolized by honorific or otherwise privileged groups but organized on the basis of democratized recruitment and promotion procedures pre-supposes the development of rational bureaucracies. In addition, the implementation of the universal franchise involves the transformation of the means of representation from collegiate clubs to bureaucratized mass political parties.

Secondly, in modern societies, although the concentration of political authority and the bureaucratic state are preconditions for the generalization of citizenship rights, they also provide the possibility of authoritarianism or the 'tyranny of the majority' of either the right or the left. As Tocqueville suggested, this is particularly likely in the context of a weakened public sphere, which creates the conditions for the acceptance of demagogic political leadership, and the willingness of the subject populations to place equality or order above liberty in their lists of priorities. Here the focus of the argument is on equality.

Perhaps Tocqueville's most astute observation of the modern age was that tyranny was not confined to the pre-democratic era. It is in this context that Weber and Tocqueville discuss the bureaucratic implications of attempts to extend the formal equalities characteristic of liberal democratic societies by using the state to facilitate the substantive equalizing of citizenship rights. As I observed earlier, this involves a critique of socialism and social democracy. For these writers, paradoxically, the absolute pursuit of equality must involve a direct threat to liberty even if 'effective liberty' is a component part of the very goal that is being pursued.

The difficulties faced by those who seek to square this circle of equality and liberty and the implications of these for bureaucracy and surveillance in modern societies can be illustrated through considering some of the recent arguments of David Held (D. Held 1987).

Held seeks to develop a practical model of democracy which transcends the competing claims of liberal democracy and socialism. The criterion of democracy is defined by the principle of 'democratic autonomy'.

> Individuals should be free and equal in the determination of the conditions of their own lives; that is they should enjoy equal rights (and accordingly equal obligations) in the specification of the framework which generates and limits the opportunities available to them, so long as they do not deploy this framework to negate the rights of others. (ibid.: 271, 290).

Consistent with the argument defended here, Held acknowledges that 'Marxism's central failure is the reduction of political power to economic power and thus to neglect . . . the dangers of centralised political power and the problems of political accountability.' (ibid.: 274)

As Weber and Tocqueville foresaw, attempts to abolish political conflict and economic scarcity through bureaucratic planning and a one-party state have simply involved the triumph of autocratic democratization or the levelling of the population beneath the party and bureaucracy.

In contrast, capitalist liberal democracies provide crucial preconditions for the flourishing of genuine democracy. For Held, these include

> the centrality, in principle, of an impersonal structure of public power, of a constitution to help guarantee and protect rights, of a diversity of power centres within and outside the state, of mechanisms to promote competition and debate between alternative political platforms.

Thus, 'the separation of the state from civil society must be a central feature of any democratic political order' (ibid.: 281).

For Held, the main weakness of liberal democracy's claim to provide the basis of a genuine democratic society lies in the centrality of capitalist appropriation in its economic and political institutions. Capitalist property relations provide the basis of a disjuncture between the formal equality of liberal democracy and glaring substantive inequalities. Held contends that democratic autonomy presupposes not just formal equality before the law and freedom to participate in capitalist markets but also

> equal rights to enjoy the conditions for effective participation; enlightened understanding and the setting of the political agenda. Such broad 'state' rights would, in turn, entail a broad bundle of social rights linked to reproduction, childcare, health and education, as well as economic rights to ensure adequate economic and financial resources for democratic autonomy. (ibid.: 285)

Furthermore,

> an equal right to material resources for men and women, in order that they may be in a position to choose among possible courses of action, would oblige the state to be preoccupied with the ways in which wealth and income can be far more equitably distributed. (ibid.)

All this would surely require the existence of a bureaucratized 'empowering legal system' of the state. It would entail a substantial increase in the state's supervisory powers over society, particularly as the state in contemporary capitalism is as yet quite unable to regulate 'civil power centres' such as large business enterprises in a way consistent with the principles of democratic autonomy. It should be evident that this line of argument does not sit at all well with those concerning Held's advocacy of a proliferation of competing power centres both within the state and in civil society nor his conviction that a crucial ingredient of a genuine democracy is the persistence of a sharp division between state and society. Indeed, Held acknowledges that as the drift of his argument involves a collapse of this very division, the whole area of the public and the private needs to be redrawn in democratic theory; but it is hardly clear what this position entails.

Nevertheless, Held's debt to liberalism is clear in his advocacy of (1) a system of constitutionally based parliamentary democracy; (2) a division between central government and local administration (an echo of Tocqueville's ideas); (3) open government in respect of freedom of information; (4) in relation to civil society, Held suggests the need for a variety of private and 'socially owned' enterprises providing goods and services to consumers. However, in this context, the demands of democratic autonomy require that economic activities take place within the overall investment priorities established by central government and that local, socially owned or co-operative enterprises are insulated from market failures by central funding. Private enterprise is not the lynchpin of the system as a whole.

In Held's attempt to square the circle of equality and liberty, it seems that the liberal items in his model of synthesis are subordinated to those which are derived from Marxism. It is difficult to see how this schema offers much in the way of an advance on corporatist and bureaucratized models of social democracy. For all the reference to liberal principles, it is still the case that, in modern industrial societies, the pursuit of equality through a tough re-distributionist state involves a fairly thorough bureaucratization of social life.

Of course, an objection to this Tocquevillean line of argument is that those who do not favour the provision of democratic autonomy for all through collective, bureaucratic means, would have much to lose from such arrangements (i.e. property and other privileges) and, at the same time, are themselves well placed to protect themselves from the vagaries of capitalist markets.

This is a telling point but there are two further replies to it. First, Held fails to acknowledge that, given the admitted rarity of genuine democracy in human history it should be noted that the social foundations of liberty in the modern west hinged in part on the division between a vigorous market capitalism on the one hand and the political authority of competing nation-states on the other. As I argued earlier, scholars like Mann and Hall echo Weber's suggestion that, in the modern age, a crucial barrier against tyranny is the division between the bureaucratic hierarchies of the nation-state and the capitalist enterprise both within and between societies. In the context of this institutional division, western societies managed to construct states equipped with both effective surveillance capacities and systems of representation responsive to the wishes of substantial sections of the subject population. Today in western Europe, with incipient processes of economic and political integration, it may well be that these historical foundations of liberty will have to be reconstructed: with the division between state and enterprise organized at the inter-state level and systems of representation structured around federal principles.

The second reply to Held's case is that the division between capitalism and the state has not only been one of the lynchpins of liberty in modern capitalist society, but also the basis of its dynamism and wealth-creating potential. On the historical evidence, it would seem that those who wish to pursue redistributionist strategies in pursuit of equality should be aware that capitalism is an institutional means of wealth creation which state socialism shows little sign of being able to emulate without shedding its core features. Both on grounds of liberty and wealth then, the axis of social democracy and liberalism would appear to provide the most fruitful basis for designing effective ways of limiting the abuses of bureaucratic systems of surveillance and adapting them for democratic ends. One implication of this conclusion should be spelt out clearly: that the problem of the relationship between equality and liberty is one of squaring the circle. The price of genuine liberty is a certain level of inequality amongst members of society even if organized as the outcome of a 'meritocratic' division of labour. The price of real equality is bureaucratic levelling.

Held seeks to transcend the division between liberal capitalism and state socialism. The view here has been that his synthesis is unstable and subject to a drift towards bureaucratic centralism. Yet this is not to deny that Held provides important insights concerning how this drift might be avoided. Nor is it to suppose that current writings on the merits of markets as the foundation of both wealth and liberty are not without their own weaknesses: in many respects these concern the placing of order above political liberty and/or liberty above equality. Thus neo-conservative or liberal writers, while discussing the respective merits of markets and bureaucracy as foundations of wealth and liberty spend far less time addressing the problem of the challenge to liberty posed by the dense and extensive nets of surveillance constructed by the strong state in so many modern societies (R. Skidelsky 1988). Meanwhile, the more libertarian of such writers appear quite unable to envisage that in a democratic age, the bureaucratic agencies of the state provide an important framework of security for those with a just claim to citizenship rights but who are not provided for through their own efforts in the market place. It is in this context that those who have sought to steer a mid course between state socialism and market capitalism, but have regarded traditional conservativism as outmoded, have sought to reconstruct corporatist models of social democracy along the lines of the social market (J. Hall 1985: 178–9).

Warfare, military power and surveillance

The final set of issues which arises out of the arguments defended here concerns war, military power and the growth of surveillance in modern societies. In sharp contrast with hitherto dominant tendencies in sociology, war and military power have figured as central themes in this book. This is in recognition of the more general claim that contemporary social analysis needs to examine the interplay between the internal and external dynamics of all social organizations not just those of nation-states. The internalist bias of many sociological discussions has always constituted a serious intellectual error but it is of particular importance to challenge it now in an era when societies are connected together through networks of truly global interdependence. As I pointed out earlier, there are signs that modern sociology is taking seriously the need to focus on the connections between internal and external dynamics and particularly on the impact of military power on social life.

A number of links have been drawn connecting warfare, military power and the growth of bureaucratic surveillance in modern western societies. These can be addressed in terms of the following broad themes.

First of all, warfare played a central part in the genesis of the infrastructure of the early modern state as a territorially bounded agency both separate from society and equipped with bureaucratic means for supervising its activities. The dominant concern of the early modern state and its principal item of expenditure related to mobilizing the material and human resources for the pursuit of power through war with other emerging states. In Europe, the foundations of the modern state were forged in wars which stemmed from a peculiarly intense level of rivalries amongst the component parts of a pluralistic geopolitical system (J. Hall 1985; M. Mann 1987; 1988; P. Kennedy 1988; C. Ashworth and C. Dandeker 1987).

Of course, the financial, organizational and industrial resources of capitalism provided the 'nerves' of the military and related administrative powers of states. This was perhaps most clearly illustrated by the military revolution of the seventeenth century and the attendant 'feedback loops' connecting capitalist development, the military and financial powers of individual western states and the global extension of the western world in general. It should be stressed that the pursuit of military and geopolitical power by states should not be attributed to the economic dynamics of class struggles. Far from the state system – and the subsequent network of nation-states – being a 'reflex' of capitalism, it was the prior existence of this pluralistic system which provided one of the major conditions for the triumph of western capitalism, and the generalization of the nation-state as the normal form of societal organization to the global context.

The second contention concerning military power and surveillance is that as war was a major and persistent feature of the early modern and modern state, military organizations were normally at the leading edge of processes of bureaucratization. The formation of military discipline, both in respect of the genesis of the officers' corps as a fusion of professional expertise and bureaucratic discipline; the creation of an organizational hierarchy connecting central authorities, officers and men; the divisional system of multi-unit organization – all of these disciplinary forms were later adapted for use in industrial capitalist organizations. Of course, not in every case did industrial capitalist enterprises look to their own state organization for models of administration; indeed the reverse was the case in the USA. In European history, if war revealed bureaucratic organization as an effective means of power and as adaptable to many other uses, it also makes the contemporary observer aware of the error in those views which seek to understand the administrative features of bureaucracy in terms of the functional imperatives of capitalist relations of production.

A third theme has been the suggestion that warfare led not only to the creation of bureaucratized military organizations but also to an extension of the state's supervisory powers over the rest of society for military objectives. There were two phases in this development: first, the formation of professional military organizations, largely separate from society as a consequence of the military revolution; second, the mobilization of national citizenries into large, bureaucratic military organizations as a result of the industrial and democratic revolutions. This was a fairly drawn out and uneven process. It stretched from the 1790s with a hiatus between 1815 and 1848 through to the two world wars of the twentieth century. National citizenries were mobilized by states in a variety of relatively 'civilianized', (liberal) or 'militarized', (autocratic) systems, ranging from the USA to Germany, Japan, Russia and later the Soviet Union. This wave engulfed even societies like the UK which succumbed to it in 1916 and again in 1939. The pressures of war and the political desire for military effectiveness certainly stimulated many societies to modernize their social structures in respect of industrial development and the extension of citizenship rights on authoritarian or liberal lines. Without a mass armed force owing allegiance to the democratized nation-state, many societies were doomed to second-class status or worse. Such calculations played a crucial part in the decisions of the political elites of Japan in the 1860s, Prussia in the early nineteenth century, and Russia in the mid-nineteenth and early twentieth centuries.

The industrialization and democratization of warfare meant that both the division between war and peace and between military and non-military became blurred. The pace of modern war meant that peace became increasingly a period of war preparation, and, particularly by the Second World War, war was a struggle between whole peoples not of specialized military organizations. The formation of extensive military-industrial complexes, the batteries of state regulatory powers over economy and society, and the proliferation of state planning agencies provided the clearest evidence of these changes.

A fourth theme addressed here concerns the ways in which, after 1945, the bureaucratized state 'techno-structure' encompassing military and society and largely created for the purpose of prosecuting war was turned to the problem of resolving some of the problems relating to the social rights of citizenship in time of peace. Of course, the effects of this shift from warfare to welfare constituted more of a shock to those societies like the UK than, say, Germany, as the former was less familiar with the ministrations of a long-established and powerful bureaucratic state. In any event, the pressure of war in the twentieth century added to and honed the administrative tools of socio-economic management possessed by states. As I pointed out earlier, these mechanisms of the bureaucratized citizenship state have remained largely intact until the resurgence of neo-liberal challenges, particularly in the Anglo-American context.

To turn to a fifth theme concerning war and military power, it is important to note that if there are now challenges to the bureaucratic citizenship state, there is also a relative decline in the significance of bureaucratized mass armed forces in the modern west. The precise outcome of this trend is still unclear. In societies such as Britain and the USA there has been a return to more professionalized military systems, although of course these remain bureaucratized structures. It is likely that this trend will be experienced by other advanced societies. The shift from mass to professional military organization can be understood in terms of the following dimensions: (a) reliance on small rather than large-scale forces in terms of numbers of personnel employed; (b) dependence upon volunteer recruitment rather than upon conscription. As a consequence of (a) and (b), the 'military participation ratio' of the societies concerned tends to decline (S. Andreski 1954); (c) Military organizations become increasingly capital intensive and consequently are characterized by a more complex division of labour. This means that in contrast with the pyramidial structures of mass armed forces, their organizational profiles tend towards the diamond shaped model (P. Manigart 1988).

As Janowitz and Van Doorn have argued, the conditions for the relative decline of mass armed forces in the west over the last few decades are first, the post-war reliance on nuclear technology as a means of deterrence; second, the difficulties of using conventional forces in Third World areas in the context of the decline of colonial empires. Not only are there legitimacy problems involved, but the nature of these small wars predisposes states to resort to professionally trained forces. This is particularly the case when viewed in the context of a third factor, the social conditions characteristic of modern capitalist societies, where affluence and the spread of education lead to a rising proportion of the population to look with disdain on the legitimacy of military service (M. Janowitz 1971; J. Van Doorn 1975; G. Harries-Jenkins 1973). As Burk has argued, this particular trend should be understood less as indicative of a decline in nationalism and more as a decline in the willingness of populations to express their national attachments in the form of commitment to military service (J. Burk 1988).

This incipient shift from mass to professionalized military systems may well be as profound a change as the ones in previous centuries which led to the formation of professionalized and national citizen armed forces. However, one must also be wary of generalizing too much from the Anglo-American context (C. Moskos and C. Wood 1988). It is also important to note that the fundamental elements of what I have referred to as the security state focused on war and war preparation remain as entrenched features of most modern capitalist societies. The forms in which the state manages to make a successful claim to a monopoly of the means of legitimate violence in a given territory may be shifting but that claim and the bureaucratized military power on which it is based remains.

A sixth theme has concerned the relationships between war, surveillance and peace. War has been a major cause of the growth of bureaucratic surveillance in both military and non-military sectors of modern societies and thus of the consolidation of nation-states. However, it should be remembered that bureaucratized military power has not only provided the material basis of war but has also been and remains one of the basic foundations of peace.

As I argued earlier, one of the central difficulties of liberal and Marxist traditions of social theory is their failure to recognize that although the potential for war is an inherent feature of a world of contending states, this is simply a particular expression of the universality of human conflict. While many liberal thinkers in the later eighteenth and nineteenth centuries regarded the 'militant' pre-industrial state as the principal source of war, later, Marxist writers levelled the same accusation at capitalist states and their military employees. The errors in their arguments are first to suppose that complex societies can do without a specialized political apparatus, or to see sufficiently clearly that without one an orderly social and economic life within and between societies would be impossible. Second, even if it were possible to do without the state, the abolition of war would simply entail the spread of unregulated violence in the field of human conflict. As Michael Howard has argued:

> war is only a particular kind of conflict between a particular category of social groups, sovereign states ... If one had no sovereign states one would have no wars as Rousseau rightly pointed out . . . but as Hobbes equally rightly pointed out, we would probably have no peace either. (M. Howard 1983: 11)

As will be recalled, one of the key components of Machiavellian social theory is the view that conflict is a perennial feature of social life and that the historical specialization of states, military organizations and the field of war are illustrations of this. As Anthony Giddens has suggested recently, 'the bulk of both archaeological and anthropological evidence leads to the conclusion that 'war' i.e. armed combat between groups in which physical violence is used by or on behalf of one community against another is present in all types of human society'. (A. Giddens 1985: 53)

The theoretical basis of the contention that conflict and the potentiality for war are inherent features of the human condition usually takes one of two forms: human aggression is biologically innate; or, as in the present view, whatever the biological predispositions, human conflict is rooted in the eternal struggles between competing absolute values. This view has been established in sociology largely through the influence of Weber. Although Anthony Giddens has offered an important critique of Weber's position, the argument here is that his case results in a qualification rather than a rebuttal of it. Giddens shows that Weber is mistaken in assuming that value disputes are only ultimately resolvable by blind faith and thus violence because both scientific and value judgements can be shown to be implicated in networks of theoretical assumptions which are always open to rational argument (A. Giddens 1977). Each field is at least as open as the other. However, the view taken here is that in all matters of conflict between human beings, one of the ways in which they resolve their disputes (and recognize them to be 'serious ones') is to ask themselves and those they are in conflict with 'Are you willing to die for what you believe in?' This is hardly an 'irrational' view of the ways in which violence may enter into the process whereby human beings judge the certainty with which contending truth claims are held.

The principal problem facing liberal and Marxist traditions of social theory is that, in the modern world, it is difficult to find a realistic alternative way of achieving peace than that based on separating the mass of the population from the means of violence and housing the latter in the bureaucratized military organizations of nation-states.

Recently, Held has argued that a series of contemporary changes are undermining the degree to which nation-states can continue to act as independent power containers (D. Held 1988a). The more important of these include the emergence of global corporations, the behaviour of which is quite beyond the power of individual nation-states to control; the spread of international organizations (although, as Giddens suggests, this development can be viewed as indicative of the continuing vitality of the nation-state (A. Giddens 1985: 263–5); the influence of international law on the conduct of states. Finally, Held, like Kennedy, points to the ways in which supra-national power blocs (particularly the emergent triad of power in the capitalist world comprising those headed by the USA, Japan and western Europe) undermine the political and military independence of individual nation-states.

These are important changes, but to consider them as heralding the end of the nation-state would be to adopt a rather premature view. For instance, trends towards economic and political integration in western Europe may well be accomapnied by somewhat contrary developments in the east, that is to say the emergence of intense national rivalries. Held accepts that even in western Europe, as elsewhere, states are extremely reluctant to give up the basis of their power which rests on the control of the means of violence. To the extent to which supra-national power blocs can be identified, these can just as well be viewed as entities comprising relations of superiority and subordination amongst nation-states. For instance, a united, federal Europe would be just such a system probably based on a hierarchy of power running from Germany and France to the UK.

In a world of global interdependence, while nation-states may well consider diplomacy as an alternative to military force as a means of resolving international disputes, their centralized control of the means of violence will be a means of ensuring that whatever agreements they make are respected by the populations they control. In addition there will always be circumstances where a state will consider force as the best way of defending its interests. By the same token, those who feel that particular states are not representing their interests may well turn to the informal sanction of terrorist violence: in short, any future decline in 'warfare' amongst states may well be linked with an increase in terrorism. The concentration of the means of violence in states provides the basis for both internal pacification and the regularization of inter-state relations even if those relations may produce wars. For many people used to living in modern nation-states based on a specialization of military and police powers and thus standing at the end of a long process of bureaucratization and internal pacification, it may be difficult to imagine the consequences of a failure by the state to maintain an effective monopoly of the means of legitimate violence within a given territory. Of course, in recent years, there have been some clear pointers in modern societies provided by the activities of numerous separatist groups and the attempts by states to use military and police agencies to quell them. Given the historical perspective offered in this book it may be well to conclude by recalling some more distant but very instructive illustrations. As Michael Howard has so acutely observed

> Those who rightly deplore the institutionalisation of war, the legitimisation of violence in the hands of political authorities, seldom consider the alternative; the use of violence as an instrument of daily intercourse in the hands of anyone strong enough to use it. The robber baron was a very familiar figure in medieval Europe, as was the unemployed knight living off the country in the intervals of more respectable forms of employment. The slow consolidation of power in the hands of a limited number of princes, the elimination of 'private war' and the fixing of a great conceptual barrier . . . between authorities who had a right to make war and those who did not was an essential step towards the creation of an orderly society. Only in such an order could there occur those developments in trade and manufacture and cultivation that brought into being a civilisation which would one day condemn as backward and barbaric the military ancestors who had made its activities possible. (M. Howard 1983: 174)

There seems little sign that, in the future, the order of modern societies both individually and collectively can do without the bureaucratized systems of military power which have played such a central role in their development.

Bibliography

Abrahamson, J. L. (1981) *America Arms For a New Century: The Making of a Great Military Power*, Collier Macmillan.

Albrow, M. (1970) *Bureaucracy*, Macmillan.

Alderson, J. C. (1985) 'Police and the Social Order' in Thomaneck J. and Roach J. *Police and Public Order in Europe*, Croom Helm.

Anderson, M. S. (1988) *War and Society in the Europe of the Old Regime*, Fontana.

Andreski, S. (1954) *Military Organization and Society*, Routledge and Kegan Paul.

Archibald, E. H. (1971) *The Metal Fighting Ship in the Royal Navy, 1860-1970*, Blandford.

Ardant, G. (1975) 'Financial Policy and Economic Infrastructure of Modern States and Nations' in C. Tilly *The Formation of National States in Western Europe*, Princeton University Press, 1975, 84-163.

Aron, R. (1965) *Main Currents in Sociological Thought*, Penguin.

Ashton D. N. et al. (1989) *Restructing the Labour Market: The Implications for Youth*, Macmillan.

Ashworth, C. E. and Dandeker, C. (1987) 'Warfare, Social Theory and West European Development', *Sociological Review* 35 (1), 1987, 1-18.

Ashworth, C. E. and Dandeker, C. (1986) ' "Capstones and Organisms: Political Forms and the Triumph of Capitalism": A Critical Comment', *Sociology* 20 (1), February 1986, 82-7.

Bailey, V. (ed.) (1981) *Policing and Punishment in Nineteenth Century Britain*, Croom Helm.

Baldwin, R. and Kinsey, R. (1982) *Police Powers and Politics*, Quartet.

Barbalet, J. (1988) *Citizenship*, Open University Press.

Barnet, C. (1963) *The Swordbearers*, Eyre and Spottiswoode.

Barnet, C. (1987) *The Audit of War*, Macmillan.

Baynham, H. (1969) *From the Lower Deck: The Old Navy, 1780-1840*, Hutchinson.

Beer, S. (1982) *Modern British Politics, Parties and Pressure Groups in the Collectivist Age*, Faber.

Beetham, D. (1985) *Max Weber and the Theory of Modern Politics*, Polity Press.

Bellamy, R. (1987) *Modern Italian Social Theory*, Polity Press.

Bendix, R. (1969) *Nation-Building and Citizenship*, Doubleday Anchor.

Benyon, J. (1986) 'Professionalism, Politics and Police in Britain', paper presented at ECPR, April 1986.

Bobbio, N. (1987) *The Future of Democracy*, Polity Press.

Bond, B. (1984) *War and Society in Europe, 1870-1970*, Fontana.

Bordua, D. (1967) *The Police: Six Sociological Essays*, Wiley.

Bourne, J. (1986) *Patronage in Nineteenth Century England*, Edward Arnold.

Brante, T. (1988) 'Sociological Approaches to the Professions', *Acta Sociologica* 31.2, 1988, 119-142.

Braverman, H. (1974) *Labour and Monopoly Capital*, Monthly Review Press.

Brewer, D. et al. (1988) *The Police, Public Order and the State*, Macmillan.

Brewer, J. and Styles J. (1980) *An Ungovernable People*, Hutchinson.

Brogden, M. (1982) *The Police: Autonomy and Consent*, Academic Press.

Brown, D. and Harrison, M. (1978) *A Sociology of Industrialisation*, Macmillan.

Burk, J. (1988) 'National Attachments and the Decline of Mass Armies', paper presented at ISA RCOI, Munich 1988.

Burnham, J. (1962) *The Managerial Revolution*, Penguin.

Burnham, J. (1970) *The New Machiavellians*, Gateway Press.

Campbell, D. (1980) 'Society Under Surveillance' in P. Hain et al., *Policing the Police*, vol. 2, J. Calder, 65-113.

Chandler, A. (ed.) (1964) *Giant Enterprise, Ford, General Motors and the Automobile Industry*, Harcourt Brace.

Chandler, A. (1965) *The Railroads: The Nation's First Big Business*, Harcourt Brace.

Chandler, A. (1977) The Visible Hand: The Managerial Revolution in American Business, Harvard University Press.

Chandler, A. and Daems, H. (1980) *Managerial Hierarchies: Comparative Perspectives on the Rise of the Modern Industrial Enterprise*, Harvard University Press.

Chapman, B. (1970) *Police State*, Pall Mall.

Child, J. (1969) *The Business Enterprise in Modern Industrial Society*, Collier Macmillan.

Child, J. (1977) *Organizations*, Harper and Row.

Cipolla, C. M. (1965) *Guns and Sails in the Early Phase of European Expansion, 1400-1700*, Collins.

Clapham, C. (1982) *Private Patronage and Public Power: Political Clientelism in the Modern State*, F. Pinter.

Clawson, D. (1980) *Bureaucracy and the Labour Process*, Monthly Review Press.

Cohen, S. (1985) *Visions of Social Control*, Polity Press.

Cohen, S. and Scull, A. (1985) *Social Control and the State*, Blackwell.

Connel, J. (1986) *The New Maginot Line*, Secker and Warburg.

Cooper, D. (1974) *The Lesson of the Scaffold*, London.

Cornish, W. R. et al. (1978) *Crime and the Law in Nineteenth Century Britain*, Irish University Press.

Cotterel, R. (1981) 'Legality and Political Legitimacy in the Sociology of Max Weber' in D. Sugarman (ed.) *Legality, Ideology and the State*, Academic Press, 69-93.

Craig, G. (1955; 1979) *The Politics of the Prussian Army*, Oxford University Press.

Creighton, C. and Shaw, M. (eds) (1987) 'The Sociology of War and Peace', *Explorations in Sociology* 24, Macmillan.

Critchley, T. A. (1967) *A History of the Police in England and Wales*, Constable.

Crouch, C. (ed.) (1979) *State and Economy in Contemporary Capitalism*, Croom Helm.

Dandeker, C. (1977) 'A Study of the Process of Bureaucratization: The Royal Navy, State and Society, 1780–1916', PhD Thesis, University of Leicester.

Dandeker, C. (1978) 'Patronage and Bureaucratic Control: The Case of the Naval Officer in English Society', *British Journal of Sociology* 29.3, 1978, 300–20.

Dandeker, C. (1983) 'Warfare, Planning and Economic Relations', *Economy and Society* 12.1, February 1983, 109–28.

Dandeker, C. (1984) 'Bureaucracy, Planning and War: The Royal Navy, 1880–1918' *Armed Forces and Society* 11.1, 1984, 130–46.

Dandeker, C. (1985) 'The Old Navy and Social Change: Discipline, Punishment and Authority in the Royal Navy, 1780–1860' in *New Aspects of Naval History*, Dept. of History, US Naval Academy, 1985, Nautical and Aviation Co., Baltimore.

Djilas, M. (1957) *The New Class: An Analysis of the Communist System*, Thames and Hudson.

Dunnigan, J. F. (1981) *How to Make War: A Comprehensive Guide to Modern Warfare*, Arms and Armour Press.

Edmonds, M. (1988) *Armed Services and Society*, Leicester University Press.

Edwards, R. (1979) *Contested Terrain*, Heinemann.

Ehrman, J. (1953) *The Navy in the War of William III, 1689–1697*, Cambridge University Press.

Eldridge, J. E. T. (1971) *Max Weber: The Social Interpretation of Reality*, Nelson.

Elger, T. (1983) 'Braverman, Capital Accumulation and Deskilling' in S. Wood (ed.) *The Degradation of Work? Skill, Deskilling and the Labour Process*, Hutchinson.

Elias, N. (1950) 'Studies in the Genesis of the Naval Profession', *British Journal of Sociology*, 1950, 291–309.

Elias, N. (1965), *The Established and the Outsiders*, Cass.

Ellis, J. (1986) *The Social History of the Machine Gun*, Johns Hopkins University Press.

Emsley, C. (1983) *Policing and its Context, 1750–1870*, Macmillan.

Emsley, C. (1987) *Crime and Society in England, 1750–1900*, Longman.

Etzioni, A. (1975) *A Comparative Analysis of Complex Organizations*, Collier Macmillan.

Feldman, A. S. (1966) *Army, Industry and Labour in Gemany, 1914–1918*, Princeton University Press.

Forsythe, W. J. (1988) *The Reform of Prisons, 1830–1900*, Croom Helm.

Foster, J. (1974) *Class Struggle in the Industrial Revolution*, Weidenfeld and Nicolson.

Foucault, M. (1979) *Discipline and Punish: The Birth of the Prison*, Penguin.

Fromm, E. (1941) *Escape From Freedom*, Holt, Rinehart and Winston.

Galbraith, J. K. (1967) *The New Industrial State*, Hamilton.

Gash, N. (1976) *Aristocracy and People: The New History of England, Britain, 1815–65*, Edward Arnold.

Gatrell, V. A. C., Lenman, B. and Parker, G. (1980) *The Social History of Crime in Western Europe Since 1500*, Europa.

Gerth, H. and Wright-Mills, C. (1970) *From Max Weber: Essays in Sociology*, Routledge and Kegan Paul.

Giddens, A. (1968) 'Power in the Recent Writings of T. Parsons', *Sociology*, vol. 2, 1968, 268–80.

Giddens, A. (1971) *Capitalism and Modern Social Theory*, Cambridge University Press.

Giddens, A. (1973) *The Class Structure of the Advanced Societies*, Hutchinson.

Giddens, A. (1981) *A Contemporary Critique of Historical Materialism*, vol. 1, Macmillan.

Giddens, A. (1982) *Profiles and Critiques in Social Theory*, Macmillan.

Giddens, A. (1985) *The Nation-State and Violence*, Polity Press.

Gilpin, R. (1988) 'The Theory of Hegemonic War', *Journal of Inter-Disciplinary History* 18.4, Spring, 591–613.

Goffman, E. (1968) *Asylums*, Penguin.

Goldstein, R. (1983) *Political Repression in Nineteenth Century Europe*, Croom Helm.

Gordon, D. M. et al. (1982) *Segmented Work, Divided Workers*, Cambridge University Press.

Gouldner, A. W. (1954) *Patterns of Industrial Bureaucracy*, Free Press of Glencoe.

Gouldner, A. W. (1970) *The Coming Crisis in Western Sociology*, Heinemann.

Habermas, J. (1976) *Legitimation Crisis*, Heinemann.

Hain, P. et al. (1980) *Policing the Police*, J. Calder.

Hall, J. A. (1985) 'Capstones and Organisms: Political Forms and the Triumph of Capitalism', *Sociology* 19. 2, May 1985.

Hall, J. A. (1986) *Powers and Liberties: The Causes and Consequences of the Rise of the West*, Pelican.

Halperin, M. (1971) *Why Bureaucrats Play Games*: Brookings Institution.

Halperin, M. (1974) *Bureaucratic Politics and Foreign Policy*, Brookings Institution.

Hannah, L. (1976) *The Rise of the Corporate Economy*, Methuen.

Hannah, L. (1980) 'Visible and Invisible Hands in Great Britain' in A. Chandler and H. Daems, *Managerial Hierarchies*, 1980.

Hardach, G. (1977) *The First World War, 1914–18*, Allen Lane.

Harding, C. et al. (1985) *Imprisonment in England and Wales: A Concise History*, Croom Helm.

Harries-Jenkins, G. (1973) *From Conscription to Volunteer Armies*, Adelphi Paper 103.

Hay, D. (1975) 'Property, Authority and the Criminal Law' in D. Hay, P. Linebaugh and E. P. Thompson, *Albion's Fatal Tree: Crime and Society in Eighteenth Century England*, Allen Lane, 17–63.

Hay, D., Linebaugh, P. and Thompson, E. P. (1975) *Albion's Fatal Tree Crime and Society in Eighteenth Century England*.

Held, D. (1987) *Models of Democracy*, Polity Press.

Held, D. (1988) 'Farewell the Nation State?' *Marxism Today*, December 1988, 12–17.

Henriques, V. (1972) 'The Rise and Decline of the Separate System of Prison

Discipline', *Past and Present* 54, 61–93.

Hirst, P. Q. (1976) *Social Evolution and Sociological Categories*, Allen and Unwin.

Hobsbawm, E. (1963) *Primitive Rebels*, Manchester University Press.

Hobsbawm, E. (1977) *The Age of Capital*, Abacus Sphere.

Holbrook-Jones, M. (1982) *Supremacy and Subordination of Labour: The Hierarchy of Work in the Early Labour Movement*, Heinemann.

Hoskin, K. and Macve, R. H. (1986) *The Genesis of Accountability: The West Point Connections: Accounting Organizations and Society*, 1986.

Howard, M. (1961) *The Franco-Prussian War*, Hart Davis.

Howard, M. (1976) *War in European History*, Oxford University Press.

Howard, M. (1981) *War and the Liberal Conscience*, Oxford University Press.

Howard, M. (1983) *The Causes of Wars*, Unwin Counterpoint.

Ignatieff, M. (1978) *A Just Measure of Pain: The Penitentiary in the Industrial Revolution, 1750–1850*, Macmillan.

Ignatieff, M. (1985) 'State, Civil Society and Total Institutions: A Critique of Recent Social Histories of Punishment' in S. Cohen and A. Scull, *Social Control and the State*, Blackwell.

Illich, I. (1975) *Medical Nemesis*, Calder.

Ingleby, D. (1985) 'Mental Health and Social Order' in S. Cohen and A. Scull, *Social Control and the State*, Blackwell, 141–90.

Innes, J. (1980) 'The King's Bench Prison in the Later Eighteenth Century: Law, Authority and Order in a London Debtor's Prison' in J. Brewer and J. Styles, *An Ungovernable People*, 250–98.

Irvine, D. D. (1938) 'The Origin of Capital Staffs', *Journal of Modern History* 10.2, 1938, 161–79.

Jackson, J. A. (1970) *Professions and Professionalisation*, Cambridge University Press.

Jamous, H. and Pelloile, B. (1970) 'Professions – A Self Perpetuating System? Changes in the French University Hospital System' in J. A. Jackson, *Professions and Professionalisation*, Cambridge University Press.

Janowitz, M. (1960; 1971 new edn) *The Professional Soldier*: Free Press of Glencoe.

Jefferey, K. and Hennessey, P. (1983) *States of Emergency: British Governments and Strike Breaking Since 1919*, Routledge and Kegan Paul.

Jelinek, M. (1981) 'Organization Structure: The Basic Conformations' in J. Litterer and R. E. Miles, *Organizations by Design: Theory and Practice*, 253–64.

Jelinek, M., Litterer, J. and Miles R. E. (1981) *Organizations by Design: Theory and Practice*, Business Publications, Plano, Texas.

Johnson, T. J. (1972) *Professions and Power*, Macmillan.

Johnson, T. J. (1976) 'Work and Power', O. U. course DE 351, People and Work Unit 12, revised for G. Esland and G. Salaman (eds), *Politics of Work and Occupations*, 1980, Open University Press.

Johnson, T. J. (1977) 'The Professions in the Class Structure' in R. Scase, *Industrial Society: Class Cleavage and Control*, Allen and Unwin, 93–110.

Johnson, T. J. and Dandeker, C. (1989), 'Patronage: Relation and System' in A. Wallace-Hadrill (ed.), *Patronage in the Ancient World*, Croom Helm.

Jones, D. (1982) *Crime, Protest, Community and Police in Nineteenth Century Britain*, Routledge and Kegan Paul.

Kaysen, C. (1957) 'The Social Significance of the Modern Corporation', *American Economic Review* 47, May, 311–19.

Kelleher, C. (1978) 'Mass Armies in the 1970s: The Debate in Western Europe', *Armed Forces and Society* 5, 1978, 3–30.

Kennedy, P. M. (1988) *The Rise and Fall of the Great Powers*, Unwin Hyman.

Kerr, C. et al. (1973) *Industrialism and Industrial Man*, Penguin.

Kieve, J. L. (1973) *The Electric Telegraph: A Social and Economic History*, David and Charles.

Kindleberger, C. (1984) *A Financial History of Western Europe*, Allen and Unwin.

Kitchen, M. (1976) *The Silent Dictatorship: The Politics of the German High Command Under Hindenburg and Ludendorff, 1916–1918*, Croom Helm.

Lambert, J. L. (1986) *Police Powers and Accountability*, Croom Helm.

Langley, H. D. (1967) *Social Reform in the United States Navy, 1778–1862*, University of Illinois.

Larson, M. S. (1977) *The Rise of Professionalism: A Sociological Analysis*, University of California Press.

Lash, S. and Urry, J. (1987) *Disorganized Capitalism*, Polity Press.

Lewis, M. (1939) *England's Sea Officers*, Allen and Unwin.

Lewis, M. (1948) *The Navy of Britain*, Allen and Unwin.

Littler, C. (1982) *The Development of the Labour Process in Capitalist Societies*.

Littler, C. (1983) 'Deskilling and Changing Structures of Control' in S. Wood (ed.) *The Degradation of Work? Skill, Deskilling and the Labour Process*, Hutchinson.

Littler, C. and Salaman, G. (1982) 'Bravermania and Beyond: Recent Theories of the Labour Process', *Sociology* 16, 251–69.

Lloyd, C. (1970) *The British Seaman*, Paladin.

Lockwood, D. (1964) 'System Integration and Social Integration' in G. K. Zollschan and W. Hirsch, *Explorations in Social Change*, Routledge, 244–56.

Lukes, S. (1974) *Power: A Radical View*, Macmillan.

Lukes, S. (1977) *Essays in Social Theory*, Macmillan.

Manwaring-White, S. (1983) *The Policing Revolution: Police Technology, Democracy and Liberty in Britain*, Harvester.

Marder, A. J. (1940) *British Naval Policy, 1800–1905*, Putnam.

Manigart, P. (1988) 'The Decline of the Mass Army in Belgium', paper presented at ISA RCOI, Munich, 1988.

Mann, M. (1984) 'Capitalism and Militarism' in M. Shaw (ed.) *War, State and Society*, Macmillan.

Mann, M. (1987) 'War and Social Theory: Into Battle With Classes, Nations and States' in M. Shaw and C. Creighton, *The Sociology of War and Peace, Explorations in Sociology* 24, Macmillan.

Mann, M. (1987a) *A History of Power, vol. 1, From the Beginning to AD 1760*, Cambridge University Press.

Mann, M. (1988) *War, States and Capitalism*, Blackwell.

Manning, P. (1977) *Police Work: The Social Organization of Policing*, MIT Press.

Marris, R. and Wood, A. (eds) (1971) *The Corporate Economy*, Macmillan.

Marshall, T. H. (1973) *Class, Citizenship and Social Development*, Greenwood Press.

Marwick, A. (1965) *The Deluge: British Society and the First World War*, Macmillan.

Mayer, J. P. (1944) *Max Weber and German Politics: A Study in Political Sociology*, Faber and Faber.

McKenna, F. (1980) *The Railway Workers, 1840-1970*, Faber.

McKeown, T. (1979) *The Role of Medicine*, Blackwell.

McNeill, W. (1983) *The Pursuit of Power, Technology, Armed Force and Society Since 1000 AD*, Blackwell.

Melossi, D. (1976) 'Institutions of Social Control and the Capitalist Organization of Work: Some Hypotheses for Research' in *La Questione Criminale* 2/3 (11): May, December, 1976.

Melossi, D. and Pavarini, M. (1981) *The Prison and the Factory*, Macmillan.

Middlemas, K. (1980) *The Politics of Industrial Society: The Experience of the British Political System Since 1911*, Deutsch.

Miller, W. R. (1977) *Cops and Bobbies: Police Authority in New York and London, 1830-1870*, University of Chicago Press.

Millet, A. R. and Maslowski, P. (1984) *For the Common Defence: A Military History of the USA*, Free Press of Glencoe.

Millis, W. (1958) *Armies and Men: A Study in American Military History*, Cape.

Mosca, G. (1939) *The Ruling Class*, McGraw Hill.

Mouzelis, N. (1974) 'Social Integration and System Integration: Some Reflections on a Fundamental Distinction', *British Journal of Sociology*, 395-409.

Munkonnen, E. (1981) *Police in Urban America, 1860-1970*, Cambridge University Press.

Nelson, D. (1975) *The Origins of the New Factory System in the United States, 1880-1970*, University of Wisconsin Press.

Offe, C. (1972) 'Advanced Capitalism and the Welfare State', *Politics and Society* 2, 4.

O'Neill, J. (1986) 'The Disciplinary Society: From Weber to Foucault', *British Journal of Sociology* 37. 1, 1986, 42-60.

Otley, C. B. (1970) 'The Social Origins of British Army Officers', *Sociological Review*, 1970, 213-39.

Otley, C. B. (1973) 'The Educational Background of British Army Officers', *Sociology* 7, 1973, 191-209.

Parkes, O. (1966) *British Battleships*, Seeley Service and Co.

Parris, H. (1974) *Constitutional Bureaucracy*, Unwin.

Parsons, T. (1964) *Max Weber: The Theory of Social and Economic Organization*, Free Press of Glencoe.

Parsons, T. (1964) *Politics and Social Structure*, Collier Macmillan.

Pearton, M. (1982) *The Knowledgeable State: War, Diplomacy and Technology Since 1830*, Hutchinson.

Perkin, H. (1969) *The Origins of Modern English Society*, Routledge.

Phillips, D. (1980) 'A New Engine of Power and Authority: The Institutionalization of Law Enforcement in England, 1780–1830' in V. A. C. Gatrell, B. Lenman, and G. Parker, *Social History of Crime in Western Europe Since 1500*, Europa.

Poggi, G. (1977) *The Development of the Modern State*, Hutchinson.

Pollard, S. (1963) 'Factory Discipline in the Industrial Revolution', *Economic History Review* 16.2, 1963, 261–9.

Pollard, S. (1968) *The Genesis of Modern Management*, Penguin.

Pratt, E. A. (1915) *The Rise of Railpower in War and Conquest*, King.

Preston, A. and Major, J. (1967) *Send a Gunboat*, Longman.

Reiner, R. (1985) *The Politics of the Police*, Harvester.

Reith, C. (1956) *A New Study of Police History*, Oliver and Boyd.

Richardson, J. F. (1974) *Urban Police in the United States*, Kennikat Press.

Roach, J. and Thomaneck, J. (1985) *Police and Public Order in Europe*, Croom Helm.

Roberts, M. (1958), *Gustavus Adolphus*, 2 vols, London.

Roberts, S. (1979) *Order and Dispute: Introduction to Legal Anthropology*, Penguin.

Rock, P. (1985) 'Law, Order and Power in Late Seventeenth and Early Eighteenth Century England' in S. Cohen and A. Scull, *Social Control and the State*, Blackwell, 191–221.

Rodger, N. A. M. (1988) *The Wooden World: An Anatomy of the Georgian Navy*, Fontana.

Rowe, C. (1986) *People and Chips: The Human Implications of Information Technology*, Paradigm.

Rubinstein, J. (1973) *City Police*, Ballantine, New York.

Rule, J. B. (1973) *Private Lives and Public Surveillance*, Allen Lane.

Rumble, G. (1985) *The Politics of Nuclear Defence*, Polity Press.

Rusche, G. and Kircheimer, O. (1939) *Punishment and Social Structure*: Columbia University Press.

Saks, M. (1983) 'A Critique of Recent Contributions to the Sociology of the Professions', *Sociological Review*, February 1983, 1–21.

The Scarman Report (1982) *The Brixton Disorders, 10–12 April 1981. Report of an Enquiry by the Lord Scarman*, Penguin.

Scase, R. (1977) *Industrial Society: Class Cleavage and Control*, Allen and Unwin.

Scott, J. (1985) *Corporations, Classes and Capitalism*, Hutchinson.

Scull, A. (1975) *Museums of Madness: The Social Organization of Insanity in Nineteenth Century England*, PhD Thesis, University of Princeton.

Shaw, M. (1984) *War, State and Society*, Macmillan.

Sheridan, A. (1980) *Michel Foucault: The Will to Truth*, Tavistock.

Silver, A. (1967) 'The Demand for Order in Civil Society: A Review of Some Themes in the History of Urban Crime, Police and Riot' in D. J. Bordua, *The Police: Six Sociological Essays*, Wiley.

Skidelsky, R. (ed.) (1988) *Thatcherism*, Chatto and Windus.

Spierenburg, P. (1984) *The Spectacle of Suffering: Execution and the Evolution of Repression: From a Pre-industrial Metropolis to the European Experience*, Cambridge University Press.

Spitzer, S. (1985) 'The Rationalization of Crime Control in Capitalist Society' in

S. Cohen and A. Scull, *Social Control and the State*, 1985.

Stammers, N. (1983) *Civil Liberties in Britain During the Second World War*, Croom Helm.

Stead, P. (1983) *The Police of France*, Macmillan.

Steedman, C. (1984) *Policing the Victorian Community: The Formation of English Provincial Police Forces, 1856–80*, Routledge and Kegan Paul.

Stone, J. and Mennel, S. (1980) *Alexis De Tocqueville: On Democracy, Revolution and Society*, University of Chicago.

Storch, R. D. (1975) 'The Plague of the Blue Locusts: Police Reform and Popular Resistance in Northern England, 1840–57', *International Review of Social History* 20, 61–90.

Storch, R. D. (1976) 'The Policeman as Domestic Missionary: Urban Discipline and Popular Culture in Northern England, 1850–1880', *Journal of Social History* 9 (4), 481–509.

Strachan, H. (1983) *European Armies and the Conduct of War*, Allen and Unwin.

Sugarman, D. (ed.) (1981) *Legality, Ideology and the State*, Academic Press.

Teitler, G. (1977) *Genesis of the Professional Officers' Corps*, Sage.

Thompson, E. P. (1967) 'Time, Work, Discipline and Industrial Capitalism', *Past and Present* 38, 56–97.

Thompson, E. P. (1975) *Whigs and Hunters: The Origins of the Black Acts*, Allen Lane.

Tilly, C. (1975), *The Formation of National States in Western Europe*, Princeton University Press.

Titmus, R. M. (1950) *Problems of Social Policy*, Longman.

Tobias, J. (1967) *Crime and Industrial Society in Nineteenth Century England*, Batsford.

Urwick, L. F. and Brech, E. F. P. (1949; 1951; 1953) *The Making of Scientific Management*, Pitman.

Useem, M. (1984) *The Inner Circle*, Oxford University Press.

Van Creveld, M. (1977) *Supplying War: Logistics from Wallenstein to Patton*: Cambridge University Press.

Van Doorn, J. A. (1965) 'The Officer Corps: A Fusion of Profession and Organization', *Archive Europeen de Sociologie*, 1965, 262–82.

Van Doorn, J. A. (1975) 'The Decline of the Mass Army in the West', *Armed Forces and Society*, 147–58.

Wallace-Hadrill, A. (ed.) (1989) *Patronage in the Ancient World*, Croom Helm.

Wallerstein, I. (1979) *The Modern World System*, Academic Press.

Weber, M. (1949) *Methodology of the Social Sciences*, Free Press of Glencoe.

Weber, M. (1956) *The Protestant Ethic and the Spirit of Capitalism*, Allen and Unwin.

Weber, M. (1961) *General Economic History*, Collier.

Weber, M. (1978) *Economy and Society*, 2 vols, University of California Press.

Weisser, M. R. (1979) *Crime and Punishment in Early Modern Europe*, Harvester.

Williamson, K. (1971) 'Managerial Discretion: Organization Form and the Multi-Division Hypothesis' in R. Marris and A. Wood (eds), *The Corporate Economy*: Macmillan.

Woloch, I. (1986) 'Napolenoic Conscription, State Power and Society', *Past and*

Present 11, 1986, 101-29.

Wood, S. (1983) *The Degradation of Work? Skill, Deskilling and the Labour Process*, Hutchinson.

Wood, S. and Kelly, J. (1983) 'Taylorism, Responsible Autonomy and Management Strategy' in S. Wood, *The Degradation of Work? Deskilling and the Labour Process*, Hutchinson, 1983, 74-89.

Wright-Mills, C. (1956) *The Power Elite*, Oxford University Press.

Zeitlin, M. (1974) 'Corporate Ownership and Control: The Large Corporation and the Capitalist Class', *American Journal of Sociology* 79.5.

Zollschan, G. K. and Hirsch, W. (1964) *Explorations in Social Change*, Routledge.

Index

238

Index by Beth Scott